Microeconomic Issues Today

Microeconomic Issues Today

Alternative Approaches

Eighth Edition

Robert B. Carson, Wade L. Thomas, Jason Hecht

M.E.Sharpe
Armonk, New York
London, England

We dedicate this edition of *Microeconomic Issues Today* to
Robert L. Heilbroner
for making the dismal science of economics
readable and understandable.

Library of Congress Cataloging-in-Publication Data

Carson, Robert Barry, 1934–
  Microeconomic issues today : alternative approaches / Robert B. Carson,
Wade L. Thomas, and Jason Hecht.—8th ed.
    p. cm.
  Includes bibliographical references and index.
  ISBN 0-7656-1502-9 (pbk.: alk. paper)
  1. Microeconomics. 2. United States—Economic policy—2001–
I. Thomas, Wade L. II. Hecht, Jason, 1958– III. Title.

HB172.C35 2005
338.5´0973—dc22   2004021684

Printed in the United States of America

The paper used in this publication meets the minimum requirements of
American National Standard for Information Sciences
Permanence of Paper for Printed Library Materials,
ANSI Z 39.48-1984.

BM (p) 10 9 8 7 6 5 4 3 2 1

Contents

Part III. Conclusion

Figures and Tables

Figures

Tables

Preface

More than a quarter century has passed since the publication of the first edition of *Economic Issues Today* (and its macroeconomic and microeconomic split versions). Needless to say, a lot of economic water has gone over the dam since 1978. Accordingly, the content of *Economic Issues Today* has undergone many changes through this, its eighth edition. Yet the underlying philosophy and pedagogical objectives of the book remain the same: to introduce those uninitiated in the ways of economists to the breadth and richness of economic reasoning.

Economic Issues Today maintains a distinctive approach with its first-person debate from Conservative, Liberal, and Radical views. The reader is advised not to approach these "ideological" positions as if they were etched in stone and not subject to change and adaptation. While each position has rather fixed philosophical foundations, the actual practice and the day-to-day politics of each has allowed appropriation of small ideological pieces from an opposing perspective on one issue or another. For example, the subject of automobile safety was a torrid debate between Left and Right twenty-five years ago. Now, it has mainstream acceptability and the debate over consumer protection has moved on to different products and problems. However, the comfortable conclusion of "issue solved" or the convenience of "score carding" which side came out ahead on a particular policy always has been fuel for this book's anticipation of the next turn of the wheel. Consider the wave of industry deregulation and other regulatory reversals that gave the impression that the bulk of regulatory institutions was on the path to oblivion. Now, corporate and accounting debacles of painful proportions have reinvigorated the public's interest in managing the ground rules for business conduct and prompted greater intrusion into lightly regulated areas such as financial reporting responsibilities and the broader accounting profession.

At the beginning of the twenty-first century and after more than twenty years of nearly uninterrupted economic prosperity, the contemporary scene is one where debates and argumentation over public policy generally have been muted. The tendency toward believing that old burning issues are solved or at least a high degree of consensus has been attained seems to have gained more traction over the past few years. Entire generations are weary of the continuing economic problems of farmers, the unemployed, environmental threats, the sustainability of the Social Security system, trade and budget deficits, poverty, and the like. These problems are supposed to be "fixed," not lingering sources of endless controversies! However, economic issues cannot be dismissed like overplayed songs and news stories or a bad season for the favorite sports team. The issues are troubling but it is more troubling when they are regarded as things too complex, too abstract, or too trivial with which to be bothered.

As it has since the first edition in 1978, *Economic Issues Today* (and the split versions) continues to plumb the depths of these debates. The book requires no background in the methods of economic analysis, and as much as possible it avoids the use of economic jargon in favor of everyday language. The eighth edition of *Economic Issues Today,* like previous ones, stresses the ideological choices that exist in economic thought and that often cause ordinary citizens to be confused about what economists *do* and what economists *believe.* As ever, it is meant to be a provocative book, more concerned with provoking discussion and thought than in presenting "right" solutions to problems. It remains committed to the belief that real economic solutions are possible in a democratic society only when all alternatives are known and considered.

Although longtime users are familiar with the text's philosophy and perspectives, new readers might benefit from an explanation of why the authors undertook this project in the first place and how the book is organized.

All too frequently, students begin their study of economics with the impression that economists are bland and monolithic when discussing important issues confronting the general society. We may as well admit that the profession sometimes exhibits a tendency to blandness in its public utterances, but surely any supposed unanimity toward social policy questions has vanished. With the rise of an influential Radical caucus within the discipline, beginning in the late 1960s, and the more recent resurgence of variations of laissez-faire ideology, any facade of consensus has clearly been broken down. The application of economic theory to issues of public policy more and more reflects a range of choice from Conservative to Liberal to Radical.

For the student struggling with basic theory and analytic tools, as well as for the ordinary citizen overwhelmed by economic data in the newspapers and on the TV evening news, it is hard to avoid confusion over what economists really think about the problems facing the nation. This book begins with the assumption that the answers economists give to policy questions can be usefully compared and analyzed according to the particular biases of their arguments and the probable outcomes of their proposals. In other words, differences in economic logic and interpretation of evidence are not so much a function of skill mastery as they are the expression of strongly held social and political opinions. The text also assumes that economics as a body of knowledge takes on greater meaning and is more readily comprehended when it is viewed in this way.

For each issue, a Conservative, Liberal, and Radical analysis and proposed solution are presented in turn as the valid approach to the problem. On one page, there may be a vigorous and unyielding defense of laissez-faire and the market economy; on another, a program for the elimination or modification of the free market. This is not the way economic analysis and theory are usually taught, but it is what the practice of economics is about. In the real world, the citizen and the economist make public policy choices that protect, attack, or modify the market mechanism. We may defend our positions in terms of economic logic, but behind our proofs lies our political and ideological view of the world. This book attempts to examine the relationship between ideological values and the economic theories and policies that are their outcome.

Since the text presents a wide range of perspectives on a number of currently sensitive issues, it should provoke disagreement, controversy, and discussion. In itself, the book does not urge a particular ideological position or a particular variety of economic analysis. The decision to select or reject this or that point of view is left—as it should be—to the reader.

Each chapter is self-contained and may be assigned in any order the instructor chooses. There are relatively few footnotes or direct references to specific economists, although the ideas of many contemporary economists and schools of economic thought will be apparent. The suggested readings at the end are offered for anyone wishing to dig a little more deeply into an issue or a particular economic perspective or approach.

What Is New in This Edition

The eighth edition represents a substantial revision over the seventh. Updating of critical changes in economic policy was undertaken for every issue. However, the introduction to the text keeps its time-tested development and explanation of the Conservative, Liberal, and Radical positions.

Microeconomic Issues Today contains the same seven problems in the marketplace of the previous edition, but each issue has been overhauled. Issue 1 keeps its informative historical basis while incorporating the new direction American agricultural policy has taken since 2002. Issue 2 is a completely modernized and revised presentation of the consumer welfare issue that extends beyond its original focus on automobile safety. The range of environmental problems in Issue 3 is modified to include more than acid rain and, along with it, greater elaboration about pollution control policies and the growing immediacy of environmental issues on an international scale. The mainstay arguments in Issue 4 on imperfect competition are largely retained in this edition, but assisted by newer and better data in support of the debate over the competitiveness of American industries. Economic regulation in Issue 5 relinquishes some of its focus on transportation deregulation in favor of examples in telecommunications, energy, and professional ethics, and considers the potential drift toward reregulation. Poverty and income distribution are more effectively addressed in Issue 6 of this edition with more complete evidence on welfare reform and the use of the Gini index to track income inequality. Issue 7 on financing government concludes the microeconomic topics with a thorough analysis of the three recent federal tax reductions from all three perspectives.

"The Market Versus Planning and Controls," takes on a new identity as a "Reprise" to all the material that has gone before it. Placing it in a stand-alone position at the end of the book acknowledges the issue's summation of comparative economic systems.

Supplements

The instructors manual for *Economic Issues Today* is available on computer disk. Key terms, multiple-choice, true-false, and essay-discussion questions are provided for each issue. Some instructors like to use *Economic Issues Today* in conjunction with their preferred principles text. The instructor's manual provides a "correlation grid" that cross-references the issues from *Economic Issues Today* with related chapters in leading principles of economics textbooks. Potential adopters can request a copy of the grid from the publisher or view it online at www.mesharpe.com. The correlation grid is reproduced for your convenience at the end of the preface.

To assist with classroom presentations, instructors can download PowerPoint slides of all figures and tables in the text from the publisher's Web site at www.mesharpe.com. The authors also maintain a portal that is a quick and easy way to link to the PowerPoint slides and correlation grid at www.EconomicIssues.com.

Correlation Grid for Using *Economic Issues Today* with Leading Introductory Economics Textbooks

EIT issues / Relevant textbook chapters	Baumol/Blinder	Case/Fair	Lipsey	McConnell/Brue	Mankiw	Mansfield/Behravesh	Miller	O'Sullivan/Sheffrin	Parkin	Ruffin/Gregory	Samuelson/Nordhaus	Schiller (one-semester text)	Stiglitz
Introduction: Alternative Economic Philosophies	1, 3, 4	1, 2	1, 2, 3	1, 2, 3, 4	1, 2	1	1	1, 2	1, 2	1, 2, 3	1, 2	1, 2	2
Issue 1: Responding to Market Outcomes: Competition or Protection for American Agriculture	5, 7, 8, 9	3, 4	4, 5, 6, 10	20, 23, 33	4, 5, 6	16, 17	3, 20	4, 5, 6	3, 4, 6	3, 4, 6	3, 4	3, 5	4, 5
Issue 2: Consumer Welfare: Is It Necessary to Protect the Consumer?	6, 7	5, 14	7	21	7, 21, 22	16, 18	19	7	19	7, 15	5	4	6, 14
Issue 3: Dealing with Externalities: How Can We Save the Environment?	8, 22	14	18, 19	30	10, 11	21	31	17	16, 19	5, 8, 20	18	5	21
Issue 4: Imperfect Competition: Is Big Business a Threat or a Boon?	10, 11, 12, 13, 20	11, 12, 13	11, 12	24, 25, 32	15, 16, 17	19	24, 25, 26, 27	10, 11, 12, 13, 14	11, 12, 13, 14	11, 12, 13, 14	9, 10	7	11, 12, 13, 14, 15
Issue 5: Economic Regulation. Which Path: Has Deregulation Worked?	14, 20		13, 18, 19	32	6, 7, 11	20	27	13, 14	14	14	2, 17	7, 9	13
Issue 6: Income Distribution: Does America Have an Income Inequality Problem?	17, 18, 19	15	15, 16	28, 29, 34	19, 20	23, 24	6, 30	19	18	17, 19	12, 19	8	19

	21	16	20	31	8, 12	26	5, 6	16	31	21, 22	16	9	16, 26
Issue 7: Financing Government: What Is a Fair System of Taxation?	23, 24	17, 21, 23	21, 23, 24	8, 9, 10	26, 28	4, 5	7, 10, 11	22, 24, 25	21, 22, 24, 30, 31, 32	23, 25, 27, 34	20, 22, 23, 24	10, 11	24, 25
Issue 8: Macroeconomic Instability: Are We Depression-Proof?	15, 24, 29, 34	19, 25, 30	25, 26, 31	8, 11, 12, 17	25, 33, 34	6, 11, 14, 25	12, 13, 18	23, 25, 26	21, 23, 24, 25	26, 27, 31, 33	20, 22, 23, 24, 27, 34	10, 11	28, 29
Issue 9: Economic Growth and Stability: Can We Maintain High and Steady Rates of Economic Growth?													
Issue 10: Balancing the Federal Budget: Should We Be Worried About the Rising Federal Deficit?	33	16, 21	32, 33	18	33, 34, 35	12	13	25	31	31, 33	34	12	36
Issue 11: Unemployment: Is Joblessness an Overrated Problem?	26, 28	26	31	16, 19	28, 33, 35	4	7	21, 29, 30, 31	22	33	31	10	24, 31
Issue 12: Inflation: Can Price Pressures Be Kept Under Control?	25, 26, 28, 31	23, 25, 26	28, 29, 30	15, 16	30, 33, 35	7, 10, 13	7	21, 28, 29, 30	27, 28, 31, 32	32	26, 32	14	30, 31
Issue 13: The New Population Problem: Can We Save Our Social Security System?	21, 33	16		36		26	6	16, 19	34	19, 21, 22	16		
Issue 14: International Economics: Where Does America Fit into the New World Order?	35, 36, 37	32, 33, 34	35, 36, 37	37, 38	3, 9, 31, 32	27, 28	17, 18, 32, 33	32, 33	33, 34	35, 36, 37	29, 30	17	3, 18, 33, 34
Reprise. The Market Versus Planning and Controls: Which Strategy Works Better?	36	11, 31	38	16, 31, 39, 40	11, 36	26	5	22, 31	5, 16	21, 22, 38, 39	33	16	37

Acknowledgments

The senior author would like to thank Michael Weber, a longtime sponsoring editor of *Economic Issues Today* at St. Martin's Press (before St. Martin's dropped its college economics line), for signing the book with its new publisher, M.E. Sharpe, Inc. And, as with each new edition, the senior author feels duty bound to note the kind and thoughtful encouragement of Bertrand Lummus, then the college editor at St. Martin's, who made it possible for *Economic Issues Today* to see the light of day in the first place. Similarly, the senior author wishes to acknowledge the efforts of Paula Franklin and Emily Berleth, whose extraordinary editorial skills in the early editions of the work have survived, both directly and indirectly, right down to the current version.

The authors want to express appreciation to several teaching professors for their suggestions and comments that have led to improvements for this edition of the text: Michael McAvoy, William P. O'Dea, and David Ring (all from SUNY Oneonta), and Amy S. Cramer, Pima Community College. We are grateful to Campbell R. McConnell for his expert advice and encouragement over the past three editions of *Economic Issues Today*. The authors also thank Lynn Taylor, economics editor, for her editorial efforts on the eighth edition.

We sadly acknowledge the passing of our good friend and mentor of *Economic Issues Today*, Robert L. Heilbroner of the New School University. Bob Heilbroner was both a teacher and colleague of coauthor Jason Hecht, and we all drew much inspiration and intellectual strength from his numerous books and writings. In particular, the influence of his most famous book, *The Worldly Philosphers,* is evident within these pages. The eighth edition of *Economic Issues Today* is dedicated in memory of Robert L. Heilbroner.

Part I

Introduction

Alternative Economic Philosophies
A Survey of Conservative, Liberal, and Radical Critiques

The ideas of economists, both when they are right and when they are wrong, are more powerful than is commonly understood. Indeed, the world is ruled by little else. Practical men, who believe themselves to be quite exempt from any intellectual influences, are usually the slaves of some defunct economist. Madmen in authority, who hear voices in the air, are distilling their frenzy from some academic scribbler of a few years back.

—*John Maynard Keynes, 1936*

As of this writing (2005), the American economy had experienced only two brief recessions (in 1990–91 and 2001) during the past twenty-two years. Add to this the fact that the American economy remains the envy of the rest of the world. By such indicators, we should be—at least with respect to economic matters—a content and happy people. Right?

Alas, economic matters rarely seem to be a solid source of shared contentment. As the outcome of the 2000 and 2004 presidential elections indicates, the country remains equally divided on the question of whether or not the American economy was headed in the right direction. This down-the-middle division leads to an obvious conclusion (and one completely independent of who won and who lost the election): A great many Americans are uncertain about their nation's economic future. In fact, the uncertainty does not end there. Each thoughtful member of either side of the great divide in opinion has to wonder about what is going on in the minds of those who went the other way on the question of the "right direction."

As with all such periods of economic uncertainty and disagreement, the citizenry becomes increasingly interested in economic matters and the observations and advice that might be offered by the keepers of economic wisdom: *economists*. Mostly ignored in good times, economists can count on getting the public's attention when worries about bad times arise. And so, economists once again find a growing popular interest in their "dismal science."

Alas, when they are thrust into the spotlight, economists invariably reveal something about their discipline that ordinary citizens tend to forget during the good times. As those recently watching economists on TV or reading op-ed pieces by economists were soon to discover (or, if old enough, *rediscover*), economists are rarely of one mind with respect to matters of deep and immediate economic impact. Some Americans suffering unease about the economy in general may experience a heightening of this malady as a result of the evident lack of unanimity in the economics profession. However, this has been an abiding characteristic of the keepers of economic wisdom for a very long time.

It is well for the reader to remember that throughout the long history of human efforts to understand and explain economic matters, disagreement rather than consensus has been the rule. In a nation that puts great stock in consensus building as the ultimate tool of governance and the principal device for sustaining social order, this may be a disconcerting fact. In any event, it is one we should understand. Even in times of considerable national economic prosperity, real differences of political and economic opinion still circulate. And, as we should know from the historical record, economic prosperity itself has always been a transitory condition; when it fades, debate over alternative economic policies often becomes heated.

When that debate takes place, squabbling among economists over policy alternatives can scarcely be hidden from the public, and such disagreement can be downright unsettling. It often comes as a rude surprise to the person on the street, who, although paying due professional respect to economists, still sees the economist as a kind of mechanic. When one's car does not start, the car owner expects (at least hopes) that the diagnosis of mechanical trouble given at one garage is exactly the same as what will be heard at any other. If there is one mechanical problem, there should be one mechanical solution. The moral of this comparison is that the study of economics is more than studying a repair manual, and economists are not mechanics.

Economics and Ideology

How is such disagreement possible? Is not economics a science? Economists' answers to that question vary. A common and reasonable enough response is simply that scientists disagree too. While there is much truth to such an answer, it really begs the question. Plainly, economics is not a science like physics. Whereas economists may sometimes talk about the laws of supply and demand as if they were eternal verities like the law of gravity, there is abundant anthropological and historical evidence that many societies have behaved quite contrary to the laws of supply and demand.

To be sure, economists employ (or at least should employ) the rigor of scientific method and quantitative techniques in collecting data, testing hypotheses, and offering reasonable conclusions and predictions. However, economists deal with different "stuff" than their colleagues in the exact sciences. Their data involve human beings, and their laboratory is a world of behavior and perception that varies with time and place. On top of this, economists, like all social scientists, are called on to answer a question not asked of those in the pure sciences: "What *ought* to be?" Astronomers, for instance, are not asked what *ought* to be the gravitational relationships of our universe. That would be a nonsensical question. Economists, however, cannot evade making some determinations about optimal prices, optimal income distribution, and so forth. Their decisions, while perhaps based on a genuine effort at neutrality, detachment, and honest evaluation of the available evidence, finally must be a matter of interpretation, a value judgment based on their own particular world views. To put the point directly: *Economics, as a study of human behavior, cannot avoid value judgments. Struggle as it may, economics as a discipline is never free from ideology.*

The early economists of the eighteenth and nineteenth centuries—Adam Smith, David Ricardo, John Stuart Mill, and especially the heretic Karl Marx—perceived economics as merely part of a broader political economy context, but this view had been largely abandoned by the end of the nineteenth century. By the middle of the twentieth century, the economics profession generally approached ideology as if it were a dirty word, unprofessional, or, at the very best, too troublesome to deal with. The emphasis was on theoretical tools, considered both universal and neutral. All this changed in the 1960s and 1970s when well-known American economists thrust themselves into the powerful debates then sweeping American society. Their views on the war in Vietnam, poverty, civil rights, the extent of government power, the environmental crisis, the oil embargo, the causes of stagflation, high technology versus smokestack industries, and much more could be heard regularly on television talk shows and miniseries or read in the columns of weekly newsmagazines. Often there was the pretension that this "talking out of church" had little impact on the body of professional theory and judgment, but the pretension was unconvincing. For good or ill, the genie was out of the bottle, and the economics profession had again become involved in politics and in recommending political courses of action to pursue economic objectives.

Initially, through the 1960s and into the early 1970s, prevailing opinion among economic reasoners upheld a Liberal perspective on political economy, advocating an active interventionism by government to correct and improve the workings of the economy. However, during the late 1970s, this consensus began to break down as the national economy slipped into a long period of sagging growth, rising unemployment, and escalating inflation. In its place, a new consensus began to build on behalf of a Conservative, minimum-government approach to political and economic matters. As the Liberals' star fell and the Conservatives' rose, the intensity and bitterness of economic and political argument sharpened. Although the shrillness of the ideological debate calmed a bit during the Reagan years—no doubt a by-product of the long economic expansion that began in late 1982—the past four decades of shifting ideological perspectives have left their mark on the economics profession. To a considerable extent, the ordinary economics textbook illustrates this point. While economics texts continue to do what such books have always done, namely, to introduce the reader to a generally agreed-on body of theoretical and analytical techniques and tools that constitute the study of economics, most have also found it necessary to identify and discuss the alternatives of Liberals, Conservatives, and, sometimes, even Radicals in the practical extension of economic analysis to actual policy-making situations.

The significance of all this should not be lost on the beginning student of economics. Though many economists may stress the value-free nature of their studies, and of economics in general, common sense and observation suggest that this is at best a vastly exaggerated claim. The content and application of economic reasoning are determined ultimately by the force of what economists believe, not by an independent and neutral logic. But to say that economics is a matter of opinion is not to say that it is just a study of relatively different ideas: Here is this view and here is that one and each is of equal value. In fact, opinions are not of equal value. There are good opinions and there are bad ones. Different economic ideas have different consequences when adopted as policy. They have different effects—now and in the future. As we confront the various policy solutions proposed to deal with the many crises now gnawing deep into our economy and society, we must make choices: this one seems likely to produce desired outcomes, that one does not. No other situation is consistent with a free and reasoning society. Granted, it is a painful situation, since choice always raises doubts and uncertainty and runs the risk of wrong judgment, but it cannot be evaded.

This book is intended to focus on a limited number of the hard choices that we must make. Its basic premise is that economic judgment is fundamentally a matter of learning to choose the best policy solution among all possible solutions. The book further assumes that failure to make this choice is to underestimate the richness and importance of the economic ideas we learn and to be blind to the fact that ideas and analyses do indeed apply to the real world of our own lives.

On Sorting Out Ideologies

Assuming that we have been at least partially convincing in our argument that economic analysis is permeated by ideological judgment, we now turn to examine the varieties of ideology common to American economic thought.

In general, we may characterize the ideological position of contemporary economics and economists as Conservative, Liberal, or Radical. These, the same handy categories that evening newscasters use to describe political positions, presumably have some meaning to people. The trouble with labels, though, is that they can mean a great deal and, at the same time, nothing at all. At a distance the various political colors of Conservative, Liberal, and Radical banners are vividly different. Close up, however, the distinctiveness blurs, and what seemed obvious differences are not so clear. For instance, there is probably *not* a strictly Liberal position on every economic issue, nor are all the economists who might be generally termed Liberal consistently in agreement. The same is true in the case of many Radical or Conservative positions as well. Unless we maintain a certain open-endedness in our categorizing of positions, the discussion of ideological differences will be overly simple and much too rigid. Therefore, the following generalizations and applications of ideological typologies will attempt to isolate and identify only representative positions. By doing this we can at least focus on the differences at the center rather than on the fuzziness at the fringes of these schools of thought.

We are still left with a problem. How do you specify an ideological position? Can you define a Radical or a Liberal or a Conservative position? The answer here is simple. As the British economist Joan Robinson once observed, an ideology is like an elephant—you cannot define an elephant but you should know one when you see it. Moreover, you should know the difference between an elephant and a horse or a cow without having to resort to definitions.

There is a general framework of thought within each of the three ideological schools by which we can recognize them. Thus we will not "define" the schools but merely describe the salient characteristics of each. In all of the following, the reader is urged to remember that there are many varieties of elephants. Our specification of a particular ideological view on any issue is a representative model—a kind of average-looking elephant (or horse or cow). Therefore, the Conservative view offered on the problem of federal deficits, for instance, will probably not encompass all Conservative thought on this question. However, it should be sufficiently representative so that the basic Conservative paradigm, or worldview, can be distinguished from the Radical or Liberal argument. Where truly important divisions within an ideological paradigm exist, the divisions will be appropriately noted and discussed.

A Brief Footnote on the Paradigms

The reader should be aware that ideological labels and categories presently are used by Americans in an increasingly flippant fashion. For example, TV journalism's efforts to "dumb down" news reporting and editorial commentary on the news has produced the well-known talking-head format where analyses of events are sifted and sorted into "from the Right" and "from the Left" perspectives. Based upon the authors' experiences, this technique of dividing up Conservative, Liberal, and Radical political-economic ideas—handy as it may be for sound-bite making—creates some awful confusion.

Neat division into "Left" or "Right" is a dangerous oversimplification of the range and variety of ideological points of view. The Left presumably includes all Liberals and Radicals, and the Right catches all Conservatives. To dump Liberals and Radicals into a presumably shared-interest category is a monumental error of the first order. True Liberals and true Radicals have been at each other's throats for a century or more. Indeed, they have been at war with each other more than either one has been at war with Conservatives.

The Left-Right designation of ideologies rests on the false assumption that political-economic belief can be neatly segregated and compartmentalized along a continuum—with Adam Smith on one end and Karl Marx on the other. Accordingly, leaning Left or Right is apparently determined by where along this continuum one is located: nearer or further from Marx and Smith. Alas, ideas are not susceptible to arrangement along a continuum. To arrange political-economic ideas as if they were part of a unified spectrum is about as useful as arranging one's personal library according to book size or one's CD collection according to the color of the disks' cases.

However, the most troublesome and misleading aspect of the Left-Right categorization of American opinion is its habit of not sorting outlooks according to the types of issues that individuals might address.

Tasteless as some may find the following "for instances," where on the Left-Right spectrum should we locate a gay or lesbian couple who regularly vote Republican but are also seeking to obtain a marriage license or the aging Pentecostal Christian who is utterly dependent on Social Security monthly checks and Medicare to support himself and his wife?

The point is that sexual orientation or religious belief are questions of personal and social values (as is the matter of one's preferred major league baseball team) and not necessarily a reflection of one's political ideology at all. To be sure, political conservatives may court those who adhere to "conservative" personal values (sometimes called "family values") and liberal ideologues may cultivate those of a "liberal" bent with respect to their personal beliefs, but that is a separate matter from the examination of competing economic ideologies.

The purpose of this "footnote" is to underscore that the following Conservative, Liberal, and Radical paradigms are generalized representations of three long-recognized schools of ideological outlook. The reader is warned that they are not easily short-handed as Left or Right nor should any of our paradigms be presumed to advocate on behalf of specific "social values."

The Conservative Paradigm

What is usually labeled the Conservative position in economic thought and policy making was not always conservative. Conservative ideas may be traced to quite radical origins. The forebears of modern Conservative thought—among them England's Adam Smith (1723–1790)—were not interested in conserving the economic order they knew but in destroying it. In 1776, when Smith wrote his classic *Wealth of Nations*, England was organized under a more or less closed economic system of monopoly rights, trade restriction, and constant government interference with the marketplace and individuals' business and private affairs. This system, known as mercantilism, had been dominant in England and, with slight variations, elsewhere on the Continent for more than 250 years.

Adam Smith's Legacy

Smith's remedy was simple enough: Remove all restrictions on commercial and industrial activity and allow the market to work freely. The philosophical basis of Smith's argument rested on his beliefs that (1) all men had the natural right to obtain and protect their property; (2) all men were by nature materialistic; and (3) all men were rational and would seek, by their own reason, to maximize their material well-being. These individualistic tendencies in men would be tempered by competition in the marketplace. There, men would have to compromise with one another to gain any individual satisfaction whatsoever. The overall effect of these compromises would ultimately lead to national as well as individual satisfaction. Competition and self-interest would keep prices down and production high and rising, as well as stimulate product improvement, invention, and steady economic progress. For this to happen, of course, there would have to be a minimum of interference with the free market—no big government, no powerful unions, and no conspiring in trade. Smith's position and that of his contemporaries and followers was known as "classical liberalism." The Conservative label now applied to these views seems to have been affixed much later, when Smith's heirs found themselves acting in the defense of a status quo rather than opposing an older order.

Thus modern capitalist economic thought must trace its origins to Adam Smith. While this body of thought has been built on and modified over the past two hundred years, the hand of Adam Smith is evident in every conventional economics textbook. Common sense tells us, however, that a lot has changed since Smith's day. Today business is big. There are labor unions and big government to interfere with his balanced free market of equals. His optimistic view of a naturally growing and expanding system is now replaced by growth problems and by a frequent dose of pessimism in some glances toward the future. Nevertheless, modern Conservatives, among contemporary defenders of capitalism, still stand close to the ideals of Adam Smith.

Modern Conservative thought is anchored in two basic philosophic ideas that distinguish it from Liberal and Radical positions. First, the market system and the spirit of competition are central to proper social organization. Second, individual rights and freedoms must be unlimited and uninfringed.

Conservatives oppose any "unnatural" interference in the marketplace. In particular, the Conservative views the growth of big government in capitalist society as the greatest threat to economic progress. Milton Friedman, Nobel laureate and preeminent figure in the Conservative Chicago school, has argued that government has moved from being merely an instrumentality necessary to sustain the economic and social order to becoming an instrument of oppression. Friedman's prescription for what "ought to be" on the matter of government is clear:

> A government which maintained law and order, defined property rights, served as a means whereby we could modify property rights and other rules of the economic game, adjudicated disputes about the interpretation of the rules, enforced contracts, promoted competition, provided a monetary framework, engaged in activities to counter technical monopolies and to overcome neighborhood effects widely regarded as sufficiently important to justify government intervention, and which supplemented private charity and the private family in protecting the irresponsible, whether madman or child—such a government would clearly have important functions to perform. The consistent liberal is not an anarchist.*

The antigovernmental position of Conservatives in fact goes further than merely pointing out the dangers to individual freedom. To Conservatives the growth of big government itself causes or worsens economic problems. For instance, the growth of elaborate government policies to improve the conditions of labor, such as minimum-wage laws and Social Security protection, are seen as actually harming labor in general. A wage higher than that determined by the market will provide greater income for some workers, but, the Conservative argument runs, it will reduce the total demand for labor, and thus dump many workers into unemployment. As this example indicates, the Conservative assault on big government is seen not simply as a moral or ethical question but also in terms of alleged economic effects.

Another unifying feature of the representative Conservative argument is its emphasis on individualism and individual freedom. To be sure, there are those in the Conservative tradition who pay only lip service to this view, but for true Conservatives it is the centerpiece of their logic. As Friedman has expressed it:

> We take freedom of the individual . . . as the ultimate goal in judging social arrangements. . . . In a society freedom has nothing to say about what an individual does with his freedom; it is not an all-embracing ethic.

---

*Milton Friedman, *Capitalism and Freedom* (Chicago: University of Chicago Press, 1962), 34.

> Indeed, a major aim of the liberal [here meaning Conservative as we use the term] is to leave the ethical problem for the individual to wrestle with.*

Modern Conservatives as a group exhibit a wide range of special biases. Not all are as articulate or logically consistent as Friedman's Chicago school. Many are identified more readily by what they oppose than by what they seem to be for. Big government, in both its microeconomic interferences and its macroeconomic policy making, is the most obvious common enemy, but virtually any institutionalized interference with individual choice is at least ceremonially opposed.

Some critics of the Conservative position are quick to point out that most modern-day Conservatives are not quite consistent on the question of individual freedom when they focus on big business. In fact, until comparatively recently, Conservatives usually did demand the end of business concentration. Like all concentrations of power, it was viewed as an infringement on individual rights. The Conservative Austrian economist Joseph Schumpeter argued that "Big Business is a half-way house on the road to Socialism." The American Conservative Henry C. Simons observed in the depressed 1930s that "the great enemy to democracy is monopoly." Accounting for the change to a more accommodating position on big business is not easy. Conservatives offer two basic reasons. First, big business and the so-called monopoly problem have been watched for a long period of time, and the threat of their power subverting freedom is seen as vastly overstated. Second, by far the larger problem is the rise of big government, which is cited as the greatest cause of business inefficiency and monopoly abuse. Another factor that seems implied in Conservative writing is the fear of communism and socialism. To direct an assault on the American business system, even if existing business concentration were a slight impediment to freedom, would lay that system open to direct Radical attack. How serious this supposed contradiction in Conservative logic really is remains a matter of debate among its critics.

The Recent Resurgence of Conservative Economic Ideas

In the United States, until the drab years of the Great Depression, what we now call "Conservative economics" *was* economics, period. Except

---

*Milton Friedman, *Capitalism and Freedom* (Chicago: University of Chicago Press, 1962), 12.

for an occasional voice challenging the dominant wisdom, usually to little effect, few economists, political leaders, or members of the public at large disagreed greatly with Adam Smith's emphasis on individual freedom and on a free market economic condition.

The Depression years, however, brought a strong reaction to this kind of political and economic thinking. Many—perhaps most—of the millions of Americans who were out of work in the 1930s and the millions more who hung on to their jobs by their teeth came to believe that a "free" economy was simply one in free fall. While most staunch Conservatives complained bitterly about the abandonment of market economics and the "creeping socialism" of Franklin Roosevelt's New Deal, they had few listeners. For thirty-two of the next forty-eight years after Roosevelt's election in 1932, the White House, and usually the Congress, was in Liberal Democratic hands. For Conservatives, however, perhaps the greater losses were in the universities, where the old free market "ideas" of Adam Smith and his disciples quickly fell out of style. In their place, a generation of professors espoused the virtues of the "New Economics" of John Maynard Keynes and the view that a capitalist economy requires government intervention to keep it from destroying itself.

Driven to the margins of academic and political influence by the 1970s, the Conservatives seemed in danger of joining the dinosaur and the dodo bird as an extinct species. However, by the late 1970s, in the aftermath of the Vietnam War and the Watergate scandal and in a period when nothing government did seemed able to control domestic inflation and unemployment problems, there developed a growing popular reaction against government in general. As more and more Americans came to believe that government economic and social interventions were the cause of the nation's maladies, the Conservative ideology took off again under its own power.

In 1980, the Conservative economic and political paradigm succeeded in recapturing the White House. Ronald Reagan became the first president since Herbert Hoover to come to office after a private sector career. There was no doubting Reagan's philosophical commitment to the principles of a free enterprise economy.

As might be expected, Conservatives found themselves facing a difficult situation. Implementing a free market policy was, of course, much easier to accomplish in theory than in the real world—especially in a world vastly more complex than that envisioned by Adam Smith.

Reaganomics, the popular catchword for the new brand of Conservative economics, was quickly and sorely tested as the economy slipped into a deep recession in late 1981. To both friendly and hostile critics, Conservatives responded that quick solutions were not possible since the economic debris of a half century needed to be swept aside before the economy could be reconstructed. Despite the fact that Reaganomics proved to be somewhat less than an unqualified success (indeed, a good many Conservatives would now call it a failure), the Reagan years were a time of moderate but sustained economic boom—the second longest peacetime boom in American history. Despite some dark clouds—the near tripling of the federal debt, a worsening international trade situation, and a precipitous stock market collapse in 1987—the Reagan-Bush 1980s remained, in economic terms, a comparatively bright period in American economic history. Meanwhile, the collapse of communism in Eastern Europe and the Soviet Union and the Soviet bloc's shift toward a more open economic and political system in the last years of the decade could only be counted as frosting on Conservatives' ideological cake. As America approached the end of the century, Conservatives basked in the sunlight of success. Important for our study is the fact that a wide range of Conservative economic ideas and political perspectives that had been shunned in serious academic debates for over forty years have again made their way back into economics textbooks.

Indeed, the rise and refurbishing of market-based economic theory— and not simply in the United States—in the last decade or two of the twentieth century is one of the most important recent developments in economics. For today's young reader, who probably believes that market-based doctrine *is* economics, it may be difficult to believe that Conservative thinking in both economic theory and policy making was, not so many years ago, without much influence in the economics profession. That fact is a good one to keep in mind. It illustrates something that is often overlooked: The prevailing ideological mood, what we might call the conventional wisdom, is ever subject to change and reevaluation.

The Liberal Paradigm

According to a national poll, Americans tend to associate the term *Liberal* with big government, Franklin Roosevelt, labor unions, and welfare. Time was, not too long ago, when Liberal stood not just as a proud appellation but seemed to characterize the natural drift of the whole country. At the height of his popularity and before the Vietnam War toppled his administration, Lyndon Johnson, speaking of the new Liberal consensus, observed:

> After years of ideological controversy, we have grown used to the new relationship between government, households, business, labor and agriculture. The tired slogans that made constructive discourse difficult have lost their meaning for most Americans. It has become abundantly clear that our society wants neither to turn backward the clock of history nor to discuss the present problems in a doctrinaire or partisan spirit.*

Although what we will identify as the Liberal position in American economic thought probably still is alive and well in the teaching and practice of economic reasoning (as we shall see, even some Conservatives have adopted elements of the Liberal analysis), the Liberal argument is undergoing considerable changes. These changes, however, are more cosmetic than basic, and the central contours of Liberal belief are still visible.

The Interventionist Faith

Whereas Conservatives and Radicals are comparatively easily identified by a representative position, Liberals are more difficult to identify. In terms of public policy positions, the Liberal spectrum ranges all the way from those favoring a very moderate level of government intervention to those advocating broad government planning of the economy.

Despite the great distance between the defining poles of Liberal thought, several basic points can be stated as unique to the Liberal paradigm. Like their Conservative counterparts, Liberals are defenders of the principle of private property and the business system. These, however, are not categorical rights, as we observed in the Conservative case. Individual claims to property or the ability to act freely in the marketplace are subject to the second Liberal principle—that social welfare and the maintenance of the entire economy supersede individual interest. In a vicious condemnation of what we would presently call the Conservative position, John Maynard Keynes directly

---

*The Economic Report of the President, 1965 (Washington, DC: U.S. Government Printing Office, 1965), 39.

assaulted the philosophy that set the individual over society. Keynes argued:

> It is not true that individuals possess a proscriptive "natural liberty" in their economic activities. There is no "compact" conferring perpetual rights on those who Have or on those who Acquire. The world is not so governed from above that private and social interest always coincide. It is not a correct deduction from the Principles of Economics that enlightened self-interest always operates in the public interest. Nor is it true that self-interest generally is enlightened; more often individuals acting separately to promote their own ends are too ignorant or too weak to attain even these. Experience does not show that individuals, when they make up a social unit, are always less clear-sighted than when they act separately.*

To the Liberal, then, government intervention in, and occasional direct regulation of, aspects of the national economy is neither a violation of principle nor an abridgement of "natural economic law." The benefits to the whole society from intervention simply outweigh any "natural right" claims. The forms of intervention may vary, but their pragmatic purpose is obvious—to tinker and manipulate in order to produce greater social benefits.

Government intervention in the economy dates from the very beginnings of the nation, but the Progressives of the early twentieth century were the first to successfully urge an extensive and systematic elaboration of governmental economic powers. In response to the excesses of giant enterprises in the era of the robber barons, the Progressives followed a number of paths in the period from 1900 to 1920. One was the regulation of monopoly power, to be accomplished either through antitrust prosecutions to restore competition or through the use of independent regulatory commissions in cases where a "break them up" policy was undesirable (for instance, railroads and other firms possessing *public utility* characteristics). A second was *indirect* business regulation, effected by such Progressive developments as legalization of unions, the passage of social legislation at both the federal and state levels, tax reforms, and controls over production (for example, laws against food

---

*John M. Keynes, "The End of Laissez Faire," in *Essays of Persuasion* (New York: Norton, 1963), 68.

adulteration)—all of which circumvented the power of business and subjected it to the public interest.

Although the legislation and leadership of the administrations of Theodore Roosevelt, William Howard Taft, and Woodrow Wilson went a long way in moderating the old laissez-faire ideology of the previous era, actual interference in business affairs remained slight until the Great Depression. By 1933 perhaps as many as one out of every three Americans was out of work (the official figures said 25 percent), business failures were common, and the specter of total financial and industrial collapse hung heavy over the whole country. In the bread lines and shanty towns known as "Hoovervilles" as well as on Main Street, there were serious mutterings that the American business system had failed. Business leaders, who had always enjoyed hero status in the history books and even among ordinary citizens, had become pariahs. Enter at this point Franklin Roosevelt, the New Deal, and the modern formulation of Liberal government-business policies. Despite violent attacks on him from the Conservative media, Roosevelt pragmatically abandoned his own conservative roots and, in a bewildering series of legislative enactments and presidential decrees, laid the foundation of public interest criteria for government regulation of the marketplace. *Whatever might work was tried.* The National Recovery Administration (NRA) encouraged industry cartels and price setting. The Tennessee Valley Authority (TVA) was an attempt at publicly owned enterprise. At the Justice Department, Attorney General Thurman Arnold initiated more antitrust actions than all of his predecessors combined. And a mass of "alphabet agencies" was created to deal with this or that aspect of the Depression.

Intervention to protect labor and extensions of social welfare provisions were not enough to end the Depression. It was the massive spending for World War II that finally restored prosperity. With this prosperity came the steady influence of Keynes, who had argued in the 1930s that only through government fiscal and monetary efforts to keep up the demand for goods and services could prosperity be reached and maintained. Keynes's arguments for government policies to maintain high levels of investment and hence employment and consumer demand became Liberal dogma. To be a Liberal was to be a Keynesian, and vice versa.

Alvin Hansen, Keynes's first and one of his foremost proponents in the United States, could scarcely hide his glee in 1957 as he described the wedding of Liberal Keynesian policies with the older government interventionist position this way:

> Within the last few decades the role of the economist has profoundly changed. And why? The reason is that economics has become operational. It has become operational because we have at long last developed a mixed public-private economy. This society is committed to the welfare state and full employment. This government is firmly in the driver's seat. In such a world, practical policy problems became grist for the mill of economic analysis. Keynes, more than any other economist of our time, has helped to rescue economics from the negative position to which it had fallen to become once again a science of the Wealth of Nations and the art of Political Economy.*

Despite the Liberal propensity for tinkering—either through selected market intervention or through macro policy action—most Liberals, like Conservatives, still rely on traditional supply-and-demand analysis to explain prices and market performance. Their differences with Conservatives on the functioning of the markets, determination of output, pricing, and so forth lie not so much in describing what is happening as in evaluating how to respond to what is happening. For instance, there is little theoretical difference between Conservatives and Liberals on how prices are determined under monopolistic conditions. However, to the Conservative, the market itself is the best regulator and preventive of monopoly abuse. To the Liberal, monopoly demands government intervention.

Varieties of Liberal Belief

As noted before, the Liberal dogma covers a wide spectrum of opinion. Moreover, the Liberal position has shifted somewhat in response to the economic disappointments of the 1970s and certain successes of the Reagan years.

On the extreme left wing of the Liberal spectrum, economists such as Robert Heilbroner and John Kenneth Galbraith have long argued that capitalism as the self-regulating system analyzed in conventional economic theory simply does not exist. Heilbroner contends: "The persis-

---

*Alvin H. Hansen, *The American Economy* (New York: McGraw-Hill, 1957), 175.

tent breakdowns of the capitalist economy, whatever their immediate precipitating factors, can all be traced to a single underlying cause. This is the anarchic or planless character of capitalist production."* For a time, this critical defect led Heilbroner to flirt with central planning as the only possible cure. However, he eventually backed away from this position, holding instead that capitalism plus government regulation to provide periodic corrections has proved to be more durable than central planning efforts.

To the left-leaning and always iconoclastic John Kenneth Galbraith, who sees problems of technology rather than profit dominating the giant corporation, a more rational atmosphere for decision making must be created. In brief, the modern firm demands a high order of internal and external planning of output, prices, and capital. The interests of the firm and state become fused in this planning process, and the expanded role of Liberal government in the whole economy and society becomes obvious. While Galbraith has in the past maintained that he was a socialist, the Liberal outcome of his program is obvious in that he (1) never explicitly takes up the expropriation of private property, and (2) still accepts a precarious social balance between public and private interest.

Although Galbraith's Liberalism leads to an economy heavily reliant on planning, most Liberals stop well before this point. Having rejected the logic of self-regulating markets and accepted the realities of giant business enterprise, Liberals unashamedly admit to being pragmatic tinkerers—ever adjusting and interfering with business decision making in an effort to assert the changing public interest. Yet all this must be done while still respecting basic property rights and due process. Under these arrangements, business regulation amounts to a protection of business itself as well as the equal protection of other interest groups in pluralist American society.

In the not-too-distant past, business itself adapted to and embraced this position. Whereas certain government actions might be opposed, the philosophy of government intervention in the economy was not necessarily seen as antibusiness. The frequent Conservative depiction of most Liberals as being opposed to the business system does not withstand the empirical test. For instance, in 1964 Henry Ford II organized a

---

*Robert Heilbroner, *The Limits of American Capitalism* (New York: Harper and Row, 1966), 88.

highly successful committee of business leaders for the Liberal Lyndon Johnson, while Conservative Barry Goldwater, with Friedman as his adviser, gained little or no support from big business. However, the extent of government regulation soon reached a level that was wholly unacceptable to the private sector. In the late 1960s and early 1970s, a blizzard of environmental, job safety, consumer protection, and energy regulations blew out of Washington. Added to what was already on the ground, the new legislative snowfall seemed to many observers at the end of the 1970s about to bring American business to a standstill. Many who a decade before frankly feared the economic freedom of the Conservative vision now embraced that position.

The distress of economic *stagflation* in the 1970s (lower growth, rising unemployment, *and* price inflation), for which the Liberals seemed to have no programmatic cures, along with a growing popular sentiment against big government in general, drove Liberals from positions of political influence. Even within universities, the Liberal consensus began to collapse, with some former Liberal theorists deserting to the Conservative camp and most others adopting a lower profile in their teaching, writing, and research. Yet by the end of the 1980s, most of the analytical and policy positions associated with Liberal economic reasoning still survived—a bit subdued from the high-flying days of Kennedy's New Frontier and Johnson's Great Society but distinguishable nonetheless. Among the more reform-minded Liberal reasoners, the old economic agenda items—income distribution, discrimination, the environment, consumer protection, monopoly abuse, labor unions, structural shifts in the economy and their resulting dislocations—remained vital concerns in any policy-making effort. However, Liberal hopes for a fairly swift and sweeping resolution of these problems had diminished greatly from the expectations of the 1960s and early 1970s. The new realities of a slow-growth economy, massive federal deficits, reduced American competitiveness in world markets, and costly entitlement programs put serious constraints on even a visionary reformer's dedication to interventionism. But this commitment had not been extinguished. When the Eastern European communist states toppled like dominoes and the long-time cold war confrontation with the Soviet Union seemed to move steadily toward a peaceful end, there was brave talk among Liberals of the prospects for a "peace dividend." The ending of the cold war was envisioned as freeing up vast sums for favored social agenda items that had long been shelved.

Meanwhile, in the business community, the old propensity to enlist government on the side of improving the stability of domestic markets was given new life in the face of rising foreign competition, the decline of certain basic industries, and the double frights provided by Black Monday (the sudden collapse of the stock market on October 19, 1987) and the savings-and-loan industry crisis. In particular, the last two events seemed to show that too much market freedom might not be as desirable as it sounded.

The present-day ambivalence of Liberals on the degree and type of intervention will be evident in our survey of economic issues in this book; nevertheless, this tendency should not be misunderstood. Specific Liberal approaches to problem solving may be debatable, but the essence of Liberal economics remains unchanged: *The capitalist economy simply requires pragmatic adjustment from time to time to maintain overall balance and to protect particular elements in the society.*

The Radical Paradigm

For most readers, specification of a Radical paradigm will seem to be a difficult and unfamiliar exercise. The identifications of Right and Left, or Conservative and Liberal, are used nightly on the television news and talk shows, and presumably these labels have self-evident political meaning to most viewers. The Radical label is not so well known, nor is it used very much by the media. For the most part, Americans are generally uninformed about the content and objectives of a Radical social outlook. Yet in a variation on the old adage about familiarity breeding contempt, we find also that ignorance breeds contempt, at least with regard to ideological matters. Quite simply, most Americans—even if they know little about a Radical ideological outlook—believe it to be essentially wrongheaded and, at bottom, un-American. Nevertheless, there is a Radical tradition in American economic thought, and it needs to be understood.

The principal litmus test for accepting the Radical position requires the rejection of production-for-profit capitalism as an economic system —both the free market capitalism of Conservatives and the regulated capitalism of Liberals. Such a minimum membership standard, needless to say, leads to the lumping of a large number of very different anticapitalist critiques into the Radical category. Nonetheless, there is an important shared outlook among true Radicals. The essence of this perspective is nicely illustrated by a comment made some years ago by Tony Benn, a political and ideological leader of the British Labour Party. Queried by an interviewer in 1992 as to what was going to happen to socialists around the world now that the Marxist-socialist regime in the Soviet Union had collapsed, Benn offered a pregnant response. "The real struggle," Benn observed, "was never between capitalism and socialism. It was and is between capitalism and democracy."

In Benn's remark lies the common core of contemporary Radical thought: Radicals espouse a social and economic order in which institutions are expected to respond to people's needs and people are to be empowered politically and economically so as to ensure democratic outcomes.

At such a general level of articulation, Radical ideology may appear deceptively benign. Who, after all, can be opposed to "empowering people?" However, the economic and political empowerment of people quickly takes on a more serious and, to some, more threatening meaning when the Radical analysis is examined in greater detail. As the Radical tradition understands the economic and social dynamic of societies, power is intricately connected to the ownership of property: Whoever owns or controls the use of a society's things invariably possesses political and economic power commensurate with such ownership or control. In capitalism, ownership of things, particularly the things (capital) that produce other things, is disproportionately held in the hands of a comparative few. These owners of the means of production are seen by Radicals as exercising excessive influence for their own personal (or class) gain in the society's decisions about what will be produced, how that output will be produced, and who will share in this output. In our Radical paradigm, empowerment necessarily leads to limiting private and individual economic power and to increasing the social ownership and control of the things within a society. For most readers, a word should spring to mind: *socialism.*

Socialism as a political, social, even religious outlook probably predates the rise of capitalism. And the term *socialism* is an umbrella that can cover a multitude of ideological tendencies. Utopian communitarians, Christian socialists, anarchists, Marxists, syndicalists, communists, guild socialists, and many other ideological variants can crowd under the socialist umbrella. The common thread to membership in any socialist tradition is acceptance of the advocacy for the social or community ownership of all, or most, of the means of production and for a societally determined standard for the distribution of the output of the society.

While it is pretty clear that all socialists would qualify as Radicals, it is by no means true that all Radicals see themselves as socialists. Partly, this is the case because socialism has long been and certainly remains a dirty word among most Americans—an ideological outlook that directly challenges the nation's historical proclivity to explain social and economic life in largely individualist terms. Partly, it reflects the fact that the term socialism is simply too big an umbrella and therefore includes a lot of ideological outlooks that, once you get past a few basic theoretical similarities, do not agree on important issues of specific programs and goals.

Moreover, many American Radicals are not political activists at all. For them, commitment to a Radical perspective is mostly an intellectual and analytical exercise aimed at attacking and revealing the deficiencies of conventional Conservative and Liberal thought. Their purpose is not to build an alternative political party, such as socialism has tended to become, but to supply an alternative critical analysis that Americans might act upon within the constraints of the existing political order. In any case, in specifying a Radical paradigm, it is wise to remember that membership includes many different marchers not necessarily listening to the same drummer, or at least not hearing the same beat even if there is a single drummer. But then again, the same can be said for Conservative and Liberal paradigms.

However, as a practical matter, an extended explanation of the Radical paradigm must be assigned an ideological starting point. And most, but surely not all, American Radicals would admit their intellectual debt to Karl Marx and his nineteenth-century critique of capitalism.

The Marxist Heritage

Since the Marxist critique is likely to be less familiar to many readers than the basic arguments of Conservatives or Liberals, it is necessary to be somewhat more detailed in specifying the Radical position. As will be quickly apparent, the Radical worldview rests on greatly different assumptions about the economic and social order than those of the Conservatives and Liberals.

According to Marx's view, the value of a commodity reflects the real labor time necessary to produce it. However, under capitalism workers lack control of their labor, selling it as they must to capitalists. The workers receive only a fraction of the value they create—according to Marx, only an amount sufficient in the long run to permit subsistence. The rest of the value—what Marx calls *surplus value*—is retained by capitalists as the source of their profits and for the accumulation of capital that will increase both future production and future profit. As the appropriation of surplus value proceeds, with the steady transference of living labor into capital (what Marx called *dead labor*), capitalists face an emerging crisis. With more and more of their production costs reflecting their growing dependence on capital (machines) and with surplus labor value their only source of profit, capitalists are confronted with the reality of not being able to expand surplus appropriation. Unless they are able to increase their exploitation of labor—getting more output for the same, or less, wages paid—they face a falling rate of profit on their growing capital investment. Worse still, with workers' relatively falling wages and capitalists' relatively increasing capacity to produce, there is a growing tendency for the entire capitalist system to produce more goods than it can in fact sell.

These trends set certain systemic tendencies in motion. Out of the chaos of capitalist competitive struggles for profits in a limited market there develops a drive toward *concentration and centralization*. In other words, the size of businesses grows and the number of enterprises shrinks. However, the problems of the falling rate of profit and chronic overproduction create violent fluctuations in the business cycle. Each depression points ever more clearly toward capitalist economic collapse. Meanwhile, among the increasingly impoverished workers, there is a steady growth of a *reserve army of the unemployed*—workers who are now unemployable as production decreases. Simultaneously, increasing misery generates class consciousness and revolutionary activity among the working class. As the economic disintegration of capitalist institutions worsens, the subjective consciousness of workers grows to the point where they successfully overthrow the capitalist system. In the new society, the workers themselves take control of the production process, and accumulation for the interest of a narrow capitalist class ceases.

The Modern Restatement of Marx

Of necessity, the modern Radical's view of the world must lack the finality of Marx's predictions. Quite simply, the capitalist system has

not self-destructed and, in fact, in a good many respects is stronger
and more aggressive than it was in Marx's day. Although the present-
day Radical may still agree with Marx's long-run predictions about
the ultimate self-destructiveness of the capitalist order, the fact is that
Radicals must deal with the world as it is. While the broad categories
of Marx's analysis are retained generally, Radical thought must focus
on real-world, current conditions of capitalist society and present an
analysis that goes beyond merely asserting the Marxist scenario for
capitalist collapse. Useful economic analysis must be offered in ex-
amining contemporary problems.

The beginning point for modern Radical critiques, as it was also for
Marx over a hundred years ago, is the unquenchable capitalist thirst
for profits. This central organizing objective of all capitalist systems
determines everything else within those systems. The Radical analysis
begins with a simple proposition about how capitalists understand
market activity:

> Total sales = total cost of materials and machinery used up in production
> + total wages and salaries paid + (– in the case of losses) total profits

Such a general view of sales, costs, and profits is, thus far, perfectly
consistent with traditional accounting concepts acceptable to any Conservative or Liberal. However, the Radical's analytic mission becomes
clearer when the proposition is reformulated:

> Total profits = total sales – total cost of materials and machinery used up
> in production – total wages and salaries paid

It now becomes evident that increasing profits depends on three general conditions: (1) that sales rise, *ceteris paribus* (all things being equal);
(2) that production costs (composed of wage costs and material and
machinery costs) decline, *ceteris paribus;* or (3) that sales increases at
least exceed production cost increases. The capitalist, according to the
Radical argument, is not simply interested in total profits but also in the
rate of profit, or the ratio of profits to the amount of capital the capitalist
has invested.

With capitalist eyes focused on raising profits or raising profit rates,
it becomes clear to Radicals which individual economic policies and
strategies will be advanced by capitalists: *Every effort will be made to*

keep costs low, such as reducing wage rates, speeding up the production line, introducing so-called labor-saving machines, seeking cheaper (often foreign) sources of labor and materials, and minimizing outlays for waste treatment and environmental maintenance. At the same time, *efforts will be made to keep prices high,* especially through the development of monopolistic price-making power on both a national and an international scale. In all of these activities, capitalists will make every effort to use government economic intervention to their own advantage—both in domestic markets and in expanding capitalist hegemony into the world.

However, taking the system as a whole, the effort of individual capitalists—either on their own or aided by government—to expand profit produces a crisis in obtaining profits. For instance, the capitalist goals of keeping wages low and prices high must lead to situations where workers as consumers simply cannot clear the market of available goods. Accordingly, the aggregate economy deteriorates into periodic recession or depression, with rising unemployment among workers and falling profits for capitalists. With capitalist support, a variety of government monetary and fiscal efforts may be employed to offset these ups and downs in the capitalist business cycle—in particular to improve the profit and profit rate of capitalist enterprises. However, so-called mixed capitalism (a mixture of private sector and government planning of the economy) cannot overcome the fundamental contradictions of a dominantly private, production-for-profit economy. And, of course, with the expansion of capitalism throughout most of the world, the capitalist crisis takes on international proportions. Quite as Marx predicted, the general economic crises deepen and occur more frequently. The search for profit becomes more frantic and more destructive to the lives of ever greater numbers of people living under capitalist hegemony throughout the world.

From the Radical point of view, periodic crisis in capitalism is not the result of excessive tinkering with the market system, as Conservatives claim; nor will the tendency toward crisis be contained by Liberal interventionism. *Periodic and deepening crisis* is *capitalism.*

Radical analysis is, of course, more penetrating than this short résumé can indicate. One further point that should be examined briefly is Marx's view of the relationship between a society's organization for production and its social relations. To Marx, capitalism was more than an economic system. Private values, religion, the family, the educational system, and political structures were all shaped by capitalist class domination and by the goal of production for private profit. It is important to recognize this tenet in any discussion of how Marxists—or Radicals with a Marxist orientation—approach contemporary social and economic problems. Marxists do not separate economics from politics or private belief. For instance, racism cannot be abstracted to the level of an ethical question. Its roots are seen in the capitalist production process. Nor is the state ever viewed as a neutrality able to act without class bias. Bourgeois democracy as we know it is seen simply as a mask for class domination.

Marx, in his early writings before his great work, *Capital,* had emphasized the "qualitative" exploitation of capitalism. Modern Radicals have revitalized this early Marx in their "quality of life" assaults on the present order. In these they emphasize the problems of worker alienation, commodity fetishism, and the wasteful and useless production of modern capitalism. The human or social problems of modern life are seen as rooted in the way the whole society is geared to produce more and more profits.

In addition to their Marxist heritage, modern Radicals derive much of their impulse from what they see as the apparent failure of Liberalism. Liberal promises to pursue policies of general social improvement are perceived as actions to protect only *some* interest groups. In general, those benefiting under Liberal arrangements are those who have always gained. The corporation is not controlled. It is more powerful than ever. Rule by elites has not ended, nor have the elites changed. Moreover, the national goals of the Liberal ethic—to improve our overall national well-being—stimulated the exploitation of poor nations, continued the cold war, and increased the militarization of the economy.

The Question of Relevance

Quite obviously, the Marxist prediction of capitalism's final collapse has not yet come to pass. In fact, Radicals—particularly those very closely associated with the Marxist tradition—are increasingly obliged to account for what many non-Radicals see as a historical turning away from all collectivist political economic alternatives with the rise of market economies in previously socialist states. These trends, along with certain internal analytical problems of Marxist analysis, are quite sufficient for most non-Radicals to consign the whole Radical paradigm to the garbage heap of worthless, worn-out ideas.

A thoughtful observer may question whether this is an entirely enlight-ened conclusion to reach. First, the tendency to lump Marxism and real-world communist systems together as one and the same, while long a habit in the noncommunist as well as the communist world, rests on a grossly inaccurate understanding of Marx's philosophy. Second, Marxism—at least as American Radical scholars have developed and used it—is more a way of looking at how our economy works than a prophecy of things to come. It is the technique of analysis rather than the truth of Marx's specific analysis that counts.

A third point might also be worth considering. Freed of the Soviet millstone, Radical critiques, which were easily evaded during the cold war epoch, might take on more meaning and appeal. Radicals no longer have to explain away the Soviet errors of authoritarian politics, decrepit bureaucracies, and failed planning before putting forth their own critique of contemporary capitalism and their own democratic-socialist programs. Moreover, and of increasing impor-tance to the relevance of Radical arguments, the post-Soviet world economy has yet to show the robustness that the victors of the cold war might have expected. Standing unchallenged in the world, capi-talism and variants of capitalism may loom as larger targets for Radi-cal attack than is generally appreciated. Consequently, it may be just a bit early to count out the Radical paradigm, as non-Radicals are presently inclined to do.

As noted before, not all Radicals subscribe to all Marxist doctrine, but Marxism in one form or another remains the central element of the Radical challenge. Marx's fundamental contention that the system of private production must be changed remains the badge of membership in the Radical ranks. This sets Radicals apart from mainstream Conser-vative and Liberal economists.

Critics of the Radical position usually point out that Radical analyses are hopelessly negativistic. Radicals, they say, describe the problems of capitalism without offering a solution other than the end of the whole system. While there is much truth to this charge, we shall see in the following sections that indeed some solutions are offered. But even if their program is vague, Radicals would argue that their greatest contri-bution is in revealing the truth of the capitalist system.

Despite lessened political influence, modern Radical economic thought still looms as a logically important alternative to the more broadly supported Conservative and Liberal paradigms. The force of an idea is not dependent on the number of true believers. Were that the case, Conservative economic doctrine would have disappeared thirty years ago.

Applying the Analysis to the Issues

We have identified the three representative paradigms; now we will put them to use. The following selected issues by no means exhaust the economic and political crises troubling the nation; nevertheless, they provide a good-sized sampling of the social agenda confronting us. The issues presented here were selected because of their immediacy and representativeness in illustrating the diverse ideological approaches of Conservative, Liberal, and Radical economic analyses.

In each of the following issues, the representative paradigms are presented in a *first-person advocacy approach.* The reader might do well to regard the arguments like those in a debate. As in a debate, one should be careful to distinguish between substantive differences and mere logical or debating strategies. Thus some points may be quite convincing, whereas others seem shallow. However, the reader should remember that, shallow or profound, these are representative political economic arguments advanced by various economic schools.

The sequence in presenting the paradigms is consistent throughout the text: first Conservative, then Liberal, then Radical. In terms of the logical and historical development of contemporary economic ideologies, this sequence is most sensible; however, it certainly is not necessary to read the arguments in this order. Each one stands by itself. Nor is any ideological position intentionally set out as a straw man in any debate.

Readers should look at each position critically. They should test their own familiarity with economic concepts and their common sense against what they read in any representative case. Finally, of course, as students of economics and as citizens, they must make their own decisions. They determine who, if anyone, is the winner of the debate.

Because of space limitations, the representative arguments are brief, and some important ideas have been boiled down to a very few sentences. Also, within each of the three major positions there is a wide range of arguments, which may sometimes be at variance with one another. Conservatives, Liberals, and Radicals disagree among themselves on specific analyses and programs. For the sake of simplicity, we have chosen not to emphasize these differences but arbitrarily (although after much thought) to select the most representative arguments. Each paradigm's discussion of an issue presents a critique of present public policy and, usually, a specific program proposal.

In all of the arguments, the factual and empirical evidence offered has been checked for accuracy. It is instructive in itself that, given the nature of economic facts, they can be marshaled to prove a great variety of different ideological positions. Different or even similar evidence supports different truths, depending on the truth we wish to *prove*.

Problems in the Marketplace

Part II focuses on issues generally accepted by economists as *microeconomic* in their analysis. Microeconomics examines specific economic units—households, firms, industries, labor groups—and the behavior of these individual units.

The focal point of formal microeconomic analysis since its nineteenth-century origins has been the market. Accordingly, Part II looks at selected problems in the marketplace. Topics include problems of agricultural supply and demand, consumer market behavior, environmental economics, firm size, government regulation, income distribution, and government finance. Each topic presents some important dimension of market performance; each has been selected for its representative qualities in developing a broadened understanding of microeconomic problems within the contemporary American economy.

Responding to Market Outcomes

Competition or Protection for American Agriculture?

Farmers should raise less corn and more Hell.
>—*Mary E. Lease, Kansas, 1890s*

We produce too much food in this country.
>—*Marty Strange, farmer advocacy group, 1982*

Because farmers are provided an incentive to make cropping decisions according to program rules rather than market signals, the [farm] programs reduce the responsiveness of U.S. agriculture to changes in world market conditions and reduce its international competitiveness.
>—Economic Report of the President, 1990

For eighteen years, the price of food has not kept up with the cost of farming.
>—*Don Taus, South Dakota farmer, 1998*

The Problem

The teaching of economic reasoning usually begins with a general examination of the market model and, more particularly, with a consideration of
how the market determines production, pricing, and resource allocation
under conditions of pure competition. Such an introduction to economics
presents the beginner almost immediately with a confusing irony. On one
hand, markets for agricultural goods would seem to be especially appropriate for illustrating the general conditions of competition because they are
dominated by many small producers selling virtually identical products to a
very broad range of consumers. Thus, agriculture should be a marvelously
useful example of the market forces of supply and demand at work, and
introductory textbooks invariably use wheat, corn, or some other farm
product when they begin constructing simple analytical models.

In the real world, on the other hand, agricultural markets illustrate a quite
contrary tendency. Here we do not find competition and free-flowing market forces, but rather some of the most elaborate efforts ever devised to
insulate an industry from the market and to employ government intervention to promote private objectives. Agricultural output and pricing decisions
actually are directly affected by a federal price support program that has been
in place in one form or another for sixty years. Meanwhile, a variety of government agencies provide emergency aid of staggering proportions. In fact,
annual payments of emergency loans and other funds in excess of $30 bil-
lion or more per year were not uncommon a decade ago, as net farm income
(in real dollars) hovered near the levels of the Great Depression.

The condition of American agriculture has not always been one of unre-
lenting crisis, but the farm problem was around, on and off again, for most of
the twentieth century. The rhythm of farm fortune and misfortune has been
like this: First, World War I created an exceptional demand for American farm
products to feed soldiers and starving European civilians. With rising prices
resulting, farmers increased their output, but in the 1920s and 1930s, after
production increased, foreign demand for American farm products declined
and prices plummeted. The deepening depression after 1930 soon transformed
the growing agricultural crisis into a full-blown catastrophe. With the coming
of the New Deal in 1933, the federal government introduced numerous market interventions aimed at artificially raising or maintaining prices. These interventions included establishing a price support system in which government
guaranteed paying farmers the difference between the market price and an
established *parity* (fair) *price* for their crops, as well as efforts to hold up the price

Figure 1.1 **Net Income of Farm Operators from Farming, 1970–2002**

Billions of dollars

Year

Current dollars

Constant (1982–84) dollars

Source: Data from *Economic Report of the President* (Washington, DC: Government Printing Office, 2004).

of farm goods by paying farmers for taking some of their land out of production. These actions laid the economic and political foundations for what was to become a long-term, if not actually permanent, government intervention in agricultural markets. World War II pumped up demand and farm prices, but peace again brought tumbling prices and reliance on government support programs. Several Russian grain deals in the 1970s returned good times for a few years; however, farmers were soon caught up in new problems—a few of which were of their own making. Figure 1.1 illustrates the roller coaster ride that American farm income has taken since 1970.

As farm exports rose in the mid-1970s and farm prices and income followed, American farmers developed a false sense of security. Planting "fencepost to fencepost" became common. Many farmers undertook considerable acquisitions of additional land and new equipment, swelling their mortgage and loan obligations. Farm debt tripled between 1973 and 1983. At first, few farmers paid much attention to the fact that interest rates on their new loans were high and rising during most of this period. The farm mood was upbeat, and many farmers thought they had finally escaped from the traditional boom-bust cycle of the agricultural economy.

But throughout the 1970s until bottom was hit in the 1980s, American farmers experienced a lot of bust and very little boom. First, inflation got in its licks, as the general price expansion of the late 1970s pushed up fuel, machinery, and borrowing costs. Unable to pass these costs on in the form of higher prices, because overseas agricultural production was increasing and the prices of foreign food products were falling, American farmers saw their profit margins and net incomes squeezed. Throughout the 1970s and into the 1980s, American farmers' overseas sales declined, and cheaper foreign agricultural goods began to penetrate domestic markets.

However, by the mid-1990s, even in the face of several years of bad weather that adversely affected American agriculture, the hard times seemed to be lifting. When a new, Republican-dominated Congress took its seat in 1994, it promised to "get government out of farming." Briefly, it looked as though the old government strategies of levying tariffs on imported goods, operating marketing boards, paying subsidies, setting output quotas, making payments for letting land lie idle, and much else that had become American farm policy suddenly would be washed away by congressional opponents of agricultural protection. But in the Federal Agriculture Improvement and Reform Act of 1996 (also known as the Freedom to Farm Act), the final phasing out of agricultural support and subsidy programs was not to take place until 2002. Scarcely two years after the act's passage, opposition was building among farmers and farm groups to the entire philosophy of the Federal Agriculture Improvement and Reform Act of 1996. Moreover, by 2001, federal farm subsidies paid to farmers still stood at about the same levels that existed before passage of this act. The 1996 statute was replaced by the Farm Security and Rural Investment Act of 2002, which marked a return to government supports, manipulation, and protectionism for American agriculture.

The debate over agricultural policy remains an important issue and a profoundly significant theoretical question, since it goes to the very foundation of American economic belief; namely, do free and competitive markets work, or do they need constant repair and support by means of government intervention? Exactly how divided economists are on this question becomes apparent when we look at the policy alternatives proposed by our three paradigms.

Synopsis

The Conservative position holds that the free operation of supply and demand is the correct and most effective determinant of agricultural prices. Liberals most frequently argue that an agricultural market left to itself is subject to wild cyclical fluctuation; thus a variety of government interventions are necessary to maintain reasonable order. Radicals see the American farm problem as a case of government being manipulated by agribusiness, with the result that government intervention has harmed both small farmers and ordinary consumers.

Anticipating the Arguments

- Why do Conservatives believe that most government efforts to help farmers by artificially raising crop prices actually hurt both farmers and consumers?
- What is the historical and economic foundation to the Liberal argument that farmers cannot depend on unregulated farm markets?
- Why do Radicals believe that most farmers have been losers under both regulated and unregulated agricultural production in the United States?

THE CONSERVATIVE ARGUMENT

Discussions of the American farm problem almost always begin with a mistaken identification of what the problem really is. Most agricultural observers, including many economists writing on farm issues, suggest that there is something inherently unstable about American agriculture. Somehow, agriculture is presented as proof that the market economy simply does not work, that the free market forces of supply and demand break down. Conservatives agree that there is indeed a farm problem; however, that problem begins and remains in Washington, D.C., not in the corn and wheat fields of the Midwest or the commodities markets in Chicago. In other words, the American farm problem is not the result of some basic failure of the market, but rather the failure of federal policy to allow the market forces to work.

Policy Failure in Times of Surplus

Although many politicians and some economists may believe and act to the contrary, supply and demand remain the only effective determinants of prices and resource allocation. Of course, it is possible to contrive desired prices and output through a manipulated agricultural policy, but regardless of short-run success, such policies must produce serious misallocations and costs in the long run.

For a considerable period of time, at least since World War I, most economists have seen the American farm problem as a matter of rising productivity with comparatively stable or modestly increasing demand. The result in the marketplace was a general and persistent downward pressure on farm prices. The economic options under such conditions were either to let prices fall to whatever level they might reach or to maintain prices artificially. Due largely to political pressure from the farm lobby in the depressed 1930s, the government devised a potpourri of farm programs to keep prices up and supposedly guarantee a living income to the American farmer. Tariffs were slapped on foreign farm products. Certain basic farm products were guaranteed a government-paid parity price well above the going market price. Bureaucrats worked out production controls and acreage allotments, with the curious economic aim of paying producers not to produce.

These tinkerings with the market forces of demand and supply, however, did not produce order in agricultural markets. Each intervention, regardless of its noble intentions, increased agricultural dependence on government price-setting efforts and, at the same time, heightened market instability. For their own part, farmers paid less and less attention to production signals from the marketplace and relied increasingly on the government to bail them out whenever farm income showed signs of falling. With the government establishing minimum price levels (using either parity price or target price mechanisms) and standing ready either to buy surplus production (before the 1970s) or, more recently, to provide loans secured by surplus output, there has been little incentive to pay attention to market forces. Except for two brief interludes—during World War II, when America virtually fed the world, and after the early Russian grain deals in the 1970s—farm prices and the income of most farmers have been held up only by government manipulation of crop prices.

The Price of Failure

The Cost to Consumers

The benefits accruing to the farm lobby from government intervention have only recently become recognized as costs to the general public. Americans have paid for government subsidies, tariffs, and production controls in two ways. First, the price of food in general has been higher than it would otherwise have been in a free agricultural market. For most Americans over most of the past sixty-five years, this higher price presented few problems. With the steady rise in American standards of living, the artificially higher food prices seemed quite tolerable, and as food expenditures declined as a share of total consumer purchases during the post–World War II years, the farm lobby met little resistance in its efforts to expand market intervention. Not until the inflationary 1970s did Americans show signs of balking at rising farm prices, and even then most of their anger was aimed at grocery chains and other middlemen.

Second, Americans, in a sense, must pay for their food *twice*. Consumers are also taxpayers, and as such they are obliged to shoulder the cost of expensive government subsidies—direct payments and low-cost loans—to farmers. Moreover, they have had to pay for the maintenance of an elaborate bureaucracy developed to administer the various farm programs. As with the higher farm product prices, this hidden second price was for a very long time ignored by most taxpayers, a cost buried in the federal budget. However, with pressure growing recently to reduce government spending and to reverse the growth of government debt, this previously concealed second charge for food became more obvious. By 2000, federal price support and other income programs for farmers were costing the average American family more than $365 per year—for an agricul-

tural program aimed in the first place at keeping tabletop food prices artificially high. The 2002 Farm Act is estimated to cost Americans $190
billion in taxes over ten years. Additionally, the provisions of the law are
expected to inflate food prices paid by consumers by $271 billion.*

Inability to Sell Overseas

Historically, American farm prices have closed off U.S. food products
from world markets. Due to climate, soil, technology, and agricultural
science, American agriculture has had an enormous advantage over the
rest of the world in food production. Programs aimed at keeping domestic prices relatively high frittered away this advantage, and the export
income it would have created. Precisely at a time when the United States
faced a worsening balance of international payments (after World War
II), the government pursued an agricultural program that denied the nation earnings it could have been making by exporting food.

The Russian grain deals of the mid-1970s brought a dramatic but brief
reversal in agricultural export habits. In 1972, the Russians negotiated the
purchase of 19 million metric tons of grain. For a number of years, Soviet
leadership had been yielding to consumer pressure to produce more meat
protein. Of necessity, this meant providing greater amounts of grain for
beef in feeding lots. When the 1971 and 1972 crops failed to reach expectations, the Soviet leaders decided not to slaughter their beef herds or tell
their people to eat potatoes and beets. They chose instead to buy U.S.
grain and to allow their "protein program" to continue.

To growers and sellers, the discovery of the Russian market was a
critical new direction for American agriculture, putting an end to the
long era of chronic excess production, depressed prices, and dependence on government subsidy programs. By selling the equivalent of
one-quarter of the 1972 crop, the Russian grain deal literally emptied American storage bins and grain elevators. This additional demand drove the prices of wheat from $1.70 per bushel in mid-1972
to $5.00 in 1973.

The trouble was, however, that commitment to free agricultural markets was unfamiliar, and when net farm income began to tumble in 1977

---

*Riedl, Brian M., *The Cost of America's Farm Subsidy Binge: An Average of $1
Million Per Farm*, Backgrounder #1510, December 10, 2001 (www.heritage.org/
Research/Agriculture/BG1510.cfm).

as the combined result of increases in production (a natural reaction to the increase in worldwide sales), a deepening worldwide recession, and worsening domestic inflation, farmers returned to their old habits. When the Food and Agricultural Act of 1977 was renewed, the farm lobby succeeded in setting target prices (the prices government would guarantee farmers through subsidies regardless of the going market prices) at about 25 percent higher than the existing world prices for most key crops. The free market experiment was over.

Insofar as government agricultural policy continues to aid farmers by artificially raising farm prices, farmers will be unable to exploit their efficiency and natural advantages in world food markets. Indeed, American farm prices are high enough to invite threats of excessive agricultural imports.

Maintaining Production Inefficiencies

Before taking up the question of production inefficiencies resulting from interventionist farm policies, we need first to square with reality the myth of the lonely and hardworking individual agriculturist. The myth of the independent family farm is deeply ingrained in American popular belief and Liberal political posturing, and is the foundation of American farm policy. The irony is, however, that the small family farm has ceased to be an important supplier of foodstuffs. Figure 1.2 tells the story very quickly.

The farm population has fallen to less than 2 percent of the total population (compare this to its 1950 level of 15 percent), while the number of farms has declined by more than half and average farm size has more than doubled over the same period. Figure 1.3 makes the point quite clearly: At present, 87 percent of the value of farm production is produced by just 18 percent of all operating farms. Moreover, about 1 percent of all operating farms produce 42 percent of our food production.

The myth of the disadvantaged, independent farmer is the basis for government subsidies—an effort to provide an income floor for the very poorest of farmers. The effect is to subsidize the least efficient farm producers at the very bottom of the agricultural ladder (two-thirds of government payments go to small farms that produce only one quarter of the nation's output) and very large farms that do not need it. This expensive agricultural welfare system has discouraged the exit of marginal agricultural producers who might better shift their resources to other productive pursuits. Worse still, subsidies paid to large and effi-

44

Figure 1.2 Changes in Farming, 1950–2002

Source: U.S. Bureau of the Census, *Statistical Abstract of the United States* (Washington, DC: Government Printing Office, 2003) and data from the U.S. Bureau of the Census.

Figure 1.3 **Shares of Total Farm Sales by Farm Size, 2002**

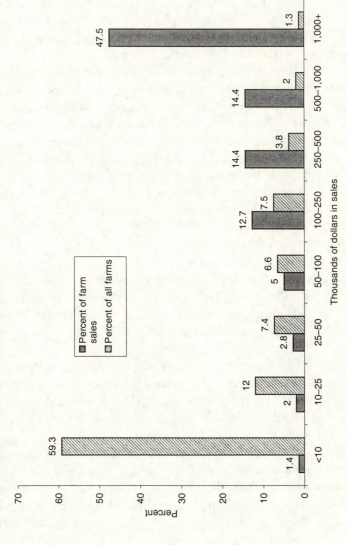

Source: U.S. Department of Agriculture, *2002 Census of Agriculture,* vol. 1.

cient farm producers act as restraints on improving their existing efficiency and productivity. Another argument against such subsidies is that farmers are not clearly the beneficiaries of agricultural supports. Rather, it is *owners* of farmland who experience the capitalization of price supports into the value of the finite amount of land available for farming. Meanwhile, governmental sponsorship of generous crop insurance provides farmers the preposterous incentive of allowing crops to fail on alternating years without serious financial penalty.

So long as we approach the farmer as if we are protecting a rare bird from extinction, we will not benefit from the practical forces of the marketplace. We will sustain at great economic cost farmers who should stop farming and, at the same time, hold back the application of business management methods and technological advances among the farm enterprises most capable of exploiting new techniques. We must recognize that farming is a business and, mythology notwithstanding, should be open to the forces of a production-for-profit economy, just like the manufacture of automobiles or personal computers.*

Toward a New Policy Direction

A Conservative program for dealing with the nation's chronic agricultural problem is easily stated: *Let markets work.* This means ending all subsidies, special loan arrangements, crop control programs, target pricing, and other arrangements aimed at setting selling prices above free market prices.

The Federal Agriculture Improvement and Reform Act of 1996 was on its way to restoring sanity to American agriculture. The phasing out of government pricing efforts by the year 2002 was intended to reduce agricultural prices and bring to an end the old and costly protectionist approach to American farming.

Falling agricultural prices (or at least a halt to their artificial rise) would have a number of salutary effects. First, it would be a direct benefit to American consumers. Second, it would expand American markets overseas. Lost revenues from lowered prices would be more than offset by expanded total sales. Third, the resulting emphasis on efficient

---

*Indeed, we should recognize the growing importance of business corporations in American agriculture. By the 1990s, 50,000 corporate farms, amounting to about 1 percent of all farms, produced more than one-fifth of farm output in the United States.

and innovative use of productive resources in agriculture would create a strong, self-sufficient, and highly productive agricultural sector where the market actually directs resource inputs.

To be sure, reliance on the market would not be without some adjustment problems. Critics would be quick to point out the effect of short-term cycles in agriculture on production and prices: This year's high prices cause next year's production to rise, increasing next year's supply faster than demand increases. The resultant lower prices lead to a reduction of supply in the next year and to a rise in prices, which in turn stimulate an increase in supply. According to many critics, this price instability perpetuates adverse effects alternately visited on consumers and then on farmers. The trouble with the argument is that no one has ever shown market-priced agricultural products to exhibit greater instability than most other goods priced according to market forces of supply and demand. In fact, demand for agricultural goods is much more stable over time than demand for steel, automobiles, or even personal computers. Moreover, a good deal of the volatility on the supply side is actually the result of government tinkering. There is a high probability that farm prices would fluctuate under a free market mechanism, but it is wrong to conclude that such fluctuations are undesirable. They are simply the market at work.

Regrettably, the Farm Security and Rural Investment Act of 2002 re-establishes the long tradition of agriculture's dependency upon government price rigging. The policy established by the 1996 Farm Act of phasing out subsidies and loans is reversed in favor of the continuation of fixed payments without regard to the crops planted or their prices. "Countercyclical payments" for specific crops to compensate for price declines are introduced. A system of "nonrecourse loans" obligates the Commodity Credit Corporation to accept agricultural commodities as payment for loans, effectively providing grants to farmers if commodity prices fall.

Because price fluctuations posed problems for farmers long accustomed to prices rigged by the government, American agriculture lobbied for a return to the security of government intervention. The less efficient will nonetheless find survival difficult, but the resumption of support programs prolongs the agony at considerable cost to consumers and taxpayers. On the other hand, efficient family farms and farm corporations are back to being deterred from applying the best production methods and determining output decisions on rational calculations of past *and* present market trends. Badly designed policy once again as-

Table 1.1

U.S. Agricultural Productivity, 1800–1950

Crop	1800	1880	1920	1950
Wheat				
yield/acre (bu)	15	13	14	17
labor hours/100 bu	373	152	87	28
Corn				
yield/acre (bu)	25	26	28	39
labor hours/100 bu	344	180	113	39
Cotton				
yield/acre (bu)	147	179	160	283
labor hours/bale	601	318	269	126

Source: U.S. Bureau of the Census, *Historical Statistics of the United States*, Series K 83–97 (Washington, DC: Government Printing Office, 1960).

sures that income will be redistributed in their favor despite the average income and net worth of farm households being much greater than that of nonfarm households. Nostalgia for preserving the family farm may have its virtues, but it cannot be trusted for efficient allocation of resources and optimal pricing of outputs.

THE LIBERAL ARGUMENT

Conservatives are quite right in stating that the American farm problem has been largely one of gains in production consistently outstripping increases in demand. Throughout most of this century, food demand was essentially a function of domestic population increase. Until recently the United States has exported large quantities of food abroad only in time of war. Meanwhile, steady advances in agricultural technology and science have produced greater output and reduced human labor needs. Table 1.1 puts these gains in perspective.

Gains in farm productivity continued to be impressive throughout the last half of the twentieth century. Output per unit of farm labor increased more than eightfold.

Rising Production and Growing Crisis

Each unit of land has been producing greater yields as a result of new fertilizers and hybrid strains. At the same time, the application of greater capital has reduced substantially the number of worker-hours needed in production. By the 1930s, American farmers were the most productive in the world—and were going broke the fastest. It is easy enough for the Conservative devotee of the laws of supply and demand to say, "Leave things alone and let the devil take the hindmost." The fact is, excess agricultural production and falling prices affected people—a great number of people.

In 1930, about 44 percent of the U.S. population was classified as rural. About 57 million people still lived on farms or in small towns dependent on agriculture. At least 31 million were full-time farmers. To adopt the Conservative proposal of letting these human resources drop out of farming if it did not pay and find alternative employment would have been inhumane and stupid. In the Great Depression decade, there was no alternative employment. The exodus from farming (which did reduce the farm population to less than 10 million by 1972) would have been faster and would have created even greater employment problems for the general economy.

With this in mind, the New Deal policies of reducing farm migration through price supports, direct payments, and other subsidies (easy credit, electrification, and so on) were created. To be sure, these programs *did* artificially hold up farm prices and, in terms of subsidy costs, *did* pass on the cost of the farm program to taxpayers at large. But they also brought a degree of order to the agricultural sector and improved the income distribution inequities between farmers and nonfarmers. For example, 1934 farm income was only about one-third that of nonfarm income ($163 per year per person compared to $469 per year per person, respectively). By 1964, after nearly thirty years of New Deal–type tinkering, annual farm income per person stood at $1,405 and nonfarm income at $2,318. By 2002, average household income for farm operators stood at $65,757 while the U.S. average household income was $57,852.

Moreover, the supposed costs of federal farm subsidy programs have been vastly overstated. For instance, subsidies and support payments paid to farmers annually amount to less than 9 percent of all federally paid subsidies to the private sector.

It must be conceded that past American agricultural policy has had its failures. For instance, the improved income level of the farm sector, a noteworthy achievement, masks some other problems. The farm programs of the 1930s, 1940s, and 1950s could not halt the eventual decline of the family farm or the regional small farm in the Northeast. With greater application of technology and changes in farm production, farm employment (mostly family workers) fell from 7 million in 1960 to barely 2.9 million in 2001. Although average farm income has improved relative to nonfarm income of the 1960s and 1970s, maldistribution of earnings within the farm sector increased. Large farms (those with annual sales of $100,000 or more) increased their share of agricultural markets from 17 percent in 1960 to almost 89 percent in 2002.

We easily can conclude, then, that the few big farms have been getting bigger, but that most remaining farmers still earn very modest incomes. In such a situation, it is quite likely that past farm subsidy programs and payments to forgo production have provided the greatest gains for the large farm producer. However, even with these shortcomings, the earlier farm policies are defensible. They did raise and maintain average farm earnings above what a purely laissez-faire solution would have produced, thus strengthening agriculture in general. They mitigated the impact of the Depression on many farmers, and when farm out-migration did occur after World War II, the displaced farmers were more easily absorbed into a growing economy. The Conservatives' laissez-faire policy would have emptied rural America sooner, encouraged the growth of only the largest farms, and led to unacceptable human costs.

While past Liberal farm policies are historically defensible, it is apparent that America has moved into a new agricultural era demanding policy changes. The capital-intensive nature of agriculture is everywhere apparent, and the day of the *small* family farm is past, but the country is still heavily reliant on the family farm. At the same time, the long-run future growth in world food demand is undeniable. The free market advocates, however, misunderstand these trends.

Failure of Market-Based Programs

Between 1972 and 1975, agricultural prices generally rose, and price supports and any effort to restrict output were unnecessary and ill advised. However, as the Agriculture and Consumer Protection Act of 1973 anticipated, high prices paid to farmers in the 1970s would not hold permanently. The 1973 act introduced the concept of *target pricing*. Under this arrangement, the government announces a target price on a specified list of commodities. If the market price is below the target price, the government pays farmers the difference between what they would receive for selling their goods in the market and the targeted figure. According to such a plan, consumers would still enjoy the benefits of the lower market price, but farmers would be guaranteed a reasonable return on their crops. To prevent the very large producers from tapping the public treasury for outrageous subsidy payments, the 1973 law specified that no farmer should receive more than $20,000 in payment for any crop.

Although subsequent agricultural acts have raised this per-farmer ceiling, the ceiling never was a very significant restriction because the larger farmers learned early on to divide their holdings among their relatives, with each smaller farm qualifying for the maximum payment. Very small farmers were virtually unaffected by the restriction on payments and continued to fail in large numbers. However, the target pricing and payment program did provide an important cushion for the middle-sized farms that are still the backbone of American agriculture.

If such payment programs, along with various loan programs, had not been in place in the middle and late 1980s, the disaster that struck American farming regions would have been much greater. More free market would have meant more farm agony. The experiment in the early 1970s with reliance on supply and demand had introduced "fencepost-to-fencepost" planting and encouraged farmers to expand debt and mortgage obligations to heighten production. Meanwhile, the collapse of demand for American farm products could be only partly blamed on high agricultural prices and the strong U.S. dollar. Quite simply, even in a hungry world, effective demand for food did not keep pace with the growth in world food supply. It should be remembered that the high interest rates and rising costs confronting farmers in the early 1980s were neither the farmers' fault nor the fault of farm policy. They were the outcome of a number of *supply shocks* (e.g., rising oil prices) that generated inflationary pressures. It was the Federal Reserve's decision to fight this inflation with a *tight money* policy that drove up interest rates and forced massive bankruptcies in American agriculture. Without standby government payments and credit and loan programs, many more than the estimated one-third of American farmers would have been facing bankruptcy in the late 1980s.

What the Market Cannot Do

Curiously, the cyclical swing of agricultural fortunes through the 1970s and 1980s was forgotten by policy makers by the 1990s. With the passage of the 1996 Farm Act, the nation adopted a farm policy that would have eliminated price supports, target pricing, and virtually all other safety nets that had evolved to protect agriculture from the violent short-run fluctuations that forever attend agricultural markets. The promise of the 1996 act after half a dozen years proved to exceed its reality. Precisely as the 2002 date for ending government support programs was to kick in, agricultural profitability stood at its lowest level in two decades. Thus, it is not surprising that agricultural policy would simultaneously switch course.

The Conservative focus on long-run trends in agricultural markets is misleading, and their argument for free agricultural markets is too simplistic. A long-run trend is nothing more than the average of a cycle of short-run highs and lows. If short-run fluctuations are extreme, especially the lows, the agricultural sector will be torn apart. Resources forced out of agriculture in bad periods will not return quickly when prices later rise. A farm is not an enterprise that can be worked for a few years and then briefly retired until a boom naturally reappears. The land blows away if it is not cultivated, and the equipment rusts and becomes obsolete. Neither the farmer nor the consumer, who would face violently fluctuating prices, should be subjected to the severity of short-run market readjustments. The laws of supply and demand, in fact, can be regulated to improve market outcomes.

Price support programs provide stability at a minimum cost. This, however, is not all that is required. Congress and the president came to grips with the failure of the 1996 Farm Act by enacting the Farm Security and Rural Investment Act in 2002, introducing a more sophisticated agricultural policy. For example, the Conservation Reserve Program has the U.S. Department of Agriculture (USDA) negotiating long-term contracts to pay farmers to refrain from cultivating land to "improve the soil, water, and wildlife resources." Wetlands preservation and other environmental quality incentives have found their place in American agricultural policy because farmers are the country's natural experts on stewardship of the land. When supplied with the proper financial incentives through markets and with the assistance of government to compensate for the uncertainties owing to markets and weather, the nation's farmers earn a fair return for their efforts while securing a stable supply of food for domestic consumption as well as for export.

THE RADICAL ARGUMENT

When conventional economics textbooks reach for an example in discussions of how supply and demand sets prices or how competition works, agricultural markets are usually cited. In the idealized models, at least, there are many small producers and consumers of homogeneous products who haggle and bargain until a fair and equitable price is established. For anyone vaguely familiar with the real-world conditions of American agriculture, the irony is heavy—nothing could be further from the truth. Perhaps because we start with such subtle deceptions when we talk about agricultural markets, we continue to deceive ourselves when we look for solutions to real farm problems. American agricultural affairs are dominated by a comparatively small number of giant producers, not by many small equal-sized farms, and prices are more the result of market power or government intervention than of the free market at work. For example, in 2000, Cargill, Archer Daniels Midland, and Zen-Noh accounted for more than 80 percent of corn exports. A similar pattern of four-firm dominance is found in beef packing, soybean crushing and exporting, flour milling, and terminal grain handling. Agriculture, as much as any sector of the economy, reveals the conflict between the professed ideal of a modified, production-for-profit system and the reality that a few benefit at the losses of many. The losers, of course, are small farmers and consumers in general.

The Old Policy: Help the Big Guys

While most farm programs from the 1920s forward were supposedly aimed at protecting the family farm and supporting the agricultural sector in general, they failed utterly to halt the concentration of agriculture into fewer and fewer hands. Programs of price supports and payments for not producing stimulated this concentration, since small farmers could not possibly reap many gains from them. Between 1930 and 1990, land under cultivation actually increased, but the number of farms declined from 6.5 million to 2 million. At the same time, acreage per farm rose. Although Liberals reluctantly note this tendency, they do not understand that it has meant higher prices to consumers, with few, if any, benefits to most individually owned farms.

The market power of individual farmers, never very strong anyway, was eroded further during the 1950s and 1960s as marketing procedures were increasingly affected by the entrance of large business corporations into agriculture—*agribusiness*. Food chains bought orchards and feedlots and integrated their operations all the way from planting and slaughtering to the store checkout counter. Cereal producers, dairy products firms, baking companies, and other farm purchasers became more concentrated. At the same time, suppliers of farm machinery became increasingly integrated and powerful such that the price of farm equipment rose relative to crop income. As a result, the real cost of farming inputs increased while farmers had to sell their produce to comparatively few buyers. Thus, it is not surprising that the share of food purchases going to farmers declined from about 40 percent in 1900 to 10 percent by the end of the twentieth century. On the other hand agribusiness was quick to exploit the most profitable linkages upstream and downstream of farming, namely input supplies, transportation, processing, and marketing.

Meanwhile, agriculture also was being "discovered" by the large industrial conglomerates. Agribusiness grew and matured as ITT absorbed Wonder Bread and Smithfield Hams, Ling-Temco-Vought took control of Wilson Meats, Greyhound joined with Armour Packing, and other similar mergers took place. Basically, this phenomenon extended and accentuated the "price taker" situation of American farmers, even large farmers. Whether selling to the government, grocery chains, or General Foods, farmers had long been accustomed to dealing with buyers who set their own prices. The consumer, however, would feel the real power of this new and rejuvenated agribusiness, as well. The new conglomerate middlemen in food production and distribution had the potential capacity to extract enormous profits. The structure for increasing food prices and middlemen's profits had been established. The Russian grain deal represents a historical example of the corruption of agricultural policy. In 1972, the United States and the Soviet Union secretly negotiated the sale of 19 million metric tons of American grain. Ironically, this sale was completed precisely as the United States was mining Haiphong Harbor in North Vietnam and bombing rail lines north of Hanoi in an effort to stop the flow of Russian goods into the war zone. Although critics were to attack the sale as the "Great Grain Robbery," Secretary of Agriculture Earl Butz defended it as a boon to the American farmer. When accused of being willing to trade with the devil if it meant a profit, Butz replied, "If he has dollars."

The New Policy: A Failed Attempt to Keep Prices Up

The Russian grain deal of the 1970s, though it may seem to be ancient history, remains an important instructional example of how capitalism really works. Conventional economists love to talk about "the market" as if it were a perfectly neutral abstraction. The Russian grain deal puts the lie to that argument. The sale of American grain to the USSR actually reflected a highly calculated effort to create super profits out of the anguish of farmers and the general public. Since the government itself lacked the legal authority to export goods, the grain sales had to be consummated by some half-dozen leading American grain trading firms. The steps in the selling process were something like this: First, the harvest came in and could not be altered by farmer action. Second, the USDA's Commodity Credit Corporation (CCC) granted the Russians exceptionally favorable credit arrangements. Third, the grain traders purchased the wheat owned and stored by the government in CCC bins and sold it to the Russians at a price significantly below the prevailing domestic price. Fourth, the grain traders, over and above their sales fees, received millions in subsidies from the government (the difference between the domestic price and the sale price).

The effects of the grain sales were injurious to practically all Americans except the grain companies and a few insiders who were able to make extraordinary profits by speculating on grain futures. Farmers were unable to take advantage of the resulting rise in wheat prices, since most had sold their grain to the government at the going market price. The American grain reserve was eliminated. Wheat prices and prices of substitute products went up, and so did the prices of beef and bread, both dependent on grain prices. Restive consumers were told it was just the law of supply and demand.

The Conservative prediction that growing world agricultural sales would eventually bring prosperity back to farming, although creating some hope in 1973 and 1974, had turned to ashes by 1978. Four years after agriculture secretary Butz promised a new era for farming by opening American agriculture to the world, farmers had become dependent on world demand to get rid of two-thirds of their wheat, one-quarter of their corn, and half of their soybeans. While American overseas grain sales remained fairly high, world grain prices (indeed, most world agricultural prices) tumbled.

And how did American consumers fare as agricultural prices fell? With large food corporations and agribusiness controlling the final goods prices for most U.S. food consumption, lowered per-unit farm prices meant higher profits, not lower prices at the grocery store. Food processors and distributors (who receive on the average 65 cents of every food dollar) saw their revenues and profits soar as farmers groaned and consumers cursed. Consumers blamed farmers. Farmers blamed unions for rising equipment costs and Arabs for higher energy and fertilizer bills. Almost no one placed the responsibility where it really belonged—with the grain trading companies and their agents at the USDA and with agribusiness monopolies, which were well represented in Washington.

What Strategy to Deal with the Problem?

From the Radical perspective, the farm problem has a number of different and troublesome dimensions. First, the chronic tendency toward overproduction and falling prices followed by underproduction and rising prices simply reflects the instability and irrationality of free markets. The vicious cycle that sometimes brings prosperity and sometimes brings crisis can be mitigated only by an effort to plan output and control prices. The trouble is that past control efforts have been biased toward helping the large farmer and agribusiness at the expense of the small farmer and the consumer. The share of government support payments going to giant enterprises has been growing. Farms with sales over $40,000 per year received 54 percent of all government payments in 1975. By 1995, they received 90 percent. Moreover, while most farmers do not receive any subsidies, the biggest farms have been garnering an ever-growing share of total subsidy payments. For example, of the $114 billion in agricultural subsidies disbursed by the USDA between 1995 and 2002, the top one-tenth—about 289,000 recipients—received 71 percent or almost $81 billion in subsidies.

Such a payment schedule encourages increased production among the large farms while at the same time pushing the small producer to the wall. By and large, it has been the small and middle-sized farmers who are going broke, not the large farmers or farm corporations. In terms of our agricultural policy, that was precisely what was supposed to happen. Shifting the direction of payments toward smaller farmers would equalize income but also encourage inefficient farm producers to continue operations. The Gordian knot can be untied only if we develop an output and pricing program that humanely moves inefficient agricultural producers out of production while curbing the ability of the giant farm enterprises to set output and prices for their own—but not the consumer's—advantage.

The USDA continues to release stylized statistics that emphasize the prevalence of small, family-operated farms while sidestepping any reference to their true economic circumstances or calling attention to the misdistribution of agricultural support in the direction of large operators. The plain fact is that a few vertically integrated transnational corporations such as Archer Daniels Midland, ConAgra, and Cargill have come to dominate *all* aspects of food production not only in the United States but worldwide as well. Moreover, joint ventures with biotechnology firms such as Monsanto and Novartis have resulted in "food chain clusters" that have furthered their hegemony in the agriculture marketplace. For example, the Cargill/Monsanto cluster has produced a "terminator gene" that causes their seeds to become sterile after a single growing season. Such technological advances will only ensure more sales for Cargill, which were about $55 billion in 2002 and "supported" with about $10 million in USDA subsidies. Even several *Fortune* 500 corporations—not well known for their agricultural products—including Chevron, Dupont, Caterpillar, and the John Hancock Mutual Life Insurance Company also received above-average crop subsidy payments from the USDA in 2002. Silly data from the Census of Agriculture about demographic diversity among farmers are prominently publicized presumably for appeal as a human interest story rather than any serious attempt at rationalizing that the market system or agricultural policy are in some mysterious and positive way influencing the numbers of female or minority farm operators.

Most Americans take eating for granted. Prices may affect our diets from time to time, but most of us have little concern about the general availability of food. This is true even though probably not one in fifty of us have the slightest knowledge of how to grow the food we eat. And so it is, of course, that we are not inclined to think very deeply about our national agricultural policies. From a Radical perspective, this is a matter of considerable shortsightedness. The emerging concentrated and centralized food production system can only result in higher food prices for consumers, lower prices paid to small farmers, and further subsidies by taxpayers to obscenely profitable agribusinesses.

In summary, the Radical agenda for agricultural reform calls for a major shift away from the support of big agribusiness, genetically engineered foods, patented life forms, and heavy pesticide and chemical use. Agricultural policy must be refocused on encouraging agricultural co-operatives through price supports, subsidies, and loans that adequately compensate farmers for production costs. Basic foodstuffs and fiber production should be emphasized along with crops and animal husbandry that yield alternative fuels.

Consumer Welfare

Is It Necessary to Protect the Consumer?

Consumption is the sole end and the purpose of all production; and the interest of the producer ought to be attended to, only in so far as it may be necessary for promoting that of the consumer.

—*Adam Smith, 1776*

The upshot of consumer protection, when it succeeds, is simply to hold industry to higher standards of excellence, and I can't see why they should object to that kind of incentive.

—*Ralph Nader, 1967*

Let me emphasize: competition does not protect the consumer because businessmen are more softhearted than bureaucrats or because they are more altruistic or because they are more generous, but only because it is in the self-interest of the entrepreneur to protect the consumer.

—*Milton Friedman, 1978*

Make no mistake: no one wants to roll the clock back on environmental, health, or safety regulations.
   —*John F. Smith Jr., Chairman, CEO, and President*
   General Motors Corporation, 1998

The Problem

Our survey of American agricultural policies illustrated the outcome of efforts to correct the market on behalf of certain producers of goods. We now turn to an example of market intervention on behalf of consumers. Just as we found that there is no free lunch when government acts to protect and promote certain sellers of goods, we now find that protecting buyers also exacts costs. While the existence of costs associated with such intervention is not a matter of much disagreement among economists and economic observers, there remains much disagreement on whether the costs are justified by the direct benefits obtained.

For ordinary citizens, consumer protection today is far less turbulent a debate than twenty to thirty years ago. The comparative calm is explained by the greater acknowledgement and acceptance of government's involvement in the more prominent concerns posed by consumer protection efforts. Consumers have come to expect protection from exposure to injury or death when purchasing and using products and services. Government has increasingly assumed the role of compensating for incomplete knowledge on the part of consumers, policing health and safety matters, and generally assuring that markets are a fair game for consumers. However, the appropriateness and extent of government intervention on behalf of the consumer remains a source of considerable controversy.

The time-honored doctrine of *consumer sovereignty* maintains that the final authority in determining production and prices is the consumer. The consumer, according to this doctrine, always is aware of *caveat emptor* (buyer beware) constraint as he or she makes consumption decisions. Consumers vote with their dollars in the marketplace. Their decisions are expressed by their final selection and willingness to pay for goods. In theory, at least, consumer sovereignty further presumes that buyers' tastes are given and unchanging, that buyers are expert and fully informed about products they are purchasing and the range of alternative products they might buy, and that prices are efficiently set in fully competitive markets. In the real world, however, many economists view such expectations about buyers' knowledge to be unrealistic. Consider that a consumer's attempt to acquire the necessary knowledge to act expertly involves sampling foods and drugs that in fact could prove fatal. Thus, as early as 1906, the federal government passed the Pure Food and Drugs Act to protect consumers from adulterated food and unsafe drugs.

The publication of Ralph Nader's *Unsafe at Any Speed* in 1965, an effective muckraking attack on a popular General Motors car, the Corvair, marked the beginning of a full-blown consumer protection movement. Nader argued persuasively that the sporty rear-engine auto had a number of defects, among them a dangerous habit of flipping over when turning corners, even at low speeds. He also claimed that General Motors engineers and managers knew about the car's engineering deficiencies but had kept quiet about them. Corvair sales dropped after Nader's attack, although General Motors disputed his influence. The company made its last Corvair in 1969.

Spurred by Nader and his activists and by the sobering fact that auto fatalities had grown by about 40 percent since 1960, Congress enacted the National Traffic and Motor Vehicle Safety Act in 1966. This legislation required that the auto industry begin to install certain specific safety features in all new cars. The first requirements (which went into effect in 1968) specified seatbelts for all occupants, energy-absorbing steering columns, increased windshield resistance, dual braking systems, and padded instrument panels. Over the years, additional safety requirements have been mandated by the National Highway Traffic Safety Administration.

Fast forwarding to the present, the public attitude toward consumer protection and safety has undergone a major transformation: safety sells products. Airbags, antilock brakes, and comparative crash testing data are high in the minds of consumers when purchasing automobiles. The National Highway Traffic Safety Administration has the expanded role of testing the effectiveness of safety devices such as airbags and children's car seats.

The consumer protection movement expanded beyond automobile safety with the passage of the Consumer Protection Act of 1972 and its creation of the Consumer Product Safety Commission. The commission claims authority to regulate the safety of some 15,000 products, including household appliances, toys, household products, and recreational products. By 1980, more than four hundred separate units in forty different government agencies were operating to advance consumer interests or protect consumer rights.

Most Americans believe that an active consumer-protection effort by their government is proper public policy. Certainly the general popularity of the government's recent assault on the tobacco industry and the drift toward criminalizing smoking supports such a conclusion. Regardless of the economic consequences or the various contradictions involved, most citizens expect their government, at least to some degree, to "protect" them from the consequences of consumer sovereignty. However, consumer protection is not a free item. As producers are aware (and consumers *should be*), consumer protection increases production costs. And sometimes protection can cause *real* pain as millions of users of the painkiller Vioxx discovered in late 2004 when—under pressure from the Food and Drug Administration—the manufacturer removed it from the market.

Synopsis

Conservatives argue that consumers are best able to determine for themselves what they should buy and that efforts to improve on consumer rationality diminish satisfaction, raise prices, and lower economic efficiency. Liberals maintain that consumers do not have enough strength to protect themselves from the manipulative power of giant enterprises. Radicals go beyond mere consumer protection, raising questions about uncritical consumption as an end in itself.

Anticipating the Arguments

- How do the Conservative, Liberal, and Radical views differ regarding the consumer's rationality and ability to choose freely and intelligently?
- In what ways do the Liberal and Conservative views of calculating the cost of goods differ?
- Why are Radicals suspicious of all efforts to protect consumers in a production-for-profit economic system?

THE CONSERVATIVE ARGUMENT

Early seeds of the consumer movement were planted at the start of the twentieth century, when a variety of state and federal laws aimed at maintaining the purity of food and drug products were passed. A second thrust developed in the 1930s with the passage of disclosure legislation that was intended to protect consumers from mislabeled or fraudulently labeled merchandise and false advertising. In the late 1960s and throughout the 1970s, consumer protectionism developed along a third line: specifying product standards for the alleged purpose of making all consumer products safer. Taken together, these three efforts, as they have developed over the past eighty years, constitute the contemporary American consumer protection movement.

Obviously, the consumer protection movement is neither a passing nor an inconsequential attempt by social engineers to correct and improve on the workings of the market. In fact, few efforts at market intervention have been so assiduously nourished as the belief that government is better able to protect and advance the interests of the consumer than anyone else—naturally enough, better than business, but even better than consumers themselves. Indeed, this idea sounds so sensible to many citizens that the irony of the last sentence will be lost entirely on many readers. Consumers have been abused to a much greater extent in the name of consumer protection than is generally appreciated.

Free Markets and the Freedom to Choose

To understand the Conservative position in the consumer protection debate, recall that all Conservative arguments start from the presumption that each individual's economic and political freedoms must be preserved—that free men and women making their own rational choices in the production and consumption of goods in free markets is the ideal social condition. While the exercise of individual freedom of choice may not always produce perfect economic and social consequences, free market conditions are ultimately preferable to those that arise in regulated or protected markets. Consequently, the underlying logic of Liberal consumer protectionists must be rejected out of hand since it rests on the view that individuals are not capable of making free choices affecting their own lives, or that if they do make such choices, there will be disastrous results. Such a dim view of people's abilities to reason and to choose, of course, inevitably leads to the conclusion that more thoughtful individuals must act to protect the ignorant majority. It is on such a rock of authoritarianism that Liberals build their arguments on behalf of social tinkering of all types, whether in the area of consumer affairs or in other realms of economic behavior.

Having said this, however, we must qualify our position in the case of consumer protection. Conservatives believe that sellers of goods, free though they may be, do not have the right individually or collectively to undertake conscious actions intended to do harm to consumers. Indeed, fraudulent sellers of shoddy products may be held responsible for damages resulting from their products, and damaged individuals must be able to recover losses resulting from sellers' fraudulent activities. Conservatives also recognize that the complexities of products present the modern consumer with problems in rationally evaluating and choosing among goods offered for sale. Consumers will be well served if a hidden hazard is brought to their attention, either by the government or by private agencies, so they can make purchases based on rational risk calculation, such as in the case of potential side effects of certain medicines. As Milton Friedman has accurately observed: "Insofar as the government has information not generally available about the merits or demerits of the items we ingest or activities we engage in, let it give us the information. But let it leave us to choose what chances we want to take with our own lives." Such a two-pronged effort on behalf of consumer protection goes a long way toward redressing the possible market imperfections that adversely affect consumers without destroying the market in the process. The freedoms of individual consumers to choose from among a broad range of alternative goods will not be impaired, as they invariably are under a Liberal protectionist scenario. The Conservative solution also avoids the unnecessary restrictions that excessive consumer protectionism ultimately produces. After all, it takes little imagination to see that government efforts to insulate us from all risks associated with goods we might voluntarily choose to consume must require the elimination of a wide range of useful or pleasurable goods— from stepladders to bicycles—that even in their ordinary use might cause us harm.

The High Cost of Safety

The Conservative approach is simple and rational, but it has not been the strategy adopted at a national level. Over the past eight decades or more, Americans have come to accept the philosophy and practices of an ever-growing body of consumer protection legislation, apparently on the premise that more protection will lead to fuller, more satisfying lives. The premise, however, fails on a number of grounds. The level of consumer protection we have been drifting toward imposes very heavy costs not fully appreciated by consumers. The costs of protection are levied in two ways. First, as taxpayers we must absorb the administrative overhead of operating numerous consumer protection agencies.

A second cost burden, and one of monumentally greater proportions, is the higher price of products, caused by the increased production costs that consumer protection efforts produce. For instance, the Consumer Product Safety Commission (CPSC), with jurisdiction over fifteen thousand products, requires manufacturers to keep detailed records on the performance of all products and even more substantial records of testing and evaluation on any product that may be deemed to "create a substantial risk of injury"—a category that has come to include everything from power mowers and stepladders to bathrobes and infant back carriers. The CPSC also has the power to recall products, demand their redesign, and, ultimately, to ban them altogether. The manufacturer absorbs all these costs. To these costs, arising in extreme but not uncommon cases, firms must add the ordinary costs of keeping abreast of the blizzard of CPSC paperwork and hiring professional safety experts, recall managers, public relations specialists, and the like. Of course these business costs are then passed along to consumers. Incidentally, these costs may be spread among a whole array of a firm's products; consequently, certain products not directly affected by consumer protection activities or made safer by protection may actually bear some of the protection costs associated with other goods.

How large the final bill is for consumers is uncertain, but one study of auto safety requirements legislated between 1968 and 1982 placed direct costs at about 10 percent of manufacturers' total costs (and this does not count another 13 percent of production costs required to cover mandated environmental protection measures).

Is It Worth It? The Cost-Benefit Question

Liberals justify the high and escalating costs of consumer protection by appealing to cost-benefit analysis. This conventional method of economic analysis justifies protectionist endeavors as long as the net money amount of social gains or benefits exceeds all private and social costs resulting from such requirements. (Or, to put it in the stricter terms of economic jargon, up to the point where marginal social costs equal marginal social benefits.) Nowhere has this technique of calculating the gain from required safety been so extensively applied as in auto safety. Needless to say, the protectionist advocates have been able to prove to their own satisfaction that the money value of safety costs is but a small fraction of the money value of social gains obtained from safety requirements.

The key, however, to any cost-benefit analysis is the calculation of benefits and costs. Benefits roughly equal the private and social outlays that would have to be made if the degree of protection required *was not* required. Naturally, benefits look impressive when lost earnings, property damage, medical costs, and the like, attributable to a presumably preventable hazard, are estimated quite high and less impressive if lower estimates are applied. The problem is that benefit and cost estimations are not an exact science, and the estimates or the use of the estimates can be self-serving.

The controversy surrounding the use of cellular phones while driving provides a compelling example. The Harvard Center for Risk Analysis issued studies in 2000 and 2002 concerning the cost-effectiveness and benefits of banning cell phones while driving. The first study rejected cell phone restrictions as premature and inefficient compared to other safety measures such as mandatory seatbelt use and daytime running lights. The net cost to society of cell phone prohibition was estimated to be about $23 billion.* The subsequent study in 2002, presumably using better data and methods, concluded that banning cell phones while driving would cost society roughly $43 billion (the economic value of banned calls), which was approximately equal to the benefits of a ban (averted property damage, medical costs, pain, suffering, and death). **

The newer estimate increases the justification for states to criminalize talking on a cell phone while driving because the benefits realized at least match the costs imposed upon society. This is easily construed to mean that such extreme measures are worth it. Yet, the monetary estimates in these studies are divined from a wide range. That is, the benefits could be as low as $9 billion or as high as $193 billion. On the other hand, costs are between $17 billion and $151 billion. This imprecision did not deter Liberal interventionists from acting upon their routine assumption that the individual should be safeguarded from his or her own shortsightedness, lack of agility, potential lapses in judgment, inattentiveness, or sloppy driving skills to the greatest extent possible by government. New York enacted the first cell phone ban in 2001. New Jersey and Washington, D.C., followed in 2004. Several other states have partial bans, most banning school bus drivers and persons with learner permits (inexperienced drivers) from using a cell phone. No one knows if

---

* K.S. Lissy, J.T. Cohen, M.Y. Park, and J.D. Graham, "Cellular Phone Use While Driving: Risks and Benefits," in *Risk in Perspective*, vol. 8, no. 6 (Boston, MA: Harvard Center for Risk Analysis, 2000).

** Joshua T. Cohen, and John D. Graham, "A Revised Economic Analysis of Restrictions on the Use of Cell Phones While Driving," in *Risk Analysis*, vol. 23, no. 1 (Blackwell Publishing, 2003).

the highways are safer as a result, but we do know that another revenue stream from the citizen's pocket to the state coffers has been established through the traffic citations issued.

One should not lose sight of the fact that each mandated safety cost is an *opportunity cost*—dollars diverted from other potentially higher valued purposes. For instance, what if the billions of dollars spent by automakers to meet safety standards (and presumably passed on to auto buyers) were spent on driver education? Would the social benefits be greater or less? No one really knows—most certainly not the Liberals who use cost-benefit analysis to justify, rather than to objectively evaluate, consumer safety actions.

For Conservatives, quite apart from the challenge of calculating social costs and benefits, cost-benefit analysis fails for more fundamental reasons. It simply defies the logic of the free market, replacing it with political value judgments. Accordingly, cost-benefit method is an instrument of presuppositions and fraught with statistical uncertainties. The results, therefore, can be inefficient and unfair. Individuals, rather than purchasing units of *safety* according to their preferences and willingness to pay, are forced to pay for levels of safety they do not want or need. Rational suburbanites who keep their fingers out of their lawnmowers must pay for protection devices they do not need. Although mental midgets who might, out of perverse curiosity, put a finger into the mower blades are protected (thus providing some alleged social gain), the thoughtful operator who gains nothing must pay more. In effect, efforts to obtain an uncertain, elusive degree of greater social benefits require that private cost-benefit considerations—the very heart of free markets in operation—be disregarded.

The search for greater net social benefits may actually produce the opposite—people acting against their own interests. For instance, higher-priced but safer cars may force some consumers to drive older, unsafe ones. But, most important, such an approach toward consumers attacks the fundamental freedom of choice and therefore compromises the liberty —even the liberty to act foolishly—that Conservatives consider so essential to a free society and a free economy.

THE LIBERAL ARGUMENT

The classical economic assumption—that buyers and sellers bargain equally in the marketplace and that buyers, acting with restraint and wisdom, are sovereign—falls into the same intellectual category as belief that the world is flat. As in the case of the flat-worlders, a great many compelling reasons can be mustered in an attempt to prove the argument, but they fly in the face of virtually all available evidence.

The Need for Intervention

From the Liberal viewpoint, protectionist interference in the private production of goods is justifiable and necessary for several reasons. First and foremost, products have become more complex. They present potential risks and hazards that consumers are simply unprepared to evaluate and act on rationally. If a product simply fails to function as promised in its advertising and labeling, the loss is limited to its purchase price plus whatever incidental expenses were associated with acquiring it. But sometimes the product is risky to use or outright dangerous. The consumer may not have sufficient expertise to judge the risk or may be completely unaware of the hazards inherent in certain products. Without government intervention, how would we have learned of thalidomide causing birth defects or the cancer risks of red dye no. 2, cyclamates, certain pesticides, and other commodities that have been removed from the market or restricted in their use? Dangerous products pose the threat of injury or death. Such losses are colossal compared to those associated with a defective ballpoint pen or a washing machine that does a poor job of cleaning clothes.

Second is the matter of *external costs*—costs paid by society that may not be accounted for in the selling price of a good. Conservatives emphasize the private cost of goods: in the case of an automobile, how much an individual must pay in the marketplace for a minimally equipped transportation vehicle. Additional costs for safety features are seen as purely private purchasing decisions: Buy safety if *you* want it. This misses an important point in understanding real costs. Social costs go beyond merely the production, assembly, and sales expenditures and the expected profits of the automaker. The private decision to drive an unsafe but cheaper car or to be distracted by a phone conversation imposes upon society the additional costs of automobile accidents, injuries, and fatalities. In turn, this leads to higher insurance rates, greater court costs, and heavier expenditures on roads, accident prevention, and enforcement. Nor are injuries or deaths simply personal matters. These human losses mean the loss of present wage earnings and the loss of productive workers (now and in the future). Thus, insufficient attention to safety results in an unnecessary burden to the whole society in the form of social costs.

The Conservatives' argument against safety standards on the grounds that they unfairly raise consumer costs is misguided. Higher-priced autos, and many other commodities, are necessary to cover all the costs certain goods generate. As we shall see, it is still a good bargain.

Restraining Sellers

The extraordinary growth of giant enterprises over the past century, along with the development of huge advertising budgets and sophisticated selling techniques, has created immense power on the sellers' side of the market. Economic concentration has given producers great freedom in establishing and maintaining their own price and quality standards. Mass advertising, meanwhile, has moved well beyond an informational function to one of actually creating and manipulating consumer wants. In such a situation, it is essential that government intervene on behalf of consumers to protect them from false advertising and poorly made or dangerous merchandise.

The efforts in automobile safety since the 1966 National Traffic and Motor Vehicle Safety Act demonstrate how governmentally supported consumer protection actions can improve the quality of an important consumer good. With 95.7 million cars on the road in 1966, the country saw more than fifty thousand fatalities from auto accidents and an accident rate of five and one-half per 100 million miles traveled. By 2003, the National Highway Traffic Safety Administration estimated that fatal accidents had dropped to 43,200 and the accident rate had fallen to one and one-half. Impressive gains in auto safety prevailed despite the fact that there were now 230 million registered vehicles.

Government and its protection agencies led to the development of more crashworthy vehicles, mandatory safety belt use, airbags, bumper improvements, window defrosters, stronger glass, and the like. Careful monitoring of autos has led to massive recalls to remedy specific safety deficiencies. And, of course, the CPSC's and Food and Drug Administration's monitoring in other product areas has similarly contributed to the improvement of product quality and consumer safety throughout the economy.

The Savings from Safety

Government safety requirements have no doubt added to the price of what we buy, although much less than Conservatives have argued. Safety belts, for instance, which (when used) have radically reduced serious injuries in collisions, add less than 1 percent to the price of a $20,000 automobile. The problem, of course, is to measure the increases in costs to consumers against the savings to society from reduced auto hazards. It is a distortion to stress only increased auto prices in a survey of auto safety costs and benefits.

Literally dozens of cost-benefit studies have been undertaken since the early 1970s in an effort to compare actual costs paid by the consuming public for auto safety devices and the actual benefits thereby obtained. No reasonably thoughtful study has ever demonstrated that the aggregate private safety costs exceed the aggregate social and private safety benefits obtained. Practically all studies indicate that a dollar in safety outlays produces at least two dollars in benefits, with most showing a vastly larger ratio of benefits to costs. The benefits are measured principally by calculating the reductions in lifetime or short-term earnings and associated medical costs that would have been lost in auto fatalities and injuries but were saved by the employment of auto safety devices. To these actual dollar losses, we could also add—if a figure were actually calculable—the value derived from the psychological satisfaction a driver or rider obtains from knowing (even if they are never involved in an accident) that theirs is a safer automobile.

To say, as Conservatives do, that such a cost-benefit argument is Liberal hooey is nonsense. Proof of that fact can be discovered by looking at one's own auto insurance policy. Quite simply, insurers would not provide the specific premium discounts they do for optional safety items if such items did not in fact reduce injury claims against the insurer.

Manufacturers may complain that enforced recalls of cars to remedy defects constitute an assault on their profits, and there is probably some truth to this. The answer, however, is better workmanship and engineering on the industry's part, not relaxed consumer protection. The cost for shoddy construction must be borne by industry, not by society at large.

If there is any serious defect in the government's efforts to protect consumers, it is that not enough has been done. The National Highway Traffic Safety Administration, for instance, operates on a yearly budget of about $430 million and employs a staff of about 660. The Consumer

Product Safety Commission is expected to regulate safety on everything from toasters to lawnmowers to roller coasters with 480 employees and a budget of just $60 million. That is a very small bureaucracy indeed to watch over safety standards in a broad swath of the nation's largest consumer-oriented industries.

The recent trend toward deregulation and reducing government interference in business decision making will cost the nation dearly if it continues. Conservatives are right in saying that withdrawing safety and consumer protection standards (and environmental and job safety standards as well) could lead to lower priced goods or, more realistically, greater industry profits. But these are cruel and false gains obtained only through creative accounting—by shifting the social or external cost of goods onto certain groups in the society. Greater efforts in consumer safety are essential. Consumer protection will not be attained until *caveat emptor* (let the buyer beware) is replaced by *caveat venditor* (let the seller beware) as the dominant motto of the marketplace.

THE RADICAL ARGUMENT

The relevant issues in the controversy over improved consumer safety are rarely raised. Conservatives approach the question as a matter of maintaining free markets and free choice while Liberals argue for the improvement of market conditions and the protection of buyers; but these are really evasions of what the consumer safety question highlights. Why, in an advanced and supposedly civilized society such as ours, is consumer safety a problem at all? Is it that we lack the resources and technology to manufacture safe products? On the contrary, we all know that technology has nothing to do with the problem. Unsafe autos, like unsafe food and dangerous drugs, are just "there." They are part of our economic and social systems—to be tolerated or, when things get bad enough, to be reformed. They are the necessary but unwanted effects of an irrational social order.

Why "Consumer Sovereignty" Does Not Exist

Capitalist economic systems are organized to make profits, not to make people happy or to make life safer. For a capitalist enterprise to make large profits, it has to sell in great quantity, and must obtain as great a surplus over costs as possible. Obviously that calculation nowhere contains any estimate of social costs and benefits. Insofar as the production-for-profit system is concerned, satisfaction is maximized simply if we have *more*. Irrespective of the time-honored tradition of consumer sovereignty, it is not really the consumer's power to choose among goods that is important. In fact, capitalism has succeeded in focusing people's attention on their relationships with goods rather than with other people. Owning and consuming the "right" goods is advertised to raise social status, win friends, improve sexual performance, and so forth.

The populace is turned into walking billboards of corporate logos and trademarks, with mass consumption as the arbiter of social relations and economic well-being. What is important is consumption, period. Citizens in a capitalist society are taught from birth to accept uncritically that the object of life is to obtain goods: the more goods, the better their lives.

Looked at this way, it is easy to see why modern capitalism periodically becomes absorbed in such developments as the consumer protection issue. The social costs of the mass consumption of dangerous products as well as private concerns about safety have finally developed to a point where reformist action must be taken. The auto safety movement, for instance, is merely another step in the long progression of product reform movements. It differs very little from the public outcry against adulterated food and unsafe or ineffective drugs that resulted in the passage of the Pure Food and Drugs Act in 1906 and the eventual establishment of the Food and Drug Administration. The FDA certainly improved food cleanliness; just as the modern consumer movement has made cars safer to drive (or at least we all believe so). However, the *success* of such reforms deflects us from questioning the reasonableness of an economic system that sells poisoned food or hazardous vehicles in the first place.

Conservatives and Liberals may bicker over whether consumer sovereignty is best expressed in free or regulated markets, but both are committed to encouraging high levels of essentially irrational consumption. No traditional economist has ever proposed that the users of goods define consumer sovereignty as the rational, coordinated control of production. That, of course, would lead to the abolition of the capitalist system. No matter how strongly Conservatives and Liberals seem to disagree on the extent of government interference with production, both hold firmly to the principle of maintaining high levels of output as well as the primary goal of production for profit.

The Self-Serving Use of the Safety Idea

Americans have been misled about the high costs of safety. Conservatives emphasize that safety features increase product prices. Liberals admit that price increases are an outcome but that the costs are worth it given the social benefits obtained. The thrust of both arguments is that safety costs money—and corporations have not missed their cue. With a public prepared by the media and the economics profession to accept higher prices as the cost of greater protection, business has used the safety argument to push product prices ever higher. Back in 1977, as extensive safety requirements were being built into American autos, General Motors reported a record-breaking net income of $4 billion on sales of $55 billion. At the same time, this firm, supposedly racked by the costs of expensive safety features, managed to rank thirty-seventh among the top five hundred American corporations in income as a percentage of shareholders' equity. And paid earnings per share were two-thirds higher than stockholder earnings a decade earlier, in preconsumerist 1966. Ford and Chrysler also ranked in 1977 among the top two hundred firms in earnings ratio, with their earnings-per-share record better than a decade earlier (Ford's had increased almost 100 percent). Such evidence seems to suggest that, initially at least, the safety boom of the 1970s may have been a ploy for digging even deeper into consumers' pockets and, of course, hiding the action.

Only later, as the economy stagnated in the late 1970s and early 1980s, did corporate management begin to push energetically against many previously accepted safety mandates. Faced with declining domestic demand and rising imports of foreign-made products, it became expedient to use safety costs as a contributing factor in the profit squeeze felt by many American firms. In the auto industry especially, consumer, environmental, and job safety programs *and* workers' salaries were obvious targets. Automakers quickly mounted a highly successful public relations and political lobbying effort to "take back" on all these fronts. Once a boon to profit making, auto safety was now depicted as a threat to profits as well as to the continued strength of a basic American industry. In the new political and economic setting, many consumers even became convinced that we could no longer afford rigorous auto safety standards. Accordingly, during the 1980s and early 1990s, many previously approved safety and environmental requirements for automobiles were rolled back.

Putting the Debate in a Radical Perspective

No doubt the Radical position seems hopelessly negativistic and irrelevant to the specific question of protecting the consumer; indeed it is if Radicals are expected by conventional economists to offer long-run remedies that do not consider the underlying philosophy and social organization of consumption activities in a capitalist society. Radicals understand that capitalism is propelled by the private search for profit and that profits increase, *ceteris paribus*, either by increasing sales or by keeping costs down. Profits by themselves are not tied to intrinsic social concerns about safety—unless, of course, safety can be used as a gimmick to raise prices. Similarly, Radicals understand that Liberal efforts to improve product safety, regardless of their posturing on behalf of consumers, cannot seriously assault the profit prerogatives or the rights of capitalists in a production-for-profit economy. Liberal actions on behalf of the abused in a production-for-profit system can never be so massive that they damage the basic profit-maximizing arrangements. The failure of the FDA to seriously test and monitor pain relievers that later proved to induce heart attacks and strokes is a perfect example of regulation based on corporate rather than social interests.

Given the constraints of a system that depends on private profit making, on one hand, and, on the other, requires the political pretense of repairing the more egregious functional shortcomings and social atrocities resulting from such a system, Radicals are inclined to ask a broader philosophical question: *Why is it that we do not have a more rational approach toward the production and use of goods?* Such a question requires one of Radical outlook to approach the issue of consumer welfare in a very different way than Liberals and Conservatives. First, from a Radical perspective, it is immediately obvious that consumer behavior (aggregate or individual) is not disconnected from the realities of consumer incomes. The chief determinant of what goods an individual consumes is, of course, that individual's level of income and preexisting wealth. American income distribution is examined in Issue 6; suffice it to say at this point, however, that *American consumers are not equal when they enter the marketplace.* Consumers with lesser incomes are excluded as purchasers of certain goods (a fact of free market economic life that does not trouble Conservatives) and they are afforded fewer of the consumer protections Liberals have successfully advocated. Safer automobiles and roads, lead- and asbestos-free housing, truth-in-lending laws, and electric shock- and fire-resistant appliances are luxuries mostly unknown to the poorest 25 percent of Americans.

However, the obvious fact that Americans have unequal access to either consumer sovereignty or consumer protection pales before an even larger problem: The mix of goods the nation chooses to consume—regardless of whether the goods are safe or not—is, from a social perspective, wasteful. For instance, in the case of the privately owned automobile and the enormously expensive system of roads and ancillary services needed to make auto ownership feasible, most Radicals see an incredibly irrational, polluting, and wasteful transportation mode. Accordingly, Radicals view the debate over private automobile safety and the virtual absence of any discussion about devising an environmentally friendly, efficient system of mass transportation as a good example of how we never address the basic questions in our analysis of consumer behavior.

Mere recognition of the broader questions of what and why we consume is not part of the present economic agenda. Radicals, in addressing the current consumer protection problem concretely, embrace most protectionist objectives: the maintenance of quality and purity in product manufacture, the accurate dissemination of information about a product's uses and limits, the recall of dangerous products, and the ability of the consumer to gain redress for damages and defrauding. *Caveat venditor* (seller beware) is an acceptable short-term strategy, but it scarcely goes to the root of our problems as long as production for profit drives the nation's economic and political engine.

Dealing with Externalities

How Can We Save the Environment?

These pollutants originate in the Midwest, eastern Canada, and western New York State; rain and snow wash them out of air passing over the state [of New York] to fall on our forests, lakes, and cities. Because some of these air pollutants become sulphuric acid, nitric acid, and other acids when dissolved in the precipitation carrying them to earth, this whole process has been dubbed "acid rain."
—*John Hawley*, The Conservationist, 1977

When we calculate all the costs to everyone, on balance, we will save money when we pass this [the Clean Air] bill.
—*Senator George Mitchell, 1990*

Kyoto is, in many ways, unrealistic. Many countries cannot meet their Kyoto targets. The targets themselves were arbitrary and not based upon science. For America, complying with those mandates would have a negative economic impact, with layoffs of workers and price increases for consumers. And when you evaluate all these flaws, most reasonable people will understand that it's not sound public policy.
—*President George W. Bush, 2001*

Prices at the pump are skyrocketing; jobs are being lost to countries with lower natural gas costs. And through it all, some in Washington still continue to stubbornly ignore the potential of a vital domestic source of energy: Arctic National Wildlife Reserve.
—*Gale A. Norton, Secretary of the Interior, 2004*

The Problem

They began to notice the problem in the Adirondack Mountains of up-
state New York more than two decades ago. Plant and aquatic life in many
of the region's lakes began to undergo a significant change, reflecting a
general degradation of lake water quality. Within a few years the problem
rapidly worsened as dozens of lakes became dead—virtually void of fish
and plants. The cause, at least as far as New Yorkers were concerned, was
acid rain. Precipitation containing high levels of sulfuric and other acids
was altering nature's balance, not only killing lakes but showing signs of
damaging the trees and ground cover as well. The source of the acid rain
was, to most scientists, easily explained: The burning of fossil fuels unleashed sulfur dioxide, nitrogen dioxide, and other chemicals and particulates into the atmosphere. These returned to earth with falling rain and
snow and, combined with water, became highly acidic. Since northern New
York had no significant fossil fuel burning, the source of the problem was
determined to be the industrial Midwest. There, manufacturing plants and
electric generating facilities belched large quantities of chemicals into the
air from high smokestacks, to be carried northeastward and deposited by
the prevailing wind and weather systems.

In general terms, economic theory offers both a theoretical explanation
and a potential remedy to the problems posed by acid rain and other types
of environmental pollution. The theoretical tool employed is the concept
of *externalities*. The analysis runs like this: Under free market conditions,
the interaction of all individual sellers (supply) and all individual buyers
(demand) establishes a market price for a product. Yet the market price
may not reflect all the incidental costs or benefits associated with the good.
For instance, a student may value (in terms of his or her estimated private
benefits) a college education at around $80,000 or $90,000, but society in
general may derive benefits of much greater value from individuals who
obtain college educations. A better-educated public may be more creative,
more efficient, and harder working, thus producing a larger economic pie
for everyone, not just the solitary student. These additional gains are spillover
or external *benefits* (sometimes called *external economies*) beyond the actual
market price paid for the commodity.

Acid rain or pollution represents spillover or external costs (also known
as *external diseconomies*). In a market economy, output decisions are based on
calculations of direct production costs. Air, water, and even the land itself
may be viewed as free goods in the production process. Insofar as the

atmosphere and the earth are free sewers and dumping grounds, the producer enjoys lower production costs by polluting. Society, living in a dirtier world, however, is saddled with the social costs of pollution. The market price of the good does not reflect the social costs of manufacturing the good. Obviously, to be efficient prices of goods need to accurately incorporate all costs, both private direct production costs and social costs. The objective of an efficient environmental policy is to internalize the social costs of pollution in the price of the goods so that preventive or remedial action is included.

However, the step from theory to practice is big. From the viewpoint of New Yorkers (and New Englanders and Canadians, too, who have been living with acid rain for some time), it is essential to attack acid rain at its source by restricting Midwestern industrial emissions. At the same time, naturally enough, Midwesterners have an interest in keeping their industries operating at low costs and in obtaining cheap coal-generated electricity.

Maintaining environmental quality has been a highly popular social priority with Americans for more than three decades, but acid rain has been a tough problem. Unlike most pollution, which affects the immediate surroundings of the polluter and usually inspires community pressure on the polluter, acid rain's apparent source and its effects are a thousand miles and many state lines separated from one another. In fact, the general problem of air pollution and global climate change is now widely regarded as an issue of international proportions. A United Nations convention grappling with the threat of greenhouse gas emissions resulted in the Kyoto Treaty of 1997, the enactment of which has been stalled by its rejection by several key countries, including the United States.

Just as conflicting regional interests make it difficult to comprehend any solution to the acid rain problem below the federal level, the transnational consequences of all sorts of pollution have commanded that solutions be sought on an international scale. Just as resolution at that national level infers that the Environmental Protection Agency's powers would have to be increased in scope and application, efforts to address international pollution problems such as greenhouse gas emissions infers the use of mechanisms and enforcement presiding above the discretion of sovereign nations. But beyond the politics of maintaining environmental safeguards, there remain important economic questions. How, precisely, does one determine the social cost of pollution? How is its source to be pinpointed? And even if the cost and the specific polluters are identified, what means should be undertaken to internalize the social cost?

Conservatives, Liberals, and Radicals come to quite different policy conclusions in answering these three questions, even when they start from an agreement about the existence of pollution, its threat, and its source. The issue, of course, is not simply acid rain or greenhouse gases, but a strategy that will be effective in dealing with all environmental problems.

Synopsis

Conservatives recognize the *neighborhood effects* of pollution and advocate a cost-benefit technique in determining the amount of environmental cleanup outlays. They favor use of market mechanisms such as emissions fees and cap-and-trade programs as the best way to allocate cleanup costs. Liberals place less trust in market-based schemes and favor direct government controls or even the use of a subsidy policy to clean up the environment. Radicals argue that most efforts to protect the environment are doomed to failure since actual environmental damage is always underestimated. Production-for-profit systems simply do not find it to their advantage to undertake truly effective actions to protect the environment.

Anticipating the Arguments

- On what grounds do Conservatives favor market-based approaches over direct government controls in eliminating pollution?
- On what grounds do Liberals believe that emissions fees and cap-and-trade schemes are insufficient in dealing with pollution problems?
- Why do Radicals believe that conventional market-directed or government-directed efforts are likely to be insufficient in protecting the environment?

THE CONSERVATIVE ARGUMENT

The debate over pollution and acid rain raises a somewhat different set of economic and theoretical questions from those considered in the earlier discussion of consumer safety. Owning and wearing seatbelts is (or at least should be) a purely voluntary matter directly affecting no one but the party involved. Pollution, on the other hand, focuses directly on third-party effects—damage done to individuals who have no economic stake in the polluting action and who can exercise no voluntary control over the effects of pollution.

According to Milton Friedman and most others who have looked at the pollution issue, there is a neighborhood effect that must be calculated and accounted for. According to Friedman:

> A . . . general class of cases in which strictly voluntary exchange is impossible arises when actions of individuals have effects on other individuals for which it is not feasible to charge or recompense them. This is the problem of "neighborhood effects." An obvious example is the pollution of a stream. The man who pollutes a stream is in effect forcing others to exchange good water for bad. These others might be willing to make the exchange at a price. But it is not feasible for them, acting individually, to avoid the exchange or to enforce appropriate compensation.*

Neighborhood Effects and the Role of Government

Clearly, in this situation, it is appropriate to expect the community to establish some technique for determining the costs that one individual imposes on another and to develop a mechanism for allocating the costs. Admitting to such occasional needs to remedy market failures, however, should not be construed as a total condemnation of the market or as a license to introduce all manner of "benevolent" tinkering with the market. Indeed, it becomes quite important that the community action chosen to deal with neighborhood effects be as neutral and nonbureaucratic as possible. Quite simply, the object is to develop a policy that makes a firm internalize all of its costs (social as well as private) in its production decisions.

In our time, magnificent government structures have been created in the name of protecting the innocent from the polluters. Yet society's gains from expensive and creative antipollution efforts have been few— and often obtained only at an unacceptable burden to everyone's voluntary rights and to economic well-being and efficiency in general. Consider the ruthless application of antipollution standards in the 1970s. With the creation of the Environmental Protection Agency (EPA) in 1970 and the passage of the Clean Air Act in the same year, the EPA was given authority to (1) determine national air quality standards; (2) set emission levels for old and new plants; (3) set motor vehicle emis-

---

*Milton Friedman, *Capitalism and Freedom* (Chicago: University of Chicago Press, 1962), 30.

sion standards; (4) establish which fuel substances may be burned in motor vehicles; and (5) establish standards in emergency situations (including the power to close down industrial polluters presenting an immediate danger to public health).

With great zeal and little contemplation of the consequences, the EPA wrote standards and enforced them vigorously. Murray Weidenbaum of the Center for the Study of American Business has estimated that between 1979 and 1986, public agencies and private firms spent nearly three-quarters of a trillion dollars in efforts to meet the EPA requirements. Looking at the data another way, Weidenbaum estimates that meeting EPA direct control standards absorbed 14 percent of the paper industry's capital outlays and 20 percent of the steel industry's new investment. Before the Reagan administration began to relax EPA direct pollution controls in the early 1980s, nearly two hundred plants employing over two hundred thousand workers had closed as the direct result of imposed pollution abatement costs.

Did such antipollution costs produce benefits? The answer is a qualified yes. National urban air quality has improved fairly steadily since 1974. The Great Lakes and the Far West have experienced significant environmental improvements. The expected national rate of environmental damage that would have occurred without pollution controls has slowed, with actual damages falling in recent years. However, it is a matter of some debate whether the benefits, in dollar terms, came anywhere close to the dollar costs imposed by the EPA.

The problem in dealing with acid rain and other pollution problems lies in establishing a method for bringing costs of control and benefits into balance. It is patent nonsense to argue, as Radicals and some Liberals do, that an absolutely clean environment is essential *whatever its cost*. To begin with, there is no technically feasible way to return the environment to its unspoiled, pre–fossil-fuel-era condition regardless of the cleanup outlays that might be undertaken. Given that some level of environmental damage is inevitable, society must establish reasonable cleanup expectations that are based on (1) the value of real benefits actually attainable and (2) the community's willingness to pay the cost of obtaining such benefits. Government-imposed cleanup costs vastly in excess of antipollution benefits that the community deems reasonable lead to a serious misallocation of resources, resulting in closed plants, inadequate new capital investment, failing world competitiveness, lost jobs, and other consequences.

The Possibility of Private Approaches

From a Conservative perspective, the most useful techniques for abating pollution employ minimal social tinkering and a greater reliance on forces of the market to bring social and private benefits into line with social and private costs. Although reliance on the market to deal with neighborhood effects has its limitations, two private (nongovernment) means of assigning the costs of pollution to polluters are possible: negotiation among affected parties and setting specific liability rules.

Negotiation of pollution costs between polluters and damaged parties is feasible where one person's property rights are clearly damaged by a second party's polluting—for instance, a city's loss of its water supply or added costs in preparing its drinking water because of a single identifiable upstream polluter. The damaged party may sue in court, which gives an incentive to the polluter to clean up its emissions. In fact, the polluter and the damaged party may sit down and bargain rather than go to court. Presumably, the pollution fee or the extent of cleanup agreed upon reflects both parties' balancing of benefits and costs.

Failing negotiation, liability rules depend on use of the courts to establish private costs resulting from pollution. Once the court sets particular damages for polluting actions, the firm must calculate such damages as a fairly certain cost of any production having polluting side effects. If the firm pollutes more, it pays more; if it pollutes less, it pays less. The incentive—without any government directives—is on the side of reducing pollution.

The obvious difficulty with relying on negotiations and liability rules is that they do not work well when the specific effects of a specific polluter are uncertain or where specifically damaged parties are either hard to determine or have difficulty establishing clear property rights. How, in fact, does a New York fisherman establish the level of personal damage from acid rain and determine who actually caused the acidity in the first place?

Collective Action

Given the shortcomings of purely private approaches to environmental issues, collective action is the sole alternative. Collective action comes in three general forms: direct controls, emissions taxes (fees) or permits, and subsidies.

Conservative opposition to direct controls was already noted. When government sets specific emissions standards backed with the force of fines or the power to close plants, government wields a dangerous degree of power. Even if used cautiously, there is no certainty that this power will produce the desired effect of balancing cleanup costs and benefits. As a matter of practice, government has tended to overvalue the benefits of halting or slowing pollution while underestimating the costs of attainment. To a considerable degree, direct controls reflect imperfect pollution-measuring standards that vary widely from firm to firm, industry to industry, and region to region.

Most important, however, direct controls provide little monetary incentive for the marginal polluter (at or just below the accepted emission standard) to reduce pollution at all. Direct controls can, at best, establish only an acceptable minimum; they have no effect in bringing about a general improvement in environmental quality as a function of a market economy's constant drive to lower costs.

Subsidies paid to firms as inducements to installing antipollution devices may sound attractive but are hopelessly inefficient. Like direct emissions controls, government-imposed problem solving looks better than it really is. Subsidies provide no market-based inducement for firms to take antipollution actions; they do not cause firms to internalize the social costs of polluting. Ironically, they simply lower polluters' costs, possibly increasing levels of pollution in the long run. If the government installed scrubbers in the smokestacks of Midwestern coal-burning plants, which are allegedly the source of acid rain, the effect would be to lower production costs (in terms of the alternative of the firm's internalizing its own pollution costs). This might encourage more coal burning, wholly offsetting the initial clean air gains.

A more acceptable method for repairing the neighborhood effects of pollution is levying an emissions fee. The fee is levied on polluters to offset the environmental damage they are causing. Relying on the firm's desire to maximize profit, cleaning up its emissions will lead to reductions in its pollution fee burden. Firms most able to adapt to antipollution requirements will respond most quickly, thus holding down their expenditures on fees. On the other hand, inefficient or poorly managed enterprises that do not act to reduce emissions will find their profits adversely affected by having to spend greater amounts on emission fees. The emissions fee essentially requires firms to pay a price for each unit of pollution emitted. Government regulators can cause a reduction in emissions by raising the fee.

Technical problems remain in metering the amount of an individual firm's emissions and translating this into a dollar value of social damages that would be the basis for estimating the correct fee level to deliver the optimal reduction in pollution. Nevertheless, emissions fees are more attractive than direct intervention and rely on the firm's basic incentive to maximize profits and minimize costs to make environmental protection work.

The question of how an emissions charge should best be levied remains a matter of some debate, but Conservatives favor the use of *marketable emissions permits*. Under such an arrangement, a scientific determination of the environment's capacity to absorb pollutants over a given area would be determined. Then a responsible public authority would auction off pollution permits totaling the permissible annual volume. Firms with high abatement costs (the costs of cleaning the air or water affected by their operations) would be inclined to pay higher prices for an emissions permit sold at auction. Those with low abatement costs might find it cheaper to do their own cleanup—as they would be required to do without acquisition of an emissions permit. Once issued, the permits would develop their own market, with firms buying and selling permits among themselves according to which is least expensive: paying their own abatement costs or buying a permit that allows a specified quantity of annual emissions from their manufacturing sites.

In practice, the EPA administers a cap-and-trade system to control acid rain. A nationwide cap is set on the sulfur dioxide (SO_2) emissions and enforced by the issuance of a limited number of emission permits called emissions allowances by the EPA. One emissions allowance is required to emit one ton of SO_2. Plants that find it easier to reduce output of SO_2 can sell unused allowances to plants that are less able to abate pollution.

The market-based approach to reducing pollution by requiring polluters to buy the right to pollute establishes incentives to curtail emissions at lower compliance costs than with command-and-control regulation. The cap-and-trade program for SO_2 has been so successful that other nations have adopted similar approaches, and a mechanism of international emissions trading worked its way into the Kyoto Protocol for reducing greenhouse gases.

The merits of marketable emissions permits are clear. Government intervention is kept to a minimum. And everyone relies on market signals rather than social control in the everyday direction of resources toward a cleaner environment. This system avoids the inefficiency and inequity of direct controls.

THE LIBERAL ARGUMENT

Although Conservatives may seem reasonable enough in their concession that pollution involves neighborhood effects that the community has the right to regulate, their actual track record with regard to environmental protection is a poor one. Their less-than-enthusiastic embrace of federal government action to control pollution stems from their blind commitment to a free market. Moreover, the pollution problem goes a long way toward demonstrating that free markets may not always ensure society's well-being.

The Failure of the Market to Allocate Externalities

As noted earlier, externalities arise when, beyond the market price of a good, there is either a calculable *external cost* (detrimental externality) or *external gain* (beneficial externality) to the individuals consuming the good or to society as a whole. Externalities are not, as Conservatives might suggest, merely interesting exceptions to the theory of markets in which the free play of supply and demand establishes prices and allocates resources accordingly. Instead, they reflect a serious market failure and are ample justification for the Liberal assertion that the market can very often be improved upon.

Externalities reveal two types of problems in allocating resources purely according to market dictates. First, there is the problem of external benefits or economies. A firm that perhaps inadvertently supplies substantial benefits to a community—say, by laying out attractive park-like playgrounds around its production site—has little monetary incentive to continue such investment in this site because it receives no gains in sales from such activity. Although the community derives esthetic and health benefits, there is no market incentive for the firm to allocate resources to such objectives (hence it is not surprising that many places of production are so drab). Second, there is little incentive to invest in good things that produce no private market gains, but there is considerable incentive to spin off certain costs onto the community rather than internalize them as part of the firm's own production costs. Thus, the rivers and the air have been viewed as free sewers by firms spewing chemicals out into the community. Left to its own devices, the free market's allocation of resources can be counted on to produce few beneficial externalities and many detrimental externalities.

In developing a useful economic policy, the logic of the market requires modification and redirection. The example of acid rain and the environmental problems it poses can be dealt with only through government action.

The Need for a National Environmental Policy

As a general rule, Conservatives oppose collective action, especially from the federal level. They prefer to support state and municipal intervention as more democratically responsive to local needs. Clearly, the case of acid rain demolishes their argument. Ohio simply has no incentive to lower the acidity of New York's lakes. Hence Conservatives' first consideration for voluntary agreement between polluters and damaged parties is a flawed argument. Since New Yorkers possess few powers to persuade Ohioans to voluntarily reduce emissions, and since there is no economic advantage for the polluters to comply, negotiation between these distant and differently motivated parties is most unlikely.

Nor does the prospect of enforcing property rights and liability rules in the courts seem more probable. While class action suits against the polluters are technically possible, the legal system offers infinite delaying tactics. Moreover, individuals as damaged parties have no realistic possibility of financing long legal battles against well-staffed and well-financed Midwestern corporations.

Given the shortcomings of voluntarism and the interstate nature of the acid rain problem, it becomes quickly evident that only strong federal intervention provides a possible solution. Even the Conservative argument, despite basic opposition to broad collective action, concedes this point—at least theoretically. The Conservative political record nevertheless demonstrates a different view in practice. When they came to office in 1981, the Reagan administration began undermining environmental protection and preservation. Administrators sympathetic to businesses' (read: "polluter's") needs began to wind down pollution control programs developed during the 1970s and opened more public land to commercial ventures. Few new efforts to exert federal leadership in environmental protection emerged.

During the 1990s, the Republican-controlled Congress continued the

Reagan legacy of benign neglect. And with the arrival of the George W. Bush administration in 2001, the White House obtained an occupant who, irrespective of his rhetoric, clearly was not a dedicated environmentalist. The Bush administration made certain that they wrestled funding for the EPA in 2004 down to the 1999 level of $7.6 billion. Whatever their arguments to the contrary, Conservatives have shown themselves markedly less concerned about neighborhood effects than about relaxing environmental regulations.

In fact, the Bush administration's environmental stance looks like a rerun of the Reagan years. There is a zeal for opening public lands reserved for habitat preservation to mining and oil and gas exploration. Damage to the ecosystem seems to be sidelined in favor of obtaining more fossil fuels to burn, which is the principal source of air pollution and greenhouse gases. At the same time, the Bush administration has refused to endorse the Kyoto Treaty, which is aimed at averting a global climate change disaster, citing that the costs of reducing greenhouse gases are too high for the United States to bear.

Direct Intervention versus Emissions Taxes

Lately, emissions fees and creating a market for emissions permits have become the rage among many economists. Supposedly, metering a firm's discharges and then taxing the firm on the basis of its measured pollution creates a neutral fee mechanism that internalizes the external costs or diseconomies. The fee becomes another cost of production that the profit-maximizing firm will seek to avoid by introducing emission controls. Even in the most ideal scenario—efficient fees and rational firms operating in competitive markets—emissions fees and tradable allowances are a slow process for forcing change in pollution habits.

Direct intervention, if seriously undertaken, promises a quicker short-run solution. When the government sets emission standards and enforces them with stiff fines or the threat of plant closure, a firm has an immediate incentive to introduce emission controls. If a carrot were preferred over a stick in inducing industry compliance with environmental standards, direct subsidies, either to pay for the cost of pollution control or as cash incentives to firms that voluntarily reduce emissions, could be paid. Direct controls also offer regulators the advantage of specifying the best methods and technologies that firms should use to abate pollution—the public has an interest in seeing pollution controlled in the *right* way.

The Conservative argument against direct controls and subsidies maintains that they are inefficient, creating greater total social and private costs than the value of the benefits obtained. This supposedly results from compelling too much antipollution activity too fast. While it may not be possible to restore the environment to pre–industrial-era conditions, indulging in excessive cost consciousness may produce a "rational pro-environment strategy" that does nothing at all for the environment.

THE RADICAL ARGUMENT

Over the past three decades, a noteworthy social awareness has developed about various market failures and their effect on the quality of life under a capitalist system of production. With fairly substantial popular support in the 1970s, a number of collective efforts were launched to deal with such issues as consumer protection, occupational safety, developing new sources for energy and other scarce resources, and, of course, environmental protection. Yet two points are worth remembering: First, it was erroneously believed that more government intervention to correct any market failure was all that was needed. Second, the few timid gestures undertaken produced very limited benefits, and, in fact, the past twenty years have been a march away from the minor victories of the mid-1970s. The problem is that "market failures" are not seen for what they really are: the market working precisely as it is supposed to work under a production-for-profit system.

Capitalism and the Environment

Profits, of course, are merely the revenues obtained by the capitalist after all production and distribution costs have been subtracted. To maximize profits, the rational capitalist must minimize costs. Insofar as it is cheaper (more profitable) to emit sulfur and other particulates into the atmosphere than invest in antipollution devices or nonpolluting production, acid rain and other environmental horrors are a quite rational and expected by-product of a production-for-profit system. Viewed this way, it becomes apparent that whatever the advantages to people in general from a clean environment, there are no advantages to a firm to undertake antipollution activities voluntarily. And this is also true of other socially directed objectives such as consumer protection and occupational safety.

The record of capitalist destruction of the earth, its atmosphere, and ultimately its inhabitants is obvious enough. The degradation of the land through clear-cutting hardwood timber in the nineteenth century to obtain nothing but tannic acid for boot making, the mid-twentieth-century practice of strip-mining coal, and the modern crises of acid rain, greenhouse gas emissions, habitat destruction, and radioactive waste from a vast number of nuclear production sites illustrate that the search for private profits stands in open opposition to environmental, and hence human, concerns.

The Failure of Past Environmental Efforts

Liberals and Conservatives (who, after all, cannot deny the evidence of environmental decline) concede the need for some proenvironmental activity. Liberals tend to favor direct control mechanisms implemented by a benevolent and all-seeing state, whereas Conservatives prefer the use of neutral emissions fees and marketable emissions permits that "induce" firms to reduce their polluting. Will either approach work?

The Liberal reliance on government direct controls or subsidies presumes, of course, that government is neutral—that government can determine environmental targets and develop and enforce rules that might directly threaten business enterprises' profits or continued operations. Yet the supposed neutrality of government in the marketplace has proved an illusion in practice. Even under Liberal administrations, the Environmental Protection Agency has shown softness in forcing businesses to pay cleanup costs. Effectively using their lobbying power, firms have successfully pointed out that cleanup efforts that are too energetic can lead to lost profits, diminished ability to compete abroad, and loss of workers' jobs. In fact, even the unions have joined private enterprise in going slow on acid rain and other pollution problems. Accordingly, in the last years of the Carter administration, the EPA introduced *pollution offset* programs in which newly established firms and plants could emit pollution so long as they could induce (pay) other firms to reduce emissions or, within their own company, reduce emissions elsewhere by an equal amount. Meanwhile, using a bubble concept, existing firms were given general permissible emissions limits over each plant, with the firm choosing where and how it would cut total pollution within the plant to meet the limits—more in the water and less in the air, or vice versa, if it was profitable. Such actions reflected concerns that too strenuous an antipollution policy could damage firm profitability. At best, they slowed the rate of pollution buildup without recognizing the need to undo the crimes of the past as well as the present.

Conservatives showed their practical lack of concern for pollution problems during the Reagan-Bush years. While talk of emissions taxes and the sale of emission permits characterized the writings of Conservative economists, when they actually addressed the pollution problem, no national emissions tax program was put in place. In fact, the EPA even pulled back from the limited level of effectiveness that characterized the Carter years. Meanwhile, although the avowedly Liberal administration of President Clinton showed more interest in environmental problems and, occasionally, showed more backbone in standing up to certain polluters, it did not produce a new and wide-ranging environmental effort.

To be perfectly blunt, even though surveys show that most Americans believe the environment must be protected whatever the cost, and even though the public's environmental awareness is now well over three decades old, no effective national environmental program has emerged or seems likely to emerge soon.

The Need to Get Beyond "Cost-Benefit"

For some, the Radicals' discounting of Liberal and Conservative environmental proposals will be interpreted as silly obstructionism. As in the case of consumer protection, the Radical opposition at first seems contradictory—that Radicals somehow oppose serious efforts to make safer products or to clean up the atmosphere. Such an inaccurate perception stems from a failure to grasp the basis of the Radical argument.

From a Radical perspective, failure to deal with environmental issues is not merely a capitalist oversight or some accidental consequence of a market-dominated society; it is directly traceable to capitalism's dominant feature—*the drive for profits*. Furthermore, it is not possible for capitalism to be itself (searching for profits) and to be better than itself (taking actions that reduce profits) at the same time. Capitalist (Conservative or Liberal) discussions about halting acid rain or cleaning up pollution in general are therefore nothing more than seductive deceptions.

The point becomes obvious when we peel back the Conservative and Liberal arguments to examine their real content. Both rely on a cost-benefit measurement of the extent of pollution as a problem and as an indicator of how much antipollution activity should be undertaken. The ultimate determinant of the extent of antipollution activity is, according to conventional theory, established by the point at which marginal social costs equal marginal social benefits (in other words, where the last dollar spent on cleaning up the environment is at least equal to a dollar's worth of gain from the actual cleanup). On the surface, this seems rational enough until we consider how costs and benefits are calculated. *Social costs* are seen as the sum of all private costs plus any governmental outlays for reducing pollution as determined by market-established prices. *Social benefits* are the sum of dollar benefits accruing to all individuals affected by the reduction of pollution. The bias of such an approach is always to overestimate costs and underestimate benefits, since costs are comparatively easily calculated in market terms while only a portion of benefits can be assigned a particular market value. A $10 million outlay for a scrubber (whether paid for by the firm or by tax dollars) is easily perceived as a cost. However, what is the benefit of not killing a lake? A lake is only partly a commodity to which a market value can be assigned as a piece of real estate lost to its owners for personal or business use. A lake, a stream, or, more pointedly, a sunset has a certain intrinsic value that is not calculable in current market terms.

Cost-benefit discussions under capitalism are always limited to property and commodity relationships. The *neighborhood effect* of Conservative theoreticians (and used also by Liberals) rests on calculating damages to individuals' property rights as the beginning point for offsetting spillover costs. Hence the estimated value of social benefits—which in discussions of external diseconomies are nothing more than the sum of estimable private property or market value gains—will always be lower than the real benefits to society of ending pollution.

Marauding global capitalism has turned environmental problems into a global concern. Developed countries that would have to be key players in any international attempt to address the environment predictably resorted to benefit-cost calculations that struck down the Kyoto Treaty. Other polluting nations sought exemptions from the greenhouse gas reductions contemplated by the treaty. The charade about "efficient pollution control" has simply moved to the international level with the same failed results experienced on the domestic front in the United States.

Recalling the issue of consumer safety, once it was stripped to its basics, the conventional debate over consumer protection was off target and avoided the real issue of socially irrational production and consumption choices being the natural outcome of a production-for-profit system. No remedy to irrationality could be found within even a modified capitalist system. Likewise, no remedy is forthcoming from efforts alleged to offset the market failure of external diseconomies resulting in acid rain or other pollution. Remedial antipollution actions of any consequence will take place only when social policies reflect real human needs, not the requirements and values of a commodity-dominated society. Ending pollution and maintaining a safe and humane environment, now and for the future, is a social goal that must be understood as having no ultimate cost limits with regard to what must be paid for its attainment. From a Radical perspective, society is more than the sum of each of its individual members. Society, or humankind, also has a historical dimension. We at the beginning of the twenty-first century have no right to limit the potential and blight the lives of human beings who will follow with acid rain, global warming, mass extinctions of species, and other environmental degradation. The simple fact remains that capitalism is incompatible with rational stewardship of the environment.

Imperfect Competition
Is Big Business a Threat or a Boon?

People of the same trade seldom meet together, even for merriment and diversion, but the conversation ends in a conspiracy against the public, or in some contrivance to raise prices.

—Adam Smith, 1776

Every contract, combination in the form of trust or otherwise, or conspiracy, in restraint of trade or commerce . . . is hereby declared to be illegal. . . . Every person who shall monopolize, or attempt to monopolize, or combine or conspire . . . to monopolize . . . shall be deemed guilty of a misdemeanor.

—Sherman Anti-Trust Act, 1890

Microsoft does not have monopoly power in the business of developing and licensing computer operating systems.

—Bill Gates, Chairman and CEO
Microsoft Corporation, 1998

Moreover, over the past several years, Microsoft has comported itself in a way that could only be consistent with rational behavior for a profit-maximizing firm if the firm knew that it possessed monopoly power, and if it was motivated by a desire to preserve the barrier to entry protecting that power.

—Thomas Penfield Jackson
U.S. District Court Judge, 2000

The Problem

On any list of contemporary economic problems that captures the American public's interest, *bigness in business* does not rank very high. That said, however, it would be incorrect to infer that corporate size and the business practices of giant corporations are unimportant economic issues. Indeed, in an economy preponderantly organized around free market principles, the size and power of the participants in any market must be matters of perpetual concern.

Conventional market theory distinguishes between competitive market structures and numerous imperfectly competitive alternatives (monopolistic competition, oligopoly, and monopoly). Moreover, conventional theory demonstrates that society reaps greater benefits under pure competition: Maximum output is assured, prices are lower, and excessive profit making is avoided, with all firms reacting to the dictates of a free market as *price takers*. Under imperfectly competitive conditions, firms are able to exercise some degree of *price making,* controlling prices and output for their own profitable advantage. In a textbook situation, there is little disagreement among economists about such generalizations. The trouble develops when we move from textbook examples to the real world.

A seemingly paradoxical situation appears when we examine the existing structure and organization of American business enterprise. On one hand, the official ideology of American capitalism espouses a competitive ideal of many smallish producers, no one of which can materially affect price or output. On the other hand, everyday experience tells us that most markets are dominated by a comparative handful of very large firms. Exactly how much bigness might alter or eliminate desired competitive conditions has long been a concern in American capitalism. Since the passage of the Sherman Antitrust Act in 1890, a considerable body of law has been enacted to protect competition. The essence of these accumulated laws may be summarized as follows:

1. It is illegal to enter into a contract, combination, or conspiracy in restraint of trade or to monopolize, attempt to monopolize, or combine or conspire to monopolize trade.
2. When the effect is to lessen competition or create a monopoly, it is illegal to acquire the stock or assets of competing companies, to discriminate among purchasers other than what can be justified by actual costs, or to enter into exclusive or tying contracts.

3. Under all cases, whether the effect is to monopolize or not, it is illegal to serve in the directorships of competing corporations, to use unfair methods of competition, or to employ unfair or deceptive acts or practices.

Despite the thrust of law and prevailing economic theory, the tendency toward larger market structures has persisted since the closing decades of the nineteenth century. Although bigness has sometimes been occasioned by a firm's own individual production and sales efforts, by far the most popular route to increasing corporate size is through merger and combination. The earliest merger efforts of the late nineteenth century were largely *horizontal mergers,* which combined side-by-side competitors in the same industry. Very shortly, there followed *vertical mergers,* combining suppliers and purchasers of goods involved in the same chain of production. United States Steel, General Motors, and the American Tobacco Company came into existence following the former path. The National Biscuit Company and Standard Oil (which also used horizontal combination) grew in size and influence using the latter strategy.

Three eras of horizontal and vertical mergers are easily identifiable: the 1890s, the 1920s, and the period immediately following World War II. Until comparatively recently, horizontal and vertical merger activity had slowed, in part because the really juicy combinations had already taken place and in part because antitrust law impeded greater concentration and growth of market power by existing giants. Merging, however, did not cease. Beginning in the 1960s and continuing to the present, firms have increasingly undertaken *conglomerate mergers,* uniting enterprises where no horizontal or vertical market advantages are present.

In recent years, the annual estimated value of mergers and acquisitions has increased from about $44 billion in 1980 to $1.2 trillion in 2003. Despite this tremendous rise, not all consolidations have resulted in either increased market share or profitability. Large industrial conglomerates such as General Electric and General Motors earn a growing share of their profits from financial and other nonmanufacturing operations. Other corporations such as AT&T and ITT were forced to downsize or sell off divisions they acquired but on which they could not generate an acceptable rate of return. That noted, however, we cannot fail to recognize that in the past couple of years there have been some truly gargantuan mergers including JP Morgan Chase and Banc One, Cingular Wireless and AT&T Wireless, Travelers-Citicorp, and Time-Warner and AOL.

Moreover, further combinations in the airline and technology industries clearly indicate that we are in the middle of a new and important period of corporate combination.

Since the election of Ronald Reagan, government policy toward big business has focused on promoting competition through the deregulation of industries and markets, especially where there are only a few competitors or perhaps none. Market forces, rather than government-initiated policies and antitrust litigation, have been viewed as the quickest and most efficient means for ensuring adequate price competition and consumer sovereignty. These policies have led to a significant curtailment of prosecutions by the Justice Department for price fixing, price discrimination, and other antitrust violations. Whether or not such policy might undergo change is a matter of debate.

What is the significance of growing business concentration? To what extent are large firms able to act as price makers, setting excessive prices, restricting output, and creating market inefficiency? To what degree do antitrust law, foreign competition, and other economic developments offset or negate the trend toward bigness?

While no economist, regardless of ideological preference, denies the existence of big business, there is widespread disagreement as to whether modern corporate size and increased merger activity represent a serious monopoly threat to the economic and social organization of American society.

Synopsis

The Conservative argument asserts that there are sufficient market and legal checks to make certain that big business does not act in an exploitative way but actually improves our economic well-being. Liberals accept the fact of bigness but maintain that government intervention is essential to control potential monopoly exploitation. The Radical argument holds that monopoly is the logical historical development of capitalism and that there is no way to halt this tendency without abolishing the production-for-profit system.

Anticipating the Arguments

- How do Conservatives argue that bigness in business is not proof of growing monopolistic power?
- What role do Liberals propose for government in dealing with the

rise of giant enterprises, and how does their view differ from the Conservative approach?

- How do Radicals support their claim that the growth of alleged monopolistic business behavior in the United States is merely the logical progression of capitalist development?

THE CONSERVATIVE ARGUMENT

American public policy toward big business tends to be cyclical, in some periods reflecting a strong antibusiness bias (the early 1900s and the 1930s, for instance) and in others tending to be more tolerant of large-scale enterprise. During the past couple of decades, with a few exceptions, public policy makers have shown reasonable restraint in their antitrust pursuits. The result has been beneficial to both American business and the American public. But federal judge Thomas Penfield Jackson's 2000 determination that Microsoft was a monopolist demonstrated that the unreasoned fear of bigness in business could reassert itself anytime. Accordingly, it is well to remember why such fears can lead to dangerous economic policy making.

In general, fear of bigness rests on gross misunderstandings of the structure and performance of American business. Foremost among these is the confusion of bigness with monopoly, and the resulting corollary that big is bad. The anti–big-business attitude that emerges from these views is always a serious threat to the American economic system. Far from leading to the rebirth of a competitive business society, most anti-monopoly efforts erode free enterprise itself. Ironically, an attack on big business boils down to an attack on business of all kinds. More than they realize, the owners of mom-and-pop grocery stores and the like are themselves threatened by assaults on business giants.

Bigness Does Not Equal Monopoly

Bigness in and of itself is not proof of monopoly power. Of course, there is no denying the existence of *dominant firms* in certain American industries and of the concentration of market share and capital in the hands of a few firms in others. However, a variety of real-world market forces come into play that negate or significantly diminish the price-making powers that economic theory suggests these business giants might possess. The point here is to get beyond monopoly theory and look at the world as it is. For instance, there are many cases of interindustry competition among different highly concentrated industries. Glass, aluminum, steel, paper, and plastic producers, for example, all battle each other for the food-container market. Nor should international competition be forgotten. While tariffs and shipping costs may offer some protection to American firms, the protection is not absolute—witness the 30 percent share of the auto market seized by foreign carmakers. The point is simple: Big business, far from ending competition, has heightened it. The solitary village blacksmith, barrel maker, or flour miller of a century ago had far greater monopoly power over price, quality, and output than does his present-day big business counterpart.

Those who worry about excessive monopoly power should consider one further point. In a market society, the great check against price gouging, by Microsoft or by a barrel maker, is consumer demand. If prices go too high, sellers simply cannot sell their products—or enough of them to make a profit—and prices will come down. If we can get beyond the silly but appealing logic of the "big is bad" argument, we might truly understand that the opposite is much more nearly correct: Big business has been good for America.

In Defense of Bigness

The primary reason for merger and combination among enterprises in the past has been to obtain technical *economies of scale* that lower production costs—in other words, cost reductions deriving from enlarged output. To be sure, there have been examples of firms attempting to exploit their market power as monopolistic price makers; however, such mergers are rare indeed, and when detected (as they easily are), antitrust law and civil law provide ample protections to society at large. In the meantime, big business has been the major vehicle for economic and technical advance in the United States. Few can deny that product progress and relatively falling prices for most consumer and producer goods since the beginning of the twentieth century have been the result of expensive technological advancements; these could have resulted only from the great capital concentration and large-scale marketing strategies of big enterprise.

Recently, Liberal and Radical critics of business enterprise have directed their wrath against the newer conglomerate mergers. Such attacks are also threats to business growth, since conglomerate mergers presently account for about three-quarters of all combinations. This strategy is an extension of the "big is bad" argument; however, it fails to consider that conglomerate mergers may also provide consumer benefits. By strengthening inefficient and costly businesses through improved management techniques and by providing badly needed capital, prices will be lowered. Moreover, the conglomerate merger often increases competition by resuscitating firms that otherwise would fail. And strong firms are strengthened by acquiring many diverse operations that permit the firm to avoid putting all its eggs in one basket. In this era of immense and swift technological and product change, diversification is an important strategy to manage business risk for a large enterprise.

The size and scale of the truly large American firms become a bit less threatening if two factors are considered: (1) the threat posed by giant foreign enterprises and (2) the health and abundance of small enterprises in the United States.

A policy aimed at weakening large firms simply because they are large will not protect the American consumer—and certainly not the American worker. A host of foreign giants stands ready to flood American markets with goods should large American firms fail to maintain their vitality and profitability. Indeed, the relative slippage of American producers in world competition is an important argument on behalf of reducing constraints on the size of American business.

In any case, bigness is vastly overemphasized. Of America's 17.6 million businesses, more than 99 percent of employer businesses qualify as small businesses, according to the Small Business Administration (SBA). Regardless of the size of the giant enterprises, no other economy can boast this proportion of small, independent enterprises to the entire population. The SBA reports that small business employs about half the private nonfarm workforce and accounts for about 60 to 80 percent of net new jobs created annually. Given these characteristics of American business enterprise, it becomes obvious that big business, even if it were a problem, gets undue attention from Liberals and Radicals. Smallness and competition remain the dominant characteristics of American enterprise.

Singling out big business is unfair and misleading. Even if business bigness were demonstrably bad, why isn't the same logic applied to big government or big labor unions? Those who cry "monopoly" in the business sector rarely apply that argument against the United Auto Workers or the Teamsters, nor do they see the bureaucratic state management of pricing—from hospital rooms to agricultural products—as analogous to the imagined monopoly power of big enterprise.

The Promise of a New Approach by Government

The record of government enforcement of antitrust law has, since the beginning of the century, been inconsistent and contradictory, tending always to reflect the political ideology of the current occupant of the White House. Naturally enough, the intensity of antitrust action heightens with Liberal occupancy. However, even under Conservative administrations, there remained a troublesome ambivalence about how to deal with giant enterprises. Frequently actions were initiated by both Conservative and Liberal administrations against firms purely on the grounds that they were big or too profitable. Such an approach works against the development of dynamic and thriving firms. It is rather like punishing the winning runner in a race because she ran too fast. The profitable business is not the only loser, however; so is the society that has benefited in jobs and lower product prices from the large firm's efficiency. However, two landmark antitrust cases of the 1980s restored some reason to our public policy toward big business.

In the 1982 dismissal of a government action against IBM for monopolizing the mainframe computer industry, the Justice Department agreed that despite IBM's size and its share of the market, there was no proof that the firm had acted monopolistically. The decision should stand as an important legal landmark against those who would penalize a firm thoughtlessly simply because it has been successful. In the AT&T case, decided at the same time as the IBM case, the Justice Department affirmed the doctrine of competition. AT&T's monopoly power in the buying and selling of communications equipment and services was ended. AT&T was proved guilty of using its power (provided by government as a regulated monopoly) to exclude competitors from the data and electronic transmission market. AT&T was compelled to divest itself of its purely "public utility" local phone operations and join battle fairly with competing firms in the long-distance and information systems markets. A sensible antitrust policy was put in place: *Bigness itself does not prove collusion or unfair price setting, but when such activities are proved, they will be halted.*

Paralleling and complementing the IBM and AT&T cases has been a relaxation at the Justice Department of vigorous opposition to large corporate mergers. This, of course, has sparked criticism from some Liberal critics who fail to see the advantages obtained from most of these mergers. Far from being a submission to business pressure, the more passive approach toward mergers and bigness in its many forms is a recognition of the economic gains from size that provide important benefits to the entire society, not the least of which is an improvement of American firms' ability to compete with foreign giants.

The initial determination in 2000 that Microsoft was a monopolist seemed at the time to portend a worrisome throwback to the antitrust era born out of the Alcoa decision of 1945, where the possession of a 90 percent market share was regarded as *proof* of monopoly. Fortunately, the recent resolution of Microsoft's 2001 antitrust settlement with the Justice Department will now allow the company to focus on its main problems: growth and innovation. Unlike bureaucrats, financial markets are much better judges of market power: Microsoft's four-year stagnant stock price unambiguously reflects its market weakness, not market prowess. Antitrust enforcement must get beyond confusing innovation, growth in market share, and business success with the evils and abuses of monopoly. The Microsoft settlement indicates a return to sanity at the Antitrust Division of the Department of Justice.

Conservatives do not deny the existence of monopoly abuse when it is real. Very clearly, the exercise of monopoly power is unjustifiable and injurious to individuals. It prevents efficient allocation of resources. However, aside from those cases of monopoly initiated or encouraged by the government and occasional conspiratorial endeavors by individual enterprises, the monopoly problem is mostly a phony issue. Liberals use it as a pretext for urging massive social or governmental interference with the market, while Radicals find it convenient as an excuse for their revolutionary assault on the entire system. Both groups would use the issue in a self-serving fashion to extinguish individualism and private property rights.

THE LIBERAL ARGUMENT

Traditional economic analysis since Adam Smith has argued that the "great regulator" for business activity is the market. Here, small, competitive firms struggle against each other to sell goods and gain customers. Prices and the possibility of exploitation are always regulated by what Smith called the *invisible hand*—the market interaction of supply and demand. Although we may nitpick over whether this type of pure competition ever existed outside of economists' minds, it certainly does not exist in the United States today. Just two thousand businesses in all areas of the economy produce over half of our gross domestic product; the highly visible fist of corporate power has largely replaced the invisible hand.

The Problem of Policy Selection

While most modern-day Conservatives equivocate on the issue of big business, preferring not to see any monopoly problems except in the rarest of cases, Liberals face the problem directly. *Business concentration does exist in the United States.* The scale and intensity of efforts to increase concentration through merger is growing. Nor are all merger efforts benign conglomerate combinations. The policy issue, then, is not a matter of recognizing the obvious but of determining how to deal with it.

The most rudimentary analysis of monopoly behavior tells us that, all things being equal, monopolistic firms tend to charge higher prices and produce less than might otherwise be expected under competitive conditions. They employ fewer workers at lower wages and generally foster resource misallocation. Moreover, the greater the degree of monopoly power, the greater the consumer exploitation.

The implications of this line of economic analysis are clear. The return of competition is apparently the only way to return to economic virtue. In a policy sense, this might mean the enforcement of a vigorous antimonopoly policy, leading to the restructuring of some industries into greater numbers of similar-sized units of production. Liberals are not in total agreement on this point, but most would oppose a grand breaking up of giant enterprises. First of all, the practical application of a literal "break them up" policy is not politically or legally feasible. We long ago passed the point of being able to return to some romantic eighteenth-century concept of the marketplace. This is not to say that stimulation of competition in certain industries might not be desirable or possible through the application of antitrust laws. In fact, the Justice Department must always be prepared to initiate antimonopoly legal action, but this could not be carried out on a broad scale without weakening our legal and economic structures. Second, there is no solid evidence that pure competition, enforced indiscriminately, would be beneficial, even if it could be attained without seriously wrenching society.

What these observations mean in a practical context is that Liberals approach the question of bigness in American business quite pragmatically. The degree of concentration varies from industry to industry, and concentration alone does not tell the whole story about abuses of market power. Accordingly, concentration in the oil industry might be approached differently than concentration in the auto industry. Domestic automobile production is effectively limited to just three firms, with General Motors (GM) producing about 50 percent of American output. Some years ago, GM's size and share were so large that, in the minds of many Americans, the firm appeared to be a logical candidate for "break them up" antitrust action, a situation not unlike the one in which Microsoft later found itself in the personal computer software industry. Charges that GM has worked effectively in the past as a price leader are difficult to question. However, that was a long time ago, when GM effectively controlled 70 to 75 percent of the American car and truck market. In any case, even if this sales practice still existed as an option for GM, price leadership would not necessarily mean consumer exploitation. Nor would breaking up GM necessarily lead to social improvement. Even though GM's size has probably pushed it well beyond what is necessary for attaining efficiency from the point of view of *economies of scale,* there is no assurance that forty or even a dozen smaller GMs could produce a product of similar price and quality and hire the workforce that the present firm does. And, at any rate, the once-dominant position of GM has been severely eroded by the extensive penetration of the American auto market by foreign carmakers. In this case at least, most Liberals will agree with Conservatives that concern over national concentration ratios and domestic firm size must be weighed against the realities of world competition. On the other hand, the oil industry, with less actual concentration than the auto industry, conspired during the 1970s energy crises to force up the prices of gasoline and natural gas by withholding supplies.

The point is that there are different types of giant enterprises, some highly predatory and exploitative and others reasonably responsible to the public interest. Concentration alone is no justification for applying a vigorous antitrust action against members of the American auto industry. But the behavior of the oil industry in the 1970s is the worst kind of monopolistic activity. There are no easy monopoly tests. Each case must be taken on its own merits.

Having rejected the rigid competitive argument, we are left to accept the reality of modern corporate concentration. However, though Liberals realize that bigness itself need not be proof of monopoly abuse, they do not subscribe to the policy advanced by Conservatives. The quest for greater market power is not always enlightened; it may, in fact, destroy business itself, as large firms act consciously or unconsciously to protect and expand their influence. Certainly, the current merger mania in American business has had a negative effect because it diverts funds into takeovers rather than capital investment and absorbs the brightest business minds in short-run profit objectives rather than long-run production planning.

Meanwhile, unrestrained business power may lead to the domination of government by narrow business interests and the subversion of the rights of the many for the benefit of a few. Thus Liberals believe the creation of a clear public policy toward mergers and bigness in business is essential to protect the balance of pluralistic interests in an open society. An equitable balance of labor, consumer, and capital interests must be the philosophical cornerstone of any intelligent policy toward business.

Through fair and calculated government intervention, big businesses can be made compatible with the social objectives of economic order, reasonable prices, high quality, and technological advancement. Government actions, depending on the situation, must go beyond mere antitrust enforcement. They may take the form of selective tax and subsidy arrangements, under certain circumstances exercising direct controls over pricing, hiring, and capital investment policies, and sometimes exerting some degree of intervention in the international operations of business. Monopoly policy, moreover, must not be separated from general public policy objectives directed at inflation control, maintaining full employment, and encouraging economic growth. Some people will argue that this external imposition of social objectives on the private sector is pure socialism, but they miss the point.

Social Control Is Not Socialism

Pragmatic social control of big business is not the same as social ownership. Corporate ownership today is widely dispersed and far removed from the day-to-day management decisions of American business. Excessive concern over *who* owns the productive property only clouds the important business and public issues at stake. *How* the privately owned property is performing is the really important question. Even though privately owned, most large businesses are already social institutions with social responsibilities. To put the point simply, GM, or even Microsoft, does not have the right to fail any more than they have the right to conspire against the public. To demand social responsibility is perfectly consistent with the real-world structure of business and the economy, and it does not challenge private ownership in any serious way.

Businesses, moreover, are more responsive in the area of social responsibility than is generally understood. Social concern on their part is not purely altruism but good business. Flagrant monopolistic behavior invites government scrutiny and public outrage. The old era of "the public be damned" is past. Few firms, whatever their size and market power, want long and costly antitrust litigation. Even consumer boycotts and public pressure for legislative intervention are sizable threats and induce thoughtful constraint. Moreover, there is significant pressure within the business community to police itself. Abuse of economic power disrupts markets and creates economic instability; this situation, while perhaps favorable to one or a few firms, interferes with general business activity. Social responsibility, finally, is not an ethical question but a matter of profit and loss.

These points should not be misunderstood. The Liberal fully understands that big business may indeed be a threat in its pricing, labor, international, and other policies. But big business does not *have* to be a threat to the economic system. It can be brought under social control.

Public policy toward big business, then, remains a matter of directing private enterprise toward social objectives that include reasonable prices, efficiency, high employment, and adequate profit return while also taking into consideration such broad concerns as ecology, resource conservation, and the overall performance of the economy. The creation of such a policy must be the responsibility of an enlightened federal government. Government must act as an unbiased umpire, attempting always to balance the diverse economic and social interests of the nation. Such intervention need not abridge basic property rights (which is what Radicals want). But it would set social priorities above the pursuit of selfish individualistic goals (so feverishly defended by Conservatives).

THE RADICAL ARGUMENT

One of the great evasions of economic theory is its idealized portrayal of competition as a process devoid of conflict, power, and politics. Indeed, the existence of *any* market power is defined strictly in technical terms: If market prices are observed to be above marginal cost, then actual competition is falling short of its standard of perfect competition. Microeconomic theory aside, it is well understood by citizens and CEOs alike that the tendency for businesses to become both more centralized in control and concentrated in sales and assets is, and has been, a persistent outcome of capitalist competition. Today, large corporations dominate most markets, and it is through their control of economic resources that they can command such a disproportionate and deleterious impact on American society. While both Conservatives and Liberals oppose monopoly power, neither group wants to recognize that political power has become concentrated in a relatively small capitalist class that now seeks to dominate the political process through its unchallenged economic power.

All mainstream economic theory is loath to recognize not only that firms seek to grow but that their objective is to dominate both a particular industry and the economy and greater society as well. To achieve these goals, it is crucial that a firm have the strength to impose its own price on the market in order to increase its profits. To do this, a business must have the capacity and power to engage in price gouging as well as sustain a ruinous price war. Competition cannot be managed, democratized, or negotiated—corporations are fundamentally authoritarian organizations driven by the imperatives of growth and profitability. Thus, the Radical position can be easily distinguished by its understanding of a relatively simple business strategy that *all* capitalist firms must obey: Grow or die. Unpalatable as it may be, small firms do not play a major role in the U.S. economy and also tend not to persist. Either they evolve into large units of production and distribution (whatever the product) or they are eliminated. In the final analysis, if the state truly wants to tame and manage big business, it has to change the terms and conditions under which large firms exist and operate.

Monopoly Capitalism: What Went Wrong?

Prior to the late 1970s, most economists—including many Radicals—believed that capitalism had entered a new stage where the cutthroat, predatory price competition that characterized the nineteenth-century economy would no longer be appropriate for large modern corporations. The new post–World War II era of *monopoly capitalism* was one where profitability would be ensured by collusive or monopoly pricing arrangements. Because there was little micro or macro evidence of persistent price declines, economists of all stripes had come to believe that firms no longer competed on the basis of price. Furthermore, though economists were loath to acknowledge it, an uneasy but workable arrangement between management and workers prevailed: Labor would subordinate its demands for higher wages and benefits if capital allowed living standards to rise. Indeed, inflation-adjusted income for workers generally rose from about 1950 to 1973, largely due to labor's ability to impose its demands upon capital through unions and political organizing. However, in the early 1970s most of these gains were reversed. The average real wage peaked in 1973 at about $14 per hour and has failed to recover to that level after nearly thirty years. Workers in capital-intensive manufacturing industries were especially hard hit as capitalists shifted production overseas or invested in more profitable, nonindustrial sectors. By the 1990s, so-called white-collar occupations that were thought immune to economic adversity were now facing layoffs, downsizing, and widespread job insecurity. What went wrong? Why could monopoly capital not maintain its pricing power and guarantee high levels of production and employment?

For one thing, by the early 1980s the political consensus that had held the economy together was over. Deregulation and globalization created a dog-eat-dog economy with rampant job insecurity and declining living standards for the vast majority of wage earners. These reactionary policies were actually initiated by Democratic president Jimmy Carter but were fully unleashed under the Reagan administration. While workers bore the brunt of these reactionary policies, there was a battle being fought within the capitalist class. First, industrial capitalists who had become complacent with their dominant market positions were quickly supplanted by nimbler and more efficient foreign competitors. This was partly the result of years of underinvestment and managerial incompetence and arrogance, but it also reflected the end of unchallenged military and economic dominance by the United States.

A second problem faced by capitalists was how to tame the unprecedented inflation that gripped the U.S. economy from about 1968 through the mid-1980s. Financial capital sought to reestablish profitability in their industries by breaking the back of persistent price increases and inflationary expectations. Once again, Jimmy Carter—a liberal Democratic president—rescued financial capital by appointing a conservative banker, Paul Volcker, to head the Federal Reserve Board. Volcker's high-interest-rate policies, combined with rampant deregulation of financial markets, brought about a decisive victory for the financial sector. Smokestack industries such as autos, steel, and heavy manufacturing could not survive the simultaneous onslaught of a stagnating economy, widespread inflation, foreign competition, and disaccumulation. The subsequent period of deindustrialization and disinflation that destroyed the industrial heartland set the stage for what has turned out to be the greatest increase in the value of paper assets in U.S. history.

Persistent Concentration, Persistent Competition

If firms have little choice but to grow or die, it should come as no surprise that success in the marketplace necessarily entails having a large scale of production and sizable market share. Growth, however, can be achieved in any number of ways, such as by increasing sales or by gobbling up a competitor. Since 1998, businesses have spent an astounding $12.2 trillion either to merge with or to acquire other firms. While capitalists and their apologists claim that combinations serve to cleanse the system of inefficient producers, in actuality much of this money will be used to transfer ownership from one capitalist to another. For workers, mergers and acquisitions typically result in plant closings and layoffs rather than new investment in factories and technologies. Even Microsoft announced in 2004 that it expects to cut $1 billion in expenses, especially in employee health care costs and benefits over the next year. In recent years, deregulation and global competition have undermined the largest firms' traditional strategies of price fixing and production limits in their efforts to ensure profitability. Nevertheless, large multinational corporations now seek to acquire both resources and their competitors in order to better withstand the increasingly dynamic and turbulent competitive environment. Earning high rates of return has become dependent on access to large pools of financial, technological, and human resources.

To gain some perspective on the degree of centralization in the American economy, let us examine Table 4.1, which shows the number of firms and sales receipts in the major sectors of the American economy with assets of at least $250 million (based on corporate federal income tax returns). It is clear that the distribution of receipts is profoundly unequal across sectors. In almost every sector, less than 1 percent of the

Table 4.1

Corporations with $250 Million or More of Assets in 2000

	Number (tax returns)	Receipts (millions of dollars)	Percentage of industry's firms	Percentage of industry's receipts	Percentage of total receipts
Agriculture, forestry, and fishing	19	8,764	0.01	7.48	0.07
Mining	161	111,505	0.49	70.30	0.89
Construction	137	151,642	0.02	14.42	1.21
Manufacturing	1,595	4,371,728	0.55	76.15	34.93
Transportation and warehousing	124	300,790	0.08	57.06	2.40
Utilities	158	720,404	1.98	95.19	5.76
Wholesale and retail trade	714	2,324,349	0.07	43.07	18.57
Finance, insurance, and real estate	5,773	2,563,781	0.77	81.37	20.49
Information	479	780,284	0.41	80.68	6.23
Management of companies and enterprises	1,170	650,184	2.46	93.76	5.20
Totals	10,883	12,514,715	0.22	60.74	100.00

Source: U.S. Bureau of the Census, *Statistical Abstract of the United States*, table no. 741 (Washington, DC: Government Printing Office, 2003), 501.

firms garner more than three quarters of all receipts; for utilities and management companies and enterprises, less than 3 percent of firms control well over 90 percent of industry sales. Overall, about 0.22 percent of all firms took in almost 61 percent of the 12.5 trillion in total receipts in 2000.

As mergers and acquisitions continue and concentration of sales and assets in many industries increases, large corporations will attempt to reassert their power in the market by using a variety of strategy and tactics. Rather than being a new era of manageable capitalism, we have returned to the nineteenth century, where unbridled competition wreaks havoc on anyone who works for a living. Reducing the labor content in each unit of output is the dominant objective in the internationalization of production. For example, multinational clothing manufacturers and retailers are able to achieve incredible profits by paying their overseas workers 50 cents per hour while simultaneously charging so-called competitive prices—between $20 and $100—for a pair of jeans or sneakers sold in the U.S. market. Meanwhile, the overseas workers toil under oppressive working conditions that would be illegal under U.S. labor law. Nike, Gap, and Disney have become unconscionably profitable by producing and pricing their products in this manner.

Domestic service industries are also trying to significantly reduce wage costs while seeking to grow through the development, acquisition, and consolidation of integrated delivery networks. Because it is more difficult to use foreign cheap labor in the production of services (e.g., a haircut or a heart transplant), capitalists employ a different but equally effective strategy. Initially, the goal is to quickly gain market share by offering a service well below the actual cost of production. Low prices in turn generate significant volume growth as the customer base rapidly expands. Managed health care companies, airlines, cable television, and online computer service providers have been singularly successful in pursuing this type of strategy. Once market dominance is achieved in a region, prices can be increased with little retaliation from either competitors or the government. In fact, all of these industries are subject to some form of regulatory oversight; yet there is little political will to control predatory market conduct for fear of losing valuable campaign contributions from corporate donors. What's more, the Justice Department has shown little interest in prosecuting corporations for unfair pricing policies. The relatively low inflation rates of the 1990s have also helped to shield large corporations from scrutiny of their pricing power. Nevertheless, it is quite evident that competition both within and between industries will intensify, which surely will lead to lower wages and benefits while capital acts to consolidate its position and seek to create conditions where it can continue to dominate the American economy.

Big Capital and Politics: Change the Rules

As concentration and centralization grow and industries invade each other's territory, corporations will not only use the political system to repress worker demands, but, more important, will use legal and governmental authority to gain competitive advantages. Historically, big business has always maintained legions of lobbying organizations to press their demands before legislators. While it is difficult for big business to win at the ballot box, it has had little problem in getting politicians to create fiscal and regulatory policies that are favorable to its interests. The rash of scandals related to campaign finance irregularities involved many large corporations seeking preferential treatment and/or governmental contracts. Moreover, the $350 billion settlement with the tobacco industry and the $100 million penalty paid by Archer Daniels Midland indicate the scale and depth of capital's resources to withstand any pressure from the state. Campaign contributions continue to be an extremely cost-effective method for businesses to obtain favors, preferential tax treatments, contracts, and a host of other benefits from the government. As voters become increasingly dissatisfied with the political process, corporations will wield greater power over federal and state legislatures.

The solution to the seemingly unstoppable power of big business does not lie within the framework of conventional economic analysis and policy. While worker control over investment, production, and employment is the only long-term solution to rein in big business, in the short run more specific measures are required. In particular, what is needed is a strategy to undercut corporate power by changing the legal status of corporations so they lose their privileges of unlimited longevity, due process, and limited liability granted to them under federal and state laws. Historically, courts have ruled that corporations are "individuals," entitled to all the rights and protections guaranteed under the U.S. Constitution. Following the Reconstruction Era (1865–70), corporations shrewdly used the due process clause of the Fourteenth Amendment (ratified by the states in 1868) to overturn limitations placed upon them by state governments. Rulings by state regulatory agencies and legislatures were continually overturned by the federal courts, which in effect defended the rapacity of nineteenth-century robber barons by arguing that state controls deprived a corporation of property without due process. While some states fought to limit corporate power, other states (such as Delaware) actively courted corporations by exempting them from taxes and granting them perpetual charters.

Limiting longevity and the ability to transfer risk will significantly curtail the capacity of a corporation to grow and achieve market dominance. Corporate managers will be very wary of undertaking illegal actions since their liabilities will not be limited to their equity holdings. While Karl Marx forcefully argued that capital would never accede anything to labor without a fight, he also recognized that capitalism depends upon specific juridical and legal institutions, especially property rights. Changing the legal status of a corporation would be a strategy both bold and politically practical, with a realistic chance of limiting the power of big capital. However, changing the status of corporations will not be sufficient to change the economic and social relations between labor and capital. As competition further winnows the ever-shrinking number of large firms and democracy withers under the oppression of a tiny number of megacorporations, it will become evident to all citizens that social control and ownership of the economy's asset base is the only viable solution. Planning by and for the needs of all citizens—not corporate planning—will become central to ensuring and fulfilling the political economic ideals of American society.

Economic Regulation
Which Path: Deregulation or Reregulation?

The committee has found among the leading representatives of the railroad interests an increasing readiness to accept the aid of Congress in working out the solution of the railroad problem which has obstinately baffled all their efforts, and not a few of the ablest railroad men of the country seem disposed to look to the intervention of Congress as promising to afford the best means of ultimately securing a more equitable and satisfactory adjustment of the relations of the transportation interests to the community than they themselves have been able to bring about.

*—U.S. Senate Select Committee
on Interstate Commerce, 1886*

Railroads were totally regulated for almost a century. Obviously it will take time for railroads to learn all of the things that can be done in a freer climate. It will also take shippers time to learn this as well. But already it is apparent that both can use deregulation to their respective advantages.
—Association of American Railroads, 1982

No reasonable person will lament the passing of the Interstate Commerce Commission.
—George Will, ABC News commentator, 1996

Since WorldCom's public announcement on June 25, 2002 that the company misstated its earnings for 2001 and the first quarter of 2002, there's been an understandable outpouring of anger from every quarter of American society. While the misdeeds we uncovered occurred before I became CEO, I want to apologize on behalf of everyone at WorldCom. And I want to underscore that WorldCom's new management team—and our more than 60,000 employees—share the public's outrage over these events.

—John Sidgmore
President and CEO of WorldCom, 2002

Despite the major financial collapses and growing evidence of market failure, the critics of regulation steadfastly maintain their commitment to the goal of free markets and their resistance to economic regulation.

—Harry M. Trebing
public utilities regulation economist, 2004

The Problem

Public policy with respect to the operations of American business enterprise traditionally has rested upon two very different strategies: antitrust
law and economic regulation. The objective of antitrust law and its enforcement, as discussed in Issue 4, is to maintain an acceptable degree of
competition in most markets. The second type of government intervention in the structure and performance of markets rests on the assumption
that certain markets perform best under less-than-competitive conditions,
which are strictly regulated by government agencies. In these regulated
industries, a kind of "monopoly bargain" is struck whereby one firm, or at
most a few, is granted various protections from competition in return for
surrendering to a regulatory agency power over pricing, output, and other
production, financing, and marketing decisions.

The most common example of a regulated industry and a regulatory
agency has been a regional public utility (a gas and electric company or a
regional phone company) regulated by a state public service commission.
Historically, the concept of public regulation has been applied much more
broadly than just to public utilities. The first federal venture into direct
regulation came with the Interstate Commerce Commission (ICC) in 1887
(three years before federal antitrust law was laid down in the Sherman
Antitrust Act). The ICC was charged with restoring order to the nation's
ailing railroads, an industry long characterized on one hand by periodic
episodes of financial collapse resulting from vicious rate wars and on the
other by the very worst type of monopolistic practices. Over the next century, more than a dozen independent federal agencies and commissions
were erected to bring a measure of government regulation to everything
from banking to the airwaves to nuclear power.

The logic of insulating certain industries from the forces of the market
rested on two economic considerations: (1) that there existed the economic
advantages of lower costs (*economies of scale*) resulting from a single producer or a limited number of producers and (2) that a discernible *public
interest* would be served by exempting the industry from competition and
by establishing government regulation of price, service, and output. As the
years passed, these two criteria were stretched, modified, and sometimes
neglected altogether as the extent of government regulation expanded in
many directions. The idea of "regulating private industry in the public interest" was a peculiarly American experiment. Elsewhere in the world, state
ownership has been the preferred technique for dealing with public inter-

est questions. In the course of European economic development, postal services, railways, telecommunications, and electric and gas utilities were generally state owned. In the United States, the postal service is the only industry ever entirely owned and operated "in the public interest."

For most of the past century, industrial regulation enjoyed a high degree of public support, with most practicing economists nodding their approval at the work of regulatory agencies. The regulatory high-water mark was reached in the early 1970s. However, in the economy of the late 1970s, troubled by inflation, recession, unemployment, energy crises, and growing federal budgetary problems, regulatory activity was placed under greater scrutiny.

Most Liberals, who had long been supporters of the "regulation in the public interest" philosophy, defended the practice. Conservatives, sensing the direction of a new ideological wind that was blowing, were quick to attack federal regulation of industry. Never strong supporters of regulatory efforts, most Conservatives identified the regulatory link as among the weakest in the chain of Liberal interventionism in the economy. Their attack was direct enough: Regulation produces greater costs to society through creating and maintaining market inefficiency than any benefits it might provide for the public interest. By the mid-1970s, a new buzzword had entered academic and political discussions of the regulatory process: *deregulation*.

Beginning in 1978, the deregulators (which now included a fair number of Liberals as well as most Conservatives) began a campaign that succeeded in eliminating most regulation of airlines, buses, trucking, radio broadcasting, and natural gas and electric power production and distribution. Considerable relaxation occurred in the regulation of railroads, television and cable broadcasting, and banking and financial services. Meanwhile, the splitting up of the Bell telephone system in 1984 as the result of federal antitrust action opened much of the previously highly regulated phone system to market competition. The deregulatory mood spread during the Reagan presidency to a variety of government agencies charged with overseeing broad areas of social regulation, such as the Department of Consumer Affairs and the Federal Trade Commission.

The deregulation movement lost some momentum when the financial shock of a 500-point decline in the stock market on October 19, 1987, brought forth calls for greater regulation of the securities market by the federal government. This shock was followed quickly by a monumental solvency crisis in the savings and loan industry that seemed to be the direct outcome of excessive deregulation of banking institutions. In the airlines industry, formerly hailed by antiregulation advocates as the model for successful deregulation, the initial consumer benefits of increased competition and lower fares seemed to be ebbing in favor of greater monopoly power and higher prices. At the same time, deregulation of the television industry seemed to be pointing toward a decline of over-the-airwaves television and the potential loss of a long-held American "right," that of free television programming. Such developments began to generate second thoughts about deregulation.

Yet if there were serious second thoughts about deregulation, they did not produce a marked redirection of public policy. The Interstate Commerce Commission Termination Act of 1995 eliminated the ICC. Regulatory functions were scaled back and transferred to the Department of Transportation's newly created Surface Transportation Board (STB).

New technologies in the form of broadband Internet access through cable, power lines, and wireless fidelity (Wi-Fi), and cellular phones posed new competition for conventional telecommunications providers. It is now feasible to sidestep old-fashioned hardwired telephones by using wireless communications and the alternative of voice-over-internet to complete phone calls. The forward progress of technology is an invitation for local phone service to join long distance as deregulated, but public policy has not yet caught up with technology.

The long economic boom of the 1990s also helped stifle doubts over deregulation: Good times rarely author policy redirections. However, by the summer of 2001, Californians and many other Americans braced themselves against rolling blackouts and rising electricity and natural gas prices in the new deregulated public utility environment. A huge failure of the electrical power grid in the Northeast and Midwest in the summer of 2003 led people to ponder the notion that more government regulation and intervention was needed, not less, to ensure public health, safety, and convenience. Conventional industry regulation was about to intersect with the regulation of both the financial sector of the economy and the accounting profession. The physical failure to deliver electricity was paralleled by the high-profile bankruptcy of the Enron energy corporation in 2001. Defects in the deregulation of electricity markets, relaxed accounting oversight, and apparent criminal activity had contributed to the second largest bankruptcy in U.S. history, rivaled only by the debacle surrounding telecommunications and Internet giant WorldCom in 2002.

WorldCom's operational problems were disguised by improper accounting. The result was the largest bankruptcy in U.S. history, dragging down the market value of the telecommunications sector across the board. Asset values plummeted, telecom bankruptcies rose, retirement accounts were decimated, and many jobs in the industry were wiped out. Much of the blame was laid at the doorstep of corporate governance and flawed regulatory oversight of the accounting profession. The response was the Public Company Accounting Reform and Investor Protection (Sarbanes-Oxley) Act of 2002. The act established the Public Company Accounting Oversight Board to better regulate auditors of public companies and required new Securities and Exchange Commission rules demanding that chief executive officers and chief financial officers of public companies "certify" the truthfulness and accuracy of financial reports. Clearly, the deregulation debate is not yet over.

Synopsis

Conservatives argue that regulation is counterproductive, producing more costs than benefits to both the regulated industries and the public. Accordingly, they support the drift to deregulation and advocate more. The Liberal argument defends the general performance record of most regulated industries and maintains that many recent experiments in deregulation are dangerous to the economy. Radicals see the historical development of regulation as essentially a prop to monopoly privilege and recent deregulation efforts as merely a smokescreen for doing away with what business now considers the less attractive aspects of serving the public interest.

Anticipating the Arguments

- What are some of the counterproductive results of regulation that Conservatives see, and how would their plan for deregulation end such problems?
- On what grounds do Liberals defend at least limited regulation over complete deregulation?
- Why do Radicals reject regulation and instead call for public ownership and operation of previously regulated industries?

THE CONSERVATIVE ARGUMENT

The Conservative position on regulation is based on two sturdy and now familiar principles. First, regulation—or any interference with the market—tends to create resource misallocation, inefficiency, and, ultimately, greater costs to the community. Second, left alone, the market is capable of more rational decisions about the success or survival of a firm or industry than is the voting public or its representatives and bureaucrats.

The Failure of Regulation

Except for the very limited and infrequent situations where a *natural monopoly* exists, there are no justifiable conditions for regulating industry. A natural monopolist, such as a local supplier of electric power, enjoys the advantages of large-scale distribution that can provide all of a market's output at lower unit costs than could exist if there were a number of power distributors. In such a situation, the community can obtain the lower costs only if it restrains the monopolists' natural propensity to maximize profits by setting prices at whatever the market will bear. The problem with the American application of this regulation principle, however, is that regulation has mostly been applied in situations where some degree of competition actually exists or where competition should be encouraged. The result has been that the community gets a regulated monopoly or a tight oligopoly when it would have been better served by creating and maintaining competitive conditions. Even the regulation of so-called natural monopolies has had its problems because of inefficient rulings on pricing and service by the regulatory agency, usually in the name of protecting the public interest.

Recounting the experience with the first effort at using an independent regulatory agency to supervise an industry—the ICC—is instructive. As the oldest U.S. regulatory agency, the ICC accumulated the longest list of classic regulatory errors and is a good example of all the debilitating effects age brings to commission activity. Its goal was to protect the public from railroad price collusion and to protect the railroads from one another. By the mid-1930s, ICC power extended to all surface commercial transportation in the country: rail, trucking, and barges. Specific ICC controls covered rate setting, mergers, financial issues, abandonment, and service discontinuance, as well as carrier layoffs of labor. There was virtually nothing that a rail carrier or any other carrier regulated by the Interstate Commerce Commission could do without first obtaining commission approval.

The ICC followed a narrow, two-sided strategy: first, to maintain a competitive balance between and among the different modes (trucks and railroads) of surface transportation that provided each carrier with an adequate return on its investment, and second, to provide a level of service that would accommodate broad public interest objectives and to do so at a cost that also served those objectives.

In misguided efforts to maintain competition among different transportation modes, the ICC long followed the strategy of *umbrella ratemaking,* a practice of setting a rate high enough to allow less efficient modes of transport to earn a profit on specific services. This provided a special handicap to railroads, which lost traffic to other modes simply because they were not allowed to set lower rates (prices) and use their greater efficiency in the movement of certain goods. In protecting trucks and water carriers, the ICC directed business away from the more efficient railroads. At the same time, shippers and consumers absorbed higher-than-necessary transport charges in their purchases.

Similar anticompetitive outcomes resulted from the ICC's opposition to rail mergers. This led to costly balkanization. The line-haul railroads were unable to combine to increase freight exchange and coordination and to strengthen their financial structures. By denying the industry access to these economies of scale, service remained expensive and inefficient. The ICC also prohibited intermodal mergers: Railroads were not allowed to consolidate with trucks and other carriers to improve their overall efficiency.

Meanwhile, in search of the will-o'-the-wisp "public interest," the ICC also acted to raise transport costs and reduce rail efficiency by maintaining redundant routes and little-used spurs. Permission to abandon low-density or loss-producing operations was difficult to obtain from the commission, and railroads were compelled to pour millions of dollars into expensive routes that generated only a few dollars in traffic.

By prohibiting railroads from setting their rates freely, denying them the right to develop joint rail-truck transportation companies, and demanding that they continue to operate costly and inefficient services and schedules, the ICC rendered the railroads' competitive situation virtually hopeless. ICC decisions on rates, abandonments, and mergers were presented as proof of the agency's commitment to the public interest. In point of fact, its action harmed rather than protected the nation's welfare.

The general ICC strategy was applied by other regulatory agencies with not much better success. Whether we look at railroads, airlines, long-distance telecommunications, broadcasting, trucking, or banking, we see the same dismal results from the era of public regulation. First, regulation encouraged cartel pricing. This usually meant setting a price floor that was high enough to allow the least efficient member of the cartel to survive. The industry price was usually higher than the price that would have existed under competitive conditions. Second, in the absence of any effective price competition in the industry, competition could only emerge in nonprice areas. Banks emphasized "special services." Airlines promoted themselves as "friendlier" or as offering more sumptuous in-flight meals. Few regulated firms were likely to introduce new services that produced real benefits or savings to customers. New ways of doing business were always seen as posing elements of risk and instability that neither the regulated industry nor the regulators wanted. Meanwhile, new investment and modernization lagged in regulated industries. Third, industries in a regulated cartel developed a special inertia at the management level. In fact, as deregulation became an increasingly popular idea in the 1970s and 1980s, many of its strongest opponents were the very industries that were to be deregulated.

The Market Alternative

Efforts to introduce a market alternative to regulation have posed and will continue to pose special problems. Not only are government bureaucrats unwilling to destroy their own jobs, but a number of regulated firms and many of their customers have also shown some fear of living in a free marketplace. What, in fact, can unregulated markets do better than regulated ones?

The first advantage the consuming public usually enjoys is falling prices. Except in cases where certain consumers experienced benefits from price discrimination, competitive market prices will be lower than those established for regulated cartels. Airline passengers, for instance, have learned to enjoy these benefits on long-distance routes since the start of the 1980s. However, some short-distance (and very high-cost) flights have gone up in price to reflect real rather than administered pricing conditions. Meanwhile, the downward pressure on prices caused by competition among existing firms and the entry of new firms into the market (limited if not impossible under regulated conditions) will compel enterprises to improve operating efficiency. This will spark new investment among firms that are vital and capable enough to undertake the outlays; it will also act as euthanasia for firms and industries that are inherently inefficient or historically outmoded. With market profitability now directing resource usage, the application of labor and capital in production operations will require efficient resource allocation. The artificial wages and job protections unions possessed in certain industries such as railroads and airlines will, of course, come to an end.

Meanwhile, bad business habits and indefensibly uneconomical managerial activities will cease under competitive operations. The old regulated industry mentality of avoiding anything that smacks of newness will have to be replaced by a more innovative and entrepreneurial managerial philosophy. The habit of counting on the regulatory agency or the government to bail out financially troubled firms through rate increases or direct subsidies, such as the rail industry long enjoyed, will end.

Under regulation, price discrimination was common. Usually referred to as *cross subsidization,* it appeared whenever certain customers were, with regulatory encouragement, charged considerably in excess of costs for the same service that other customers received at less than cost. In the telephone industry, before the AT&T breakup, cross subsidies existed when long-distance charges were artificially inflated to underwrite losses on local service. The result was to discriminate against business customers primarily and in favor of most residential phone users. In this case, deregulation has meant higher prices for residential phone users (but lower prices for all long-distance users). As with airline pricing, ending cross subsidies produces winners and losers. Only the shortsighted will oppose ending official price discrimination, for unless actual costs are the major determinant of rates and prices, we are employing a pricing system that is inefficient *and* unfair.

Finally, of course, a market-directed system explodes the fiction of the public interest. The notion that some bureaucratic authority can determine a transcendent public interest and then act to implement it belongs more to the realm of metaphysics than to that of sensible economic reasoning. To return to our earlier discussion of the ICC and America's railroads, we might speculate that, left to the dictates of a free market (and without an ICC), a national transportation mix might have emerged that would have allowed each transport mode to develop its inherent strengths. Instead of the artificial competition created "in the public interest" that pitted trucks and railroads against each other but provided no way of determining their relative efficiency, each form of transportation could have exploited its own advantages, dropping out of markets where it had none. The market is indeed the best determinant of the public's best interests.

Evaluating Deregulation to Date

The final test for the effectiveness of deregulation is not logic but actual performance, and here deregulation has proved an important spur to the American economy. A look at the record should be convincing enough.

The Airline Deregulation Act of 1978 was the first important effort to dismantle a regulated cartel and return it to competition. Under this law, air carriers were granted greater ratemaking freedom and greater freedom of entry and exit from airline markets. Accordingly, the Civil Aeronautics Board (CAB) (which went out of business in early 1985, the first major regulatory agency so abolished) allowed airlines to fly on a "first come, first served" basis to most American cities. The action ended the old, inefficient practice of granting virtual monopoly power to certain carriers over certain routes. As a result, dozens of existing companies altered their routes (both expanding and contracting service on specific routes). At the same time, more than a score of brand-new long-distance carriers suddenly appeared. Meanwhile, the market, rather than the CAB, was allowed to determine most airline rates. The new approach brought most long-distance airfares down. Loss-producing routes were abandoned to new specialized commuter lines, or fares were adjusted upward by the larger carriers to reflect real operating costs. The new market freedom allowed the airlines to price and operate according to actual supply-and-demand conditions and permitted passengers to enjoy the price benefits of competition.

Two years after the deregulation of the airlines, the Motor Carrier Act of 1980 brought gradual deregulation to the trucking industry (regulated by the ICC since 1930). Again the approach was the same: to allow greater freedom in ratemaking by individual truckers and the easing of entry restrictions into long-haul, interstate trucking. The benefits to the public came quickly. More than 5,200 new trucking firms entered the industry in the first eighteen months of deregulation; 20,000 new route applications were filed with the ICC; and average freight bills went down 10 to 20 percent.

In 1980, the Staggers Rail Act gave railroads some relief from ICC control. In particular, they were freed to make most rate changes without prior ICC approval and were given permission to contract directly with shippers at less-than-market rates for long-term, bulk shipments. Previously, approval for rate changes had cost the railroads up to $1 billion a year as the ICC delayed adjusting rates for inflation, and special shipper-railroad contracts had been held to be an illegal form of rebating. The Surface Transportation Board has calculated that rail rates (adjusted for inflation) fell by more than 45 percent from 1984 to 1999, and this resulted in annual savings to consumers in 1999 of $31.7 billion.*

The gains from deregulation have not been limited to transportation. The deregulation of long-distance telecommunications has produced consumer savings and a more vibrant industry. In banking and finance, most restrictions have been lifted on branch banking, bank mergers, and overseas banking operations. There is more freedom to offer greater variety of financial options to customers. The elimination of artificial limits on the operations and functions of banks and other financial institutions has promoted increased competition among commercial banks, thrifts, credit unions, brokerage firms, and insurance companies in funds markets, raising investor earnings possibilities and lowering customer charges.

Those interested in *reregulation* will doubtless cite the recent California public power crisis as evidence that deregulation does not work. Likewise, blackouts caused by unreliable power transmission are erroneously blamed on deregulation or the absence of other forms of government intrusion. According to their view, California's experiment with partial deregulation of energy prices (the separating of power generation from public utility distribution and the introduction of free market conditions in the pricing of wholesale purchases of natural gas and electric power) led to the state's energy shortage *and* to the bankrupting of the public utility deliverance of gas and electricity. It is true, of course, that the wholesale prices of gas and electricity rose after partial deregulation. *They had to.* California (like other regulated states) had for too long maintained artificially low wholesale prices under its regulated system. This was done so consumers could pay below-market retail prices. But a low return on energy supplies (even when these supplies were owned by the public utilities themselves or by the State of California) discouraged the development of new sources of supply precisely as the artificially low cost to consumers pumped up the demand for energy. Long before deregulation of energy supplies took place, California was headed for a train wreck—one caused by the regulators themselves.

---

* "Rail Rates Continue Multi-Year Decline," Office of Economics, Environmental Analysis and Administration, Surface Transportation Board (December 2000).

To argue that California's rolling blackouts and rising consumer prices were the result of price gouging by suppliers is simply not true. The price of energy had to go up one way or another. There can be no free lunch. Either California taxpayers would pay (to build state-operated or subsidized power sources) to close the gap between fixed, below-market prices and rising wholesale energy costs or, sooner or later, California consumers would have to pay. In any event, while deregulation of wholesale energy prices in California will lead to somewhat higher retail prices, higher rates will also invite more suppliers into the energy market. In the long run, prices will settle in at an acceptable level *and* California will no longer face the energy deficit that regulation forced upon the state.

Regulation and reregulation advocates continue to stake out policy positions that retard the development of new markets, curtail benefits to consumers, and extend the monopoly power of regulated firms. For example, innovations in wireless and Internet communications really obviate the need for rate regulation of wire-based telecommunications, but the Federal Communications Commission continues to regulate pricing policies and attempts to manage competition among different modes.

Those who now see certain shortcomings with deregulation forget that the gains of market-directed economic activities are not possible without occasional risks. Avoiding such risks through regulation may produce a desired orderliness, but only at an exceptionally high cost. Overall, the economic costs of regulation impose a much greater burden on society than any risks associated with market competition.

THE LIBERAL ARGUMENT

Regulatory agencies are the logical outcome of the need to improve market conditions in certain industries. Direct regulation is not essential to all markets, but in certain cases—mainly where natural monopolies tend to develop or should be encouraged—regulation by government agencies can maximize the benefits to both the consumer and the affected industry. Antitrust action, as we have discussed, is employed in cases of conspiracy to attain a socially undesirable monopoly advantage in the market, but direct regulation is a ratification of monopoly power. In exchange for this recognized monopoly position, a firm submits to close political and economic supervision.

The Rules of Regulation

Under regulation, business firms are guaranteed certain rights. For example, their property rights are legally protected, and confiscation is not a serious possibility. They are entitled to receive reasonable prices and a fair rate of return on their capital. In the specific geographic area in which it operates, a regulated firm is given partial or total protection from competition. A firm can challenge in the courts any regulatory decision made by the relevant commission.

Regulated firms also have certain obligations. Their prices and profits must not be excessive. Prices should be established that offer the greatest possible service without compelling a company to forfeit its capital through continuous losses. Moreover, the regulated firm must meet all demand at the established prices. Any change in the quantity or quality of service must be approved in advance by the regulatory agency. The final decision in such cases as petitions for abandonment of service must balance two conflicting objectives: the firm's operational benefits and the public interest. Finally, all regulated industries must be committed to high levels of performance with the highest possible standards of safety to the public. The key to regulation philosophy, developed over ten decades of experience and through sixteen independent agencies, is this: a balance of public and private (corporate) interests.

The Public Interest Revisited

The deafening roar of the Conservative crowd cheering on the recent drift toward deregulation has drowned out reason. While theoretical arguments are developed with considerable elegance to "prove" that regulation does not work and that a return to market competition for previously regulated industries would improve economic efficiency and well-being, the real issue has been papered over. What we have forgotten in our rush toward deregulation is to ask ourselves why Americans introduced the regulatory experiment in the first place. Surely regulation did not just happen accidentally. What, then, were its antecedents? It began with the long-held view that certain public interest objectives could never be well served in unregulated markets.

In the current rewriting of American economic history, Conservatives fail to recall that most ventures into regulation by independent regulatory commissions were not simply unconscious evasions of a market-dominated economy. A survey of previously or presently regulated industries shows that regulation evolved only after consistent evidence of market failure under conditions of competition.

The creation of the ICC in 1887 and its development of real regulatory power over the next twenty years came only after the excessive and irrational building of the American railroad network had brought about cutthroat competition that destabilized the industry. Periodically, bloody rate wars would break out among the giants as each tried to gain a larger share of the restricted transportation market. Consequently, there were frequent bankruptcies and breakdowns in service. Because of their critical place in the economy, as railroads went, so went the nation. Every major financial panic and recession after the Civil War—in 1873, 1884, and 1893—started with railroad bankruptcies. Attempts at private rate fixing and cartels, even before the Sherman Antitrust Act established their unconstitutionality, almost always failed. Even so, these expedients harmed farmers and other shippers. This, then, was the situation when the ICC was created. The free market operation of the rail industry could no longer be tolerated. This view was widely held by bankers, farmers, shippers, and railroad management.

Eventually all commercial surface transport enterprises came under ICC jurisdiction. The accretions of power in every case were responses to the failure of competitive market operations in the transport industry. It is important to recognize that elimination of the ICC in 1996 did not *eliminate* surface transportation regulation. Essential regulatory authority was moved to the Surface Transportation Board in practical recognition of the fact that the transportation industry's stability depends on government oversight.

The story was similar elsewhere as public regulation was employed to offset a variety of problems rooted in an overly competitive economic system. The regulation of the airwaves in the 1920s by the FCC made it possible for radio listeners to interpret the chatter coming from radios. Competitive stations had operated without license or assigned frequencies, and the public was ill served. The building of the Federal Reserve System in 1914 (following passage of the Federal Reserve Act of 1913) came after a hundred years of unregulated and chaotic competition. Banks, usually operating with the skimpiest of reserves, showed a dangerous tendency to fall off into periods of panic, which in turn drove the nation into episodes of economic depression. The Securities and Exchange Commission was created in the 1930s after the overzealous actions of securities firms and banks played a central role in the financial collapse of 1929.

The list of regulatory responses to the market failures of a purely free and competitive economy goes on and on. Regulation reflects not a situation where the nation has *not tried* competition, but rather one where it has been tried and found wanting, where the disadvantages of competition have shown themselves to be greater than the community wishes to shoulder. Conservatives attack the concept of regulation in the public interest without admitting that the public was badly served by an unreliable and frequently bankrupt transportation system, by dangerous if not fraudulent banking practices, by unscrupulous investment bankers and brokers, and by an unregulated use of the airwaves. When railroads fail and banks close or when unregulated energy prices close industries and chill homes, the nation is not simply faced with some readjustment of markets but with a threat to its very survival. Accordingly, it has been understood that certain basic sectors of the economy have responsibilities that go beyond private interest, that in fact serve a broader public interest even if they are privately owned. Europeans generally chose to deal with this conflict of interests by nationalizing or operating as public enterprises those industries that had broad public interest responsibilities. Public regulation was a less extreme response to this problem.

Another dimension of the "public interest approach" is the commitment to maintaining *universal service.* Under this philosophy, regulatory agencies frequently employ cross subsidization to ensure that certain customers who might not otherwise have obtained service if charges were based solely on costs do in fact have reasonable service. Essentially, an ability-to-pay principle is applied, with those with greater carrying capacity subsidizing those whose costs are high but capacity to pay is low. So it was that rural rail and trucking services were subsidized by long-distance shippers and that elderly, fixed-income phone users had part of their costs paid by large corporations. To Conservatives, this is price discrimination, pure and simple; however, they make no attempt to explain how society's interests would be better served if small communities atrophy for lack of reasonably priced transportation or if low-income families are left without phone service.

Finally, on behalf of the public interest, it is appropriate for the government to allocate scarce resources. For instance, regulating prices and limiting exploitation of natural resources, with a view toward rationing their use, are appropriate public policy objectives that transcend any narrow profit interests.

To be sure, regulation in the public interest is not without its costs. The costs, however, are not really the alleged costs of inefficiency so frequently cited by Conservatives. They are the costs of creating market stability and equity that would not otherwise exist. Supplying reasonably priced phone service to all users may mean higher costs for some users. A safer banking system costs more to operate than a dangerously weak and speculative one. These costs are more than offset, however, by the long-run gains achieved for the entire society. Deregulation, meanwhile, stresses only the benefit of short-run savings (profits, really) from relaxing our concern for the public interest.

The Deregulation Balance Sheet

Deregulation as an effective economic policy is now more than a quarter century old. Evidence is abundant enough to make an evaluation, and, contrary to the cheery Conservative assessment, it is not all that supporting.

In the transportation industries, the results are at best mixed. Railroads generally have benefited at the expense of the less efficient trucking competitors and of hundreds of communities that have lost rail service. Accordingly, some shippers—those able to use railroads—have gained, while others have lost. In the airlines industry, the early pricing benefits obtained by consumers under greater competition were quite temporary. Very quickly the opening of new routes and markets was followed by a wave of mergers that reduced the number of competing air carriers and consequently increased monopolistic control over passenger traffic at each of the major hub cities. Characteristically, airfares began to rise and passengers noticed a steady deterioration of service.

Although not the specific result of dismantling a regulatory agency but certainly the outcome of other public policies running in that direction, the breakup of AT&T does not stand out as a shining example of deregulatory success. The ending of cross subsidization translated directly into high and rising phone bills for virtually all residential customers. Meanwhile, the alleged benefits of competitive long-distance service seem lost in the confusion of phone bills and the selecting of one's long-distance carrier. Most average users of the telephone regularly report in opinion surveys that they feel costs have risen and service has declined since the breakup of Ma Bell.

The extent to which deregulation can produce truly catastrophic costs for society is best illustrated by the banking and finance industry. With thrifts (savings and loan associations, mutual savings banks, and credit unions) freed in 1982 to compete with commercial banks and other financial intermediaries, they found themselves compelled to pay fairly high interest rates to attract funds. Indeed, the exceptionally high interest rates of the time would have caused problems regardless of deregulation. However, now freed of earlier restraints that confined the savings and loan activities almost exclusively to mortgage markets, thrifts ventured into high-return—and high-risk—lending. Loans to speculative real estate ventures, solar energy companies, windmill farms, and the like had very high failure rates in the early 1980s. Accordingly, many banks drifted toward and finally into bankruptcy.

With depositors' savings insured, government was obliged to "socialize" the costs of the thrifts' zeal in seeking high-return investments. Some will argue that this was a unique situation, largely the result of government insulating financial institutions from market discipline by insuring their fiduciary responsibilities. However, it does not take an overactive imagination to consider that the socialization of deregulatory costs is not necessarily limited to financial markets. Should conditions resulting from deregulation demand it, government bailouts of airlines, telecommunication companies, public utilities, and the like are not unthinkable.

Of course, some criticisms of regulatory agencies—especially regarding their inflexibility in the face of changed economic and technological conditions and their habit of becoming too cozy with the very firms they regulate—are quite valid. Some regulatory agencies have outlived their usefulness. The passing of the ICC in 1996 was scarcely noticed by anyone. However, regulatory weaknesses are not causes for abandoning regulation altogether. The tumult produced by haphazard deregulation of electrical generation combined with insufficient regulation of the accounting profession resulted in severe disruptions and the largest corporate bankruptcies in history. That recent lesson calls for a reasoned and longer view of deregulation and its effects. Dismantling regulatory machinery has reintroduced the old problems that were the impetus for regulation in the first place. Liberals see little benefit from having to learn again that unregulated capitalism produces serious market failures and imperfections that must sooner or later be offset by government intervention.

THE RADICAL ARGUMENT

History readily shows that the natural inclination of production-for-profit enterprises is to acquire as much price-making power as possible. Therefore, the long-term outcome of competition is invariably the development of some degree of monopoly power. Yet monopolistic power is not always easily attained. It often requires enlisting the apparatus of the state in its behalf to be effective. Accordingly, public regulatory commissions were organized in the United States to ratify the existence of monopoly. Regardless of the intention of reformers who championed their development, regulatory agencies worked primarily on behalf of the industries they regulated. The creation of independent regulatory agencies and their performance do not support the Liberal claim that public interest is a major element in regulatory action. Neither do they support the Conservative charge that regulation has been antibusiness.

Curiously, however, the deregulation movement also has advanced the objective of creating monopoly—but, of course, not in an obvious way. From a Radical perspective, the oscillations in public policy from free market to regulation to deregulation (and recently) to reregulation are not a cycle at all, as conventional economists suggest, but are variations on the same monopoly capitalist theme. Such an argument will be unfamiliar to many non-Radicals and may initially appear to be contradictory. To make the Radical position a bit clearer, we will examine one regulatory case in considerable detail rather than undertake a broad survey of American regulatory activities. The Interstate Commerce Commission's regulation of surface transportation in the United States is an excellent representative example.

Regulation as a Creature of Industry: The Case of the ICC

Progressive-era legislative and regulatory actions, rather than being single-minded efforts to find a compromise between parties on either side of a particular market (as the then-current political rhetoric maintained), were really efforts to bring order to highly disrupted and overly competitive markets. But order was achieved on terms that supported the principles of private property and corporate profit seeking, terms that replaced competition with official recognition of limited monopolistic power and cartelization.

The ICC from its very beginning was an attempt to create an official cartel in rail transportation. This policy was steadily enlarged and elaborated on by the industry. Eventually, it also was applied to other modes of public transportation (buses, trucks, water carriers, and pipelines under the ICC and air carriers under the Civil Aeronautics Board). The development of the ICC was not a haphazard abandonment of high principles; it was the unfolding of a planned and rational policy. (It was rational at least in the sense that it consistently pursued clear ends, even though these goals might ultimately result in economic and social loss to the nation.)

Although many economic interests favored the creation of a federal railroad regulatory agency in the late 1880s, one of the most influential groups consisted of railroad leaders themselves. The closing decades of the nineteenth century had witnessed costly rate wars and other competitive difficulties, resulting largely from the enormous excess capacity built into the industry. These conflicts could not be handled through private efforts at cartelization, partly because these efforts usually collapsed of their own enforcement weaknesses and partly because other economic groups challenged such blatant attempts to build monopoly power. The railroads, therefore, turned to the federal government for official sanction of cartel creation. Progress toward this end began with passage of the Interstate Commerce Act of 1887; over the next twenty years, in the ICC and in Congress, railroads obtained important recognition as a cartel. Indeed, the Elkins Act (1903), which ended the hated competitive practice of paying rebates to certain shippers, was written in the legal offices of the Pennsylvania Railroad. The Hepburn Act (1906), which enlarged the ICC's power, supposedly at the expense of the rail monopolies, had considerable management endorsement.

"Community of interest" (informal domination of all rail operations in a region by a few large railroads) and other plans formulated to integrate rail properties for the purpose of gaining greater monopoly power were frustrated for a time, but railroads emerged from World War I, after their ignominious operational collapse and more than two years of government control, with the Esch-Cummins Act of 1920. This law, as interpreted by the ICC and the courts, firmly established the principle of railroad cartelization. The old competitive situation within the industry no longer existed and the rail network was reduced to a limited number of essentially noncompetitive systems. Most state regulatory powers over finance and operations were abolished. The old ambition of industry pooling and rate bureaus was nourished during the Depression. Throughout the disastrous 1930s, the government, at Franklin Roosevelt's insistence, officially recognized the Association of American Railroads as the industrywide policy-making body. It was a powerful lobby and a tool for encouraging collusion within the industry. At the behest of rail leaders, the government moved in 1935 to control competition from the hated trucks and buses by placing them under ICC regulatory control. Finally, with the passage of the Transportation Act of 1940, the federal government officially declared an end to any pretense of maintaining "costly competition," either between railroads or among competing transport modes.

None of these regulatory and legislative successes by the railroads could, however, insulate the industry from competition or the structural and demand dislocations that persistently wreaked havoc with railroad balance sheets through the 1950s and 1960s. The decline was not halted even by the hastily drawn Transportation Act of 1958, which took away the last effective regulatory power of the states over passenger trains, nor by the ICC's growing willingness to approve almost any kind of merger or abandonment. The railroads had succeeded in getting themselves established as a protected cartel. Though they were not totally free to undertake whatever was in their interest, the official commitment to maintaining railroads as a privately owned industry meant that railroad legislation and regulation were loaded in their favor. The industry had to be kept going—on its own terms. For society, this translated into the reduction of rail service and the steady deterioration of service that remained.

The Deregulation Phenomenon

In many respects, the emergency legislation efforts to deal with the rail crisis in the Northeast corridor reveal the actual content, past and present, of our transportation and regulatory policy. Under the 1976 Railroad Revitalization and Regulatory Reform Act, six bankrupt northeastern railroads were organized into Conrail. Two points are noteworthy in this development. First, Conrail, although federally organized, was to become a private production-for-profit corporation after it had been reconditioned by a massive infusion of government funds and by a ruthless reduction in its trackage. Second, Conrail was devised to rescue the funds of the bankrupt railroads' investors. Although the government's initial estimate of the scrap value of the bankrupt railroads was set at $621 million, the owners claimed their deteriorated rolling stock and rusting rails to be worth at least $7 billion. Under pressure from banks, insurance companies, and other holders of railroad securities, Conrail was initially granted $2.1 billion in federal funds to acquire the nearly worthless financial paper of these railroads. The prospects of monetary gain from Conrail were evident to the investors in the bankrupt lines, many of whom spoke glowingly of government ownership. There was little talk of such actions being socialistic, but economist John Kenneth Galbraith has correctly called it "socialism for the rich."

The Motor Carrier Act of 1980 and the Staggers Rail Act of the same year put the finishing touches on what had been started four years earlier. The former deregulated trucking, and the latter gave broad ratemaking and other freedoms to railroads. Deregulating surface transportation can only help the railroads, just as regulation helped in an earlier stage. With the end of ICC pricing strategies that protected the less efficient long-distance trucking industry, deregulation gives railroads a chance to utilize their major cost advantage over trucks. Regulation previously protected railroads from competition between themselves and the highly subsidized truckers. Now, with the railroad industry highly concentrated (and few new railroads likely to be built), intermodal competition will likely create rail domination of trucking. The less concentrated trucking industry is already feeling the effects as its profits fall and rail profits rise. In the railroad-truck competition, giant transportation firms can be built on the railroad stem as railroads expand trailer-on-flatcar (TOFL) and container service on long-distance routes and add their own trucking facilities at either end of their rail routes. For a while there may be an illusion of competition (more truckers, more rate freedom, etc.), but the competition only masks the development of new monopoly power in the transportation industry.

The surface transportation industry scenario, which we have examined in detail, reflects the case of other industries undergoing deregulation. Among the deregulated airlines, despite the early appearance of new entrants in the market, recent mergers are increasing the likelihood of greater concentration among long-distance carriers. Caught up in the deregulation mood of the times, the Federal Communications Commission has permitted several giant mergers and a very large number of small ones in the radio and television industries. These mergers have narrowed the number of independently owned radio and television stations and created several absolute giants in broadcasting. Deregulation in banking has meant the building of giant financial-service enterprises that combine banking and nonbanking functions as well as the enlargement of already huge banks by reducing restrictions on branch banking and interstate banking. Such developments in no way support the Conservative claim that deregulation is restoring competition. Deregulation only continues the cartelizing of certain industries that commenced in the now discredited era of regulation.

Deregulation, whatever its immediate short-term gains to particular industries, can never be a long-term strategy. The destabilizing effects of excessive monopoly power—the direct result of deregulation—must be corrected to maintain economic and social order. The potential for abuse by deregulated but monopolistic railroads and air carriers provokes pressure for reregulation from the public and from commercial shippers. Similarly, the destabilizing of American banking and finance cannot be permitted. The banking industry requires reregulation to provide orderly financial markets. The 2001 price gouging affecting California's electricity consumers is only the latest example of the destabilizing effects of deregulation. The recent appeal of controlling and cartelizing deregulated industries, while appearing to be a new public policy direction, is merely a return to the old strategy of creating officially protected cartels.

As deregulation pressures wind down and give way to calls for reregulation, we should learn this lesson: *Social ownership and control of predominantly public interest industries offers the only viable alternative.* Public ownership and operation of transportation, banking, telecommunications, and the like is a means of establishing the collective control that regulation initially promised but could not achieve and that deregulation directly opposes.

Income Distribution

Does America Have an Income Inequality Problem?

Like all other contracts, wages should be left to the fair and free competition of the market, and should never be controlled by the interference of the legislature. The clear and direct tendency of the poor laws is in direct opposition to these obvious principles: it is not as the legislature benevolently intended, to amend the condition of the poor, but to deteriorate the condition of both poor and rich; instead of making the poor rich, they are calculated to make the rich poor.

—David Ricardo, 1821

It is not to die, or even to die of hunger, that makes a man wretched; many men have died, all men must die. . . . But it is to live miserable we know not why; to work sore and yet gain nothing; to be heart-worn, weary yet isolated, unrelated, girt in with a cold, universal Laissez Faire.

—Thomas Carlyle, 1853

Here's the bottom line: welfare reform worked because single mothers left welfare and went to work in unprecedented numbers. Good for them. Good for their children.

—White House News Release, 2002

The Problem

In August 1996, Congress passed the Personal Responsibility and Work Opportunity Reconciliation Act (PRWORA) in order to "end the dependence of needy parents on government benefits by promoting job preparedness, work, and marriage." The legislation transferred much of social welfare policy making and program development to the states. Congress also imposed several new mandates including stricter work requirements and time limits on benefits. Cash payments to impoverished families are now administered under the Temporary Assistance to Needy Families (TANF) program and funded by federal "block grants" administered by the individual fifty states. The block-granting of funds to the states seemed to mean the repeal of an old covenant between the federal government and the nation's needy that could be traced all the way back to the New Deal of Franklin Roosevelt. To others, it was less a reneging on an old promise than a matter of coming to terms—"getting real"—with the mess that the nation's previous welfare system had become. For example, TANF now requires that 90 percent of a state's welfare recipients be moved into work or work-related activities within two years and there is a five-year time limit on most benefits. At its core, TANF transformed cash assistance to poor people from a right to a privilege, contingent upon the ability to perform work.

Welfare as a right was, in fact, a comparatively new idea in the United States. Its origins could not be traced back beyond the 1930s, and, some would argue, not really beyond the late 1960s. In the distant past (before the twentieth century), any welfare that existed was mostly provided by private charitable activity, sometimes by churches but most frequently by the largesse of compassionate friends and relatives. As late as 1902, combined federal, state, and local outlays for public welfare totaled only $41 million, and practically all of this came from local governments. This amounted to 0.2 percent of gross domestic product (GDP).

Until the 1930s, public assistance was always intended to address short-term instances of unemployment or poverty. Ordinarily, the recipient was required to work at some public-sector job for the assistance received. Indeed, Franklin Roosevelt followed that long-accepted pattern with his make-work Works Progress Administration (WPA) welfare programs in the 1930s. In 1934, in the depths of the Great Depression, public welfare outlays by state, local, and federal governments totaled about $1 billion, or about 2 percent of GDP. Still, public assistance was seen as a short-term measure. Unlike Great Britain, where the poorhouse and the dole had persisted for more than a century as a way of life for the truly poor, no similar arrangements were constructed in the United States to deal with chronic poverty. However, the notion that citizens had a right to public assistance began to take shape with certain New Deal programs—Aid to the Aged, Aid to the Disabled, and Aid to Dependent Children (later to be known as Aid to Families with Dependent Children, or AFDC). In the late 1960s, President Lyndon Johnson's War on Poverty efforts left no doubt that access to public assistance was a right for all needy citizens.

By 1978, with the federal government having essentially taken control of most public assistance programs (although the states still exercised some influence over the level of certain in-state payments), means-tested (or income-based) public assistance programs accounted for more than $63 billion in federal outlays and $20 billion in state outlays. Such programs included Medicaid, AFDC, Supplemental Security Income, food stamps, child nutrition, and housing assistance and opportunity grants. By the mid-1990s, federal and state cash and in-kind assistance and Medicaid had grown to more than $225 billion. Large as such a figure seems, it was still only a bit over 3 percent of GDP.

In any case, in the emerging debate about the nation's welfare program, the actual size of the public assistance outlay was always secondary to another question: What exactly was the nation buying with its welfare outlays? Even the welfare system's defenders took little pride in what had been created. True, by the mid-1990s, public assistance was only a temporary stopping spot for most of the 10 to 12 percent of the nation who were poor; but almost half of the poor, about one in every twenty Americans, were caught in chronic poverty. Among this group, public assistance, for whatever reason, had become a permanent condition. All too frequently it was accompanied by an ugly social pathology of broken families, unmarried mothers, educational failure, joblessness, high rates of substance addiction and crime, and, always, abiding personal despair.

By the 1990s, amidst an increasingly conservative political climate, the old American opposition to providing a permanent dole had resurfaced with a vengeance. Politically speaking, there was no way to oppose the growing national will to abolish welfare as a right and to place stringent restrictions upon it as a privilege. The political mood doubtless had been buoyed by the good economic times of the 1990s in which it became easy to believe that most poor people should be able to work themselves out of welfare.

While it is too early to give a definitive answer about the ultimate success or failure of the current experiment with welfare reform, certain trends are not disputed. Since 1996 there has been about a 50 percent decline in the number of families with children who receive cash compensation from public assistance. Moreover, while there was much concern over the effect of a recession on workfare participants, recent Census Bureau data suggest only very modest increases in child and female-headed household poverty rates, while the poverty rate for African American children reached an all-time low in 2001. Employment rates among TANF recipients have remained relatively stable while labor force participation rates for unmarried mothers exhibited a persistent and notable increase after 1996.

Nevertheless, the precise reasons for these changes cannot be easily disentangled from the larger economic picture. First, individual states such as Wisconsin had already been transforming their social welfare policies and programs from needs-based to work-based requirements well before federal reforms. Second, significant state-level economic growth between 1995 and 2000 reduced welfare rolls and freed up TANF funds for additional welfare benefits, especially for day care, health insurance, education, and job training. Third, the broader ten-year economic expansion generated significant gains in inflation-adjusted wages, especially for low and unskilled workers. Unemployment rates among high-school dropouts were cut in half and reached all-time lows for African American and Hispanic workers. Finally, the minimum hourly wage rose to $5.15 in 1997 while the Earned Income Tax Credit (EITC) made an additional contribution to after-tax wages through tax rebates to minimum-wage workers with children.

The significant decline in the number of families receiving public assistance since 1996 was likely due to a combination of both strong employment growth and welfare policy changes. The transformation of welfare policy continues to incite broad disagreement about its long-term effects. With the success of welfare reform hinging in a large way upon the economy's performance, the practical questions remain about financing and sustaining income security for the poor. Yet, such questions are deceivingly ordinary because the deeper ideological passions range from questioning the necessity of income redistribution to an avowed commitment to equal distribution of income.

Synopsis

Conservatives are profoundly skeptical of social welfare programs, arguing that efforts at redistributing income are bound to produce a drag on economic performance. Liberals contend that a distribution of income based upon markets is bound to generate inequitable results that can be offset only through governmental manipulation of taxes and transfers. Radicals express deep-felt rejection of capitalism's exploitative mechanism of distributing economic rewards and would make a first step in rectifying matters through aggressive redistribution of income and wealth.

Anticipating the Arguments

- On what specific grounds do Conservatives condemn the view that welfare is a right that should be guaranteed to all needy citizens?
- While Liberals may agree with Conservatives that past uses of the welfare system have failed to help the poor, how do their proposals for dealing with poverty differ from the Conservative view?
- Radicals maintain that we have attempted to get rid of welfare support only for the needy but not for the well-to-do. What do they mean by such an assertion?

THE CONSERVATIVE ARGUMENT

From the perspective of American Conservatives, the contemporary dismantling of the nation's welfare system is an undertaking that is long overdue. Whatever the good intentions of several generations of welfare advocates, their efforts placed a heavy burden on the entire society, perhaps the heaviest of all on those citizens whom they sought to help. The current shift in American social policy toward dismantling the dole and bringing the nation's poor and less fortunate population into the mainstream of economic life is to be lamented only because it took so long for common sense to be translated into actual practice. Since Congress enacted the most sweeping welfare reform program in seventy years in 1996, welfare rolls have plummeted while formerly welfare-dependent Americans have become gainfully employed. The emancipation of the nation's poor from the tyranny of the welfare state has put them firmly on the path to becoming mainstream Americans.

The Sources of the Welfare Problem

The sources of modern America's welfare problem are not difficult to determine. They reside amidst the rubble of the general economic collapse of the 1930s—the Great Depression. Poverty, of course, did not make its first appearance in the 1930s, but it was in the 1930s that America began to institutionalize poverty. Up to this point in the American experience, poverty and the joblessness that was its primary cause had been viewed as a temporary situation. Given time and their own hard work, the poor could sooner or later put the episode behind them. Indeed, by the 1920s, the record was rather clear on this. Most of those who came to America voluntarily came poor and, within a generation or two, managed to escape the clutches of poverty. Only African Americans, devastated by their experiences first with slavery and then with sharecropping, moved out of poverty slowly. But even among this group of citizens on the eve of the Great Depression, there was noticeable upward economic movement.

Whether or not the Great Depression had to be as deep or prolonged as it was is a matter of debate. Conservatives, of course, hold the view that this great rupture in American political and economic life was really worsened by the Liberal response it initially brought forth (see Issue 8). In any case, with unemployment hovering at about 25 percent, the matter of providing relief for the unemployed and the poor was an important underlying issue in the presidential contest that year between President Herbert Hoover and New York governor Franklin D. Roosevelt. The Republican and philosophically conservative Hoover took the correct but unpopular position that any federal provision of emergency funds to the needy would establish a precedent that would eventually destroy the long-held American commitment to individualism. Roosevelt won, and the die was cast for the growth of the American welfare state.

Interestingly, even Roosevelt had reservations about establishing a permanent womb-to-tomb welfare system. As late as 1935, a couple of years after introduction of his WPA make-work relief program and his Aid to Dependent Children program, Roosevelt observed: "The lessons of history, confirmed by evidence immediately before me, show conclusively that continued dependence upon relief induces a spiritual and moral disintegration fundamentally destructive to the national fiber. To dole out relief in this way is to administer a narcotic, a subtle destroyer of the human spirit. It is inimical to the dictates of sound policy. It is a violation of the traditions of America. Work must be found for able-bodied but destitute workers."

No Conservative could have stated the case any more forcefully than Roosevelt did. However, putting the toothpaste back in the tube was politically impossible. Once the Liberal solution to poverty—providing a dole for any who chose to demonstrate need—became understood as an American right, it would not be a right quickly surrendered. This became even more the case as the extent and amount of public relief continued to grow in the 1960s and 1970s. More than half a century would pass after Roosevelt's public lament before a Conservative Congress could put an end to this awful Liberal experiment in social engineering.

Toward a Just System of Rewards

As the American welfare system grew, especially in the 1960s and 1970s, so did the notion that the nation would be better served with a more equal distribution of income. More than is generally realized, this idea legitimized the expansion of the welfare system and obscured real understanding of the terrible outcomes that welfare dependence was producing. Accordingly, it is important at this point to understand where Conservatives stand on the entire matter of income distribution before taking up the particular issue of current welfare reform.

A unifying feature of all Liberal and Radical programs for the past hundred years has been the call for egalitarianism in income. The "Robin Hood" illusion is the very beginning of any collectivist's social dream. In the United States, income redistribution efforts in this century have appeared in two general forms: (1) a highly progressive income tax structure aimed at piling the expense of social spending on the upper-income members of society, and (2) a vast giveaway of these appropriations to the poor and the nonproductive groups within the nation. Both schemes rest on serious errors of economic and social thinking that deserve fuller elaboration and criticism.

Distribution of income should be governed by the simple and equitable principle that all members of a society should receive according to what they, or whatever they own, are able to produce. The abilities, tastes, and occupational interests of individuals vary. People value work and leisure differently. Some individuals are willing to forgo an assured lower income in favor of taking a risk and possibly earning more than the guaranteed level. Enforced equality of income utterly fails to consider these possibilities. It presumes that greater social satisfaction is attained by income parity rather than by letting people make their own valuations of what money means to them.

Consider, for instance, a person who is quite content to live on $500 a week. From this person's point of view, needs are satisfied and the right balance between leisure and work has been achieved. To transfer to this person one-quarter of the wages of another person who makes $1,000 a week will hardly increase the first person's welfare or happiness. At the same time, it subtracts much satisfaction from the second person, who is willing to work hard enough to earn the $1,000 wage. If we now added up the relative satisfactions of the two workers, it would be lower after redistribution than before. In other words, proof is lacking that a more equal income distribution actually maximizes community satisfaction.

At another level, egalitarianism leads to more serious troubles. Enforcing equal distribution of income penalizes the industrious and inventive and subsidizes those with less initiative. If the industrious fail to obtain rewards for their talents and work, they will naturally slacken their efforts. As a result, the total productiveness of society is lessened. In the subsequent egalitarian redistribution, everyone gets less than before. Just how far the detrimental effects of income equalization can go in destroying a society became evident in Great Britain by the 1970s. Subsidies for idleness and confiscation of earned income had lowered British output and put the nation at considerable disadvantage in world trade. The best minds and the nation's capital were fleeing overseas. A shabby equality and a culture of mediocrity enveloped the domestic economy. Only the reversal of the old welfare-state policies by the Conservative government of Margaret Thatcher in the late 1970s and early 1980s saved Britain from social and economic collapse.

While the discussion so far has been mostly concerned with individual labor, it also applies to individuals' command over capital and wealth. Appropriating the wealth of one person to support another denies the individual's right to property and will lead to inefficiency and economic contraction in the whole society. (Whether the wealth is inherited or has been earned by the individual is irrelevant.) This is not just an economic matter. Seizures of wages and property are violations of freedom. It is not such a big step from telling people what their income will be to telling them what work to do or what ideas to think.

The Basic Problems with Welfare

Conservatives have long understood that their attack on welfare is often depicted as a Scrooge-like heartlessness. In a nation of abundance and opportunity, it is natural for there to be much popular support for charity aimed at the "deserving poor." But charity involves a number of costs.

First of all, there is the cost to the giver. In the growing national economy of the 1960s, the expansion of a variety of welfare programs—AFDC, for example—provoked little taxpayer response. The programs seemed relatively small, and because the nation was enjoying an impressive annual growth in its gross domestic product, few Americans doubted that this was a charity we would someday not be able to afford. However, after thirty years of failed government welfare policies, a lot of working Americans began believing that charity should start at home. No doubt this self-concern was sharpened by the new realities of American labor markets. Corporate downsizing meant that many American workers had to take considerable pay cuts as they scrambled about for new jobs. In the new employment environment, a growing friction emerged between those choosing to work, even at considerably reduced wages or with the prospect of reduced wages, and millions of welfare recipients choosing not to work at all. That the former should continue to support the latter comfortably made less and less sense to many hard-working citizens. By the mid-1990s, public opinion polls no longer indicated that the majority of Americans supported the nation's welfare experiment.

There was also growing recognition of a second type of cost that welfare exacted, this one borne by its recipients. Aid to Families with Dependent Children, given only to mothers and children in the absence of a working father, was from its very beginning—although well-intended welfare advocates generally ignored the fact—constructed so as to fracture the families of the poor. It also encouraged out-of-wedlock childbirth. Accordingly, millions of children were denied the opportunity to grow and thrive within a conventional nuclear family. Generally, cash-assistance welfare programs required that eligible recipients have no earned income or that any earned income be subtracted from welfare payments received. Fortunately, the welfare reform of 1996 has begun to correct these destructive policies.

The overall effect of America's former welfare program was easily summarized: It created a strong disincentive to work and discouraged people from improving themselves. Recipients not only had to be poor to qualify for welfare protection but they had to remain poor to keep getting it. Thus our welfare system created a vast, permanent subculture of the disadvantaged. And, of course, overseeing this mess was a monumental welfare bureaucracy utterly lacking in incentives to solve the welfare dilemma, because their paychecks depended on the problem's continued existence. It is hard to imagine that such an irrational system could have been defended, and thereby permitted to exist, for so many years.

The Results Are In: Workfare Works!

There is no doubt that the welfare reform legislation enacted by Congress in 1996—especially the TANF program—has been an unqualified success: workfare works! Data gathered by both federal and state authorities confirm that the policy changes are achieving unprecedented results. Welfare rolls have been cut in half since 1996 and former recipients are finding gainful employment. Detailed studies from forty states show that on average most mothers leaving welfare find gainful employment. Labor force participation among unmarried mothers has increased since 1996 and Census Bureau data confirm a dramatic increase in income from wages for the bottom 40 percent of female-headed households while income from welfare declined. Finally, the objective of promoting marriage and decreasing nonmarital births is slowly being realized. This is because states have been given greater flexibility to use federal resources to reduce nonmarital and teenage births, especially through abstinence education programs and improving child support enforcement. There is ample evidence to suggest that if impoverished single mothers married the biological father of their children, most poor families would be lifted out of poverty. While Conservatives do not harbor a philosophical predisposition anchored in marital relations, from a practical standpoint encouraging and promoting marriage has proven to be a sound policy for ending welfare dependency.

Given the success of these changes in social welfare policies, Conservatives readily acknowledge that circumstances may arise from time to time that make it impossible for some citizens to find work. To the extent that an individual is disabled and unable to work at all or is too young to work, we recognize that society bears a responsibility to provide for the basic needs of those so affected. But when an individual is capable of working, it is not a cruel act by society to require that person to provide some useful labor on behalf of those providing his or her support.

Conservatives are particularly enthusiastic about welfare reform efforts that encourage welfare recipients to seek private sector employment. Restoring a sense of self-worth to former welfare recipients by means of their finding jobs is the only long-term cure for the welfare problem. However—and this is an important point to keep in mind—successfully engaging former welfare recipients in the ordinary economic life of the nation requires more than a little job training here and a little career counseling there. As a nation, we should be very careful that some of our economic initiatives—often actions that seem to have nothing to do with the welfare problem—do not work against solving that problem. For instance, the simple act of raising the legal minimum wage may seem to be a fairly benign undertaking aimed only at raising the living standards of a few million low-wage workers. In fact, such an action, or any others that raise an employer's cost in hiring additional workers, will shrink the employment opportunities of current welfare recipients and may even be the cause of a new round of joblessness and a resurgence of the old welfare cycle. Moreover, there is much that remains to be done in welfare reform: half the TANF caseload is still sitting idle while the food stamp and public housing programs are completely unreformed.

Remember, from a Conservative perspective, welfare dependency emerged in the first place as the result of undesirable tinkering with a market economy. We can reform welfare as much as we like, but the usefulness of such reforms depends ultimately on our commitment to permitting the economy to operate freely and openly, with as little social and economic interference as possible.

THE LIBERAL ARGUMENT

Conservatives are on the right track when they attack redistributive programs, but not for the reasons they present. The failure of public policy efforts is not due, as Conservatives believe, to some collectivist utopia in which a massive Robin Hood program takes from the rich and gives to the poor, simultaneously trampling on property rights, reducing work incentives, and lowering overall economic efficiency and national economic growth. Liberals maintain that public policy actually *has* failed in its professed efforts to close the gap between those at the very bottom of the income distribution and those at the top.

Conservatives are by no means troubled by this aspect of public policy failure and indeed perceive inequality as in some way incentive-inspiring and a normal outcome of well-functioning competitive markets. Liberals question the disincentives and adverse effects upon economic growth that Conservatives assert are the by-products of an oversized welfare state. Moreover, the Liberal view challenges the ability of the market mechanism to generate socially acceptable results with regard to income distribution. Conservatives turn a blind eye to the potential contagion of social problems that accompany poverty. Liberals criticize Conservatives' methods of reforming welfare as overridingly motivated by the goals of reducing the influence of central government and curtailing redistribution under the guise of cost savings—all the while chanting the popular mantra of efficiency.

Liberals are receptive to reforms that reduce costs and improve efficiency, but are realistic in our evaluation of income distribution and aware of the limitations that poorly functioning markets impose upon economic opportunity. Consequently, while adhering to the notion of personal responsibility and self-reliance, Liberals maintain that government's role in welfare can never be as small as Conservatives would hope.

Examining Income Distribution

As Table 6.1 illustrates, shares of money income received by various American income groups showed some movement toward greater equality in the New Deal era of the 1930s. The distribution was markedly stable from the 1940s to the mid-1970s. Thereafter the distribution began to exhibit greater inequality. Moreover, the quintile figures mask the fact that the share of income going to the top 5 percent climbed from under 16 percent in the 1970s to over 22 percent by 2001. Economists have also adopted another measure of aggregate income inequality, the Gini ratio, which was developed by Italian statistician Corrado Gini (1884–1965). This index measures the gap between an equal income distribution (where each share of the population has an equal share of national income) and the actual income distribution. A Gini ratio of 0 indicates zero inequality or *perfect equality*. A value of 1 is interpreted as 100 percent inequality or *perfect inequality* in the distribution of income. For example, if the column values in Table 6.1 were all equal to 20 percent, the United States would have had a Gini index equal to 0. Historically, the Gini ratio peaked around 1932 and then rapidly declined through World War II and stayed relatively flat until

Table 6.1

Share of Aggregate Income Received in Families in Each Income Quintile, 1929–2001

Income quintile	1929	1936	1947	1960	1970	1980	1990	2001
Lowest		4.1	5.0	4.8	5.4	5.3	4.6	4.2
Second	12.5*	9.2	11.9	12.2	12.2	11.6	10.8	9.7
Third	13.8	14.1	17.0	17.8	17.6	17.6	16.6	15.4
Fourth	19.3	20.9	23.1	24.0	23.8	24.4	23.8	22.9
Highest	54.4	51.7	43.0	41.3	40.9	41.1	44.3	47.7

Source: U.S. Bureau of the Census.
*Lowest and second quintile combined.

1968. Figure 6.1 shows the actual Gini index for the United States beginning in 1970 when income inequality began an almost uninterrupted increase. Thus, both sets of data strongly suggest that the economic situation of those at the bottom of the income distribution has not appreciably improved. Since the late 1960s, individuals in the highest quintiles in the income distribution were claiming an even larger share of money income. Clearly, such evidence does not support the Conservative suggestion that we have been on a long and dangerous slide toward egalitarianism.

Liberals concede that the sources of the rise in income inequality are numerous and elusive. Experts cite the impact of technological change that has handsomely rewarded particular types of skills, adverse effects of international competition that happened to be more pronounced for those at the bottom of the income distribution, decline in the purchasing power of the minimum wage, lower levels of unionization in the labor force and weakening of union influence over wages, and an influx of low-skill, low-wage immigrants who shrink the income share figures at the bottom of the distribution. However, these explanations have little to do with the Conservative assault upon government's efforts to redistribute income via the welfare system. And despite these explanations, one must bear in mind that the principal focus of redistributive efforts has not been to significantly alter the distribution of income. Specifically, the evolution of welfare programs has been a response to the inadequacies of a market system and the experiencing of the actual consequences of those inadequacies.

Figure 6.1   **Rising Income Inequality**

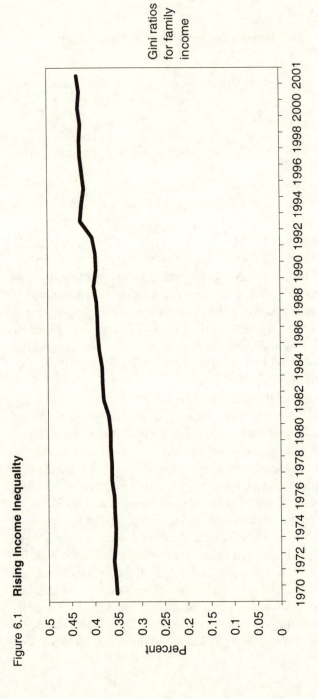

Source: Data from the U.S. Bureau of the Census.

Belief versus Reality

In its strictest embodiment, the Conservative view has a terribly difficult time reconciling the predictions of its most honored models with actual phenomena. This is particularly true when models of competitive markets are compared against real-world results. While acknowledging that theoretical models of *perfect* markets suffer from a strained relationship with their real-world counterparts, Conservatives are reluctant to acknowledge that the problems of monopoly power, the absence of complete information—or the presence of distorted information—for consumers to make intelligent choices, and the serious failures of markets (as in the case of pollution) are serious enough to warrant much intervention on the part of government. Likewise in the cases of poverty and income inequality, Conservatives are unwilling to find the justification for government intervention.

Experience finds this perplexing. The depths of the Great Depression motivated Franklin Roosevelt, a fiscally and ideologically conservative president, to discard Conservative claptrap in favor of Liberal policies that might at the very least finesse the problem. Similarly, the enviable, burgeoning production economy of the United States was tormented in the post–World War II period by a legacy of high poverty rates, in excess of 20 percent. These rates began to fall with the onset of a combination of economic growth and redistribution policies—both instilled through government intervention—that improved the economic lot for not only the citizenry at the bottom of the income distribution but everyone else as well. On the subject of economic growth, both Conservatives and Liberals agree: The best way out of poverty is a job. However, the contingency is economic growth. Here, as on other matters, Liberals must part company with the Conservatives.

The Basis for Intervention

Although the landscape of reasons is expansive and can become highly detailed, the Liberal argument for intervention and income maintenance programs rests mainly upon the following foundations:

- Competition in markets is not universal, and the existence of monopoly power and other market imperfections necessitates government corrective action on several fronts, including redistribution of income.

- Private markets fail and cannot insure people against the uncertainty of economic downturns that throw people out of work and into poverty.
- Egalitarianism is not at odds with economic growth.
- Government policies should be crafted to fight poverty and promote fairness in the income distribution—not just to unload or shift around the financial burden of paying for the nation's poor.

Market Imperfections

Theories of competitive product markets and resource markets presume certain ideal conditions that dodge practical complications. Conservatives maintain that such models strongly represent economic reality, and Radicals reject them outright. Liberals reside in between, with well-founded concerns about the magnitude of imperfections in real-world markets. These imperfections are bound to influence the fairness of the game and, therefore, the fairness of the results. Recognize that Conservatives do not perceive imperfections as a very large problem and that Radicals believe the game is rigged.

The competitive model promoted by Conservatives is countered by the existence of monopoly power in product markets and the results must be reflected in the income distribution. In short, the monopolist gets rich at the expense of society as whole.

Likewise, inequality in bargaining power in labor markets places the employee in a weaker position relative to the employer when striking the wage bargain. Other imperfections such as geographic and sociological immobilities impair the performance of labor markets by denying people ready access to improved economic opportunities just because they are unaware, too far away, or can be had only after insurmountable personal adjustments. Other citizens experience lack of opportunity and access to proper education, training, and experience—what economists call *human capital*. Hence, insufficient investment in human capital yields paltry returns in the form of income earned in the labor market, which in turn leads back to low investment, trapping the poor in a vicious circle of poverty.

Poverty and inequality are further cultivated by circumstances that are beyond the control of individual choices and relative efforts in the labor market. Some may suffer from the limitations imposed by disabilities. Others are the victims of accidents and misfortune. Still others must tangle with labor market discrimination. Certainly society could not be intent upon ignoring or punishing these people.

Welfare as Social Insurance

Conservatives are well aware that economic activities for certain sectors of the economy would be greatly retarded or nonexistent were it not for the development of insurance. Insurance offsets the discouraging effects imparted by random accidents, bad weather, fire, flood, or other adverse events where, based upon past experience, an insurer can estimate the expected frequency and severity with which such events will occur. Private insurance works quite well within a particular domain. However, private insurance markets do not provide adequate (or any) insurance against the uncertainties of the business cycle and consequent unemployment. Nor have private insurance markets found it financially feasible to extend coverage to the chronically ill or to develop income security insurance for low-wage workers with spotty employment histories. The development of social insurance programs, including antipoverty programs, is a response to this particular failure of markets.

Egalitarianism, Incentives, and Growth

Liberals do not subscribe to Conservatives' reasoning about the adverse impact of income redistribution upon economic incentives and economic growth. Conservatives' assertion that taxes levied upon productive efforts and transferred to unproductive individuals are a disincentive to being productive seems to make sense. However, this proves to be a matter of degree or the *threshold* at which extremely high taxes and bountiful welfare benefits truly discourage work effort, saving, and investment. In fact, there is no discernible, systematic relationship to support the idea that greater equity is accompanied by a pronounced loss of economic efficiency. Many European countries engage in far more vigorous tax and transfer efforts than the United States. Yet this does not seem to impinge upon economic progress. Greater economic security may actually improve the outlook for economic growth! Consider the examples of less developed countries with highly unequal distributions of income, coupled with marked inefficiency and abysmal records of economic growth. Indeed, income redistribution does confront society with a dilemma. However, the trade-off is not so pointed that we must agonize about whether future economic growth is dangerously jeopardized by trying to help the poor.

Throw Them Overboard?

Liberals advocate government policies to fight poverty and promote an equitable distribution of income. This overarching objective does not obstruct exploring the most expeditious and inexpensive means of dealing with the poverty problem. However, Conservative prescriptions for cost cutting and efficiency are worrisome. When likened to the allegorical overcrowded lifeboat, Conservative policies seem bent upon shrinking the size of the boat and heaving passengers overboard.

Although the Conservative agenda may be honestly dominated by the desire to shrink government and its influence, there is certain mean-spiritedness to their methods. Liberals are, therefore, skeptical of efforts that merely shift the responsibility for, and burden of, the poverty problem from one level of government to another. Historical experience with the failure of "poor laws" that held local governments accountable for providing for their resident indigents is instructive: The approach was to make it legally difficult to be poor *and* be a resident, or for governmental provision for the poor to be parsimonious. The purpose of this strategy was to chase the undesirables into some other political jurisdiction where tolerance and provision for the poor were greater.

Inequities are certain to grow if each state establishes its *social minimum.* In the 1930s, some states denied voting rights to those on public assistance. In the 1950s, welfare in some Mississippi townships consisted of $75 and a one-way bus ticket to Detroit. Inevitably, local governments would be prompted to adopt in common the worst of restrictions and frugality lest they be overwhelmed by legions of paupers. Understanding the problem of ceding responsibility to local authority prompts reasoned caution about policy reforms—especially if they reverse decades of progress in reducing poverty.

Success in Reducing Poverty Rates

Figure 6.2 shows the trend in poverty rates since 1959. There are some cyclical ups and downs because poverty rates rise during economic contractions and fall during periods of prosperity. The rate of economic growth is clearly a powerful force in determining poverty rates. A rising tide of economic growth lifts all boats—or nearly all. Conservatives are fierce advocates of work rather than welfare. However, suf-

Figure 6.2 **Poverty Rates, 1959–2002**

Source: Data from U.S. Bureau of the Census, *Historical Poverty Tables–Persons.*

ficient employment opportunities depend on the economy's performance. Even then, growth has never been a foolproof remedy for poverty and income inequality.

The 1960s brought the onset of expanded social insurance programs, which had impressive results. Propelled by President Lyndon Johnson's vision of the Great Society, poverty rates took a nosedive, from more than 22 percent of the population to slightly more than 11 percent by 1973. Much of the improvement can be attributed to more generous Social Security benefits and the creation of Medicare in 1965, providing medical and hospitalization insurance to the aged. A companion program, Medicaid, was also initiated to pay the health care costs of the indigent. Social Security, Medicare, and even Medicaid, to the extent that it pays for nursing home and home health care for the elderly, have escaped the notoriety of being "welfare." The beneficiaries, many of Conservative persuasion, fervently refuse to allow that *they*, with *their* transfer payments from government, bear any resemblance to the recipients of payments from AFDC or food stamps. While older Americans could claim victory in the War on Poverty, beginning in the 1970s poverty rates rose at an alarming rate for persons under eighteen. Poverty continued to exhibit a disparate impact upon minorities and female heads of household.

Nonetheless, the overall poverty problem would be far worse without government redistribution programs. In the *Economic Report of the President, 1997,* the president's Council of Economic Advisors estimated that cash transfer payments held the official poverty rate in 1995 to 13.8 percent; otherwise, it would have been 21.9 percent! Furthermore, the effect of the Earned Income Tax Credit (EITC) as discussed below and the value of *in-kind* transfers (such as subsidized housing and health care services) effectively reduce the poverty rate to 10.3 percent.*

The Liberal Agenda

The Liberal agenda for addressing the problems of poverty and income inequality is not based upon attempting to preserve the "welfare state" or the welfare bureaucracy. Rather, Liberals are guided by sound

---

Economic Report of the President (Washington, DC: Government Printing Office, 1997), 186.

principles of where and when government should intervene as well as the desire for a humane and civil society. Let us translate that into a plan of action.

Increase the Minimum Wage

A straightforward way to raise income and encourage work is to raise the minimum wage and index it to automatically rise with consumer prices or in tandem with other wages in the economy. The inflation-adjusted value of the minimum wage is 24 percent lower than it was in 1979. Conservatives who argue that minimum-wage laws restrict the demand for labor cannot claim it is due to its lower real cost: The number of workers demanded should increase as its price falls. If the minimum wage had simply kept up with inflation since 1968 when it was $1.60, it would stand at $8.46 in 2003.

Maintain and Expand the Earned Income Tax Credit

The Earned Income Tax Credit permits low-income families to receive as much as 12.5 percent of earned income as refundable tax credit, depending upon family size. The EITC is a version of a guaranteed annual income (GAI) or negative income tax (NIT) for the working poor. Even Conservatives such as Milton Friedman have advanced some support for a GAI or NIT. The EITC is not a full remedy, but it can be credited with greatly increasing employment among unmarried mothers (34 percent increase from 1992 to 1996) and lifting 4.1 million individuals (including 2.3 million children) out of poverty in 1999.*

Fostering Economic Opportunity and Personal Responsibility

Welfare is not the real solution to poverty or income inequality. Programs designed to pacify the poor create a permanent poor. Federal programs must attack the root of the problem through job creation, training, and education. Although Liberals are not fully enthralled with workfare as an alternative to unrestricted grants to the poor, it is the only viable long-run strategy for eliminating chronic poverty. Since the enactment of the 1996

Economic Report of the President (Washington, DC: Government Printing Office, 2001), 200.

welfare reform there has been a decline in both welfare caseloads and poverty rates. Nevertheless, whether this was due to a change in welfare policies or a booming economy is unclear. The Federal Reserve Bank of New York evaluated the progress and prospects of the 1996 legislation.* A critical question was whether a strong economy, by itself, "pulled" the most "job-ready" welfare recipients off the welfare rolls, but left the least-skilled recipients behind. Alternatively, a decline in the welfare caseload could also be due to the indiscriminant "pushing" off of indigent citizens from the welfare rolls by cold-hearted caseworkers.

From a Liberal perspective, the recent changes to reform the welfare system should be commended. Unfortunately, disadvantaged recipients remain in large numbers—primarily women with very young children—who have experienced significant hardship after leaving the welfare system. Therefore, the Liberal program still requires devoting additional resources to the pursuit of eliminating poverty. Not all of these resources need to be marshaled by government. However, private enterprise cannot sit idly by regarding this social problem as principally one for government to solve. Private businesses profess a strong interest in reforming welfare and must participate as a quintessential partner to that end. Alas, Liberals must concede that the Conservative program to reform the welfare system has had some success; however, much more support is needed to build on these limited gains. The Liberal approach is predisposed to what Conservatives would call social engineering, *but there is no other way.*

THE RADICAL ARGUMENT

The welfare reform bill that was passed by Congress and signed into law by President Clinton in 1996 codified and justified a brutal attack waged by the right wing on the poor and working class of America. Conservatives have been phenomenally successful in implementing their agenda to criminalize poverty and stigmatize the poor in order to eliminate any and all remaining social protections such as unemployment insurance and Social Security. While Senate and House Republicans are unabashed and un-apologetic about implementing these changes, Liberals are somewhat more cautious regarding their likely success. Nevertheless, both view poverty as a *personal* failure of character or circumstance. To the Conservative, a

---

Welfare Reform Four Years Later: Progress and Prospects, Economic Policy Review, vol. 7, no. 2, Federal Reserve Bank of New York, September 2001.

low income or the absence of any income at all reflects the market-determined value of an individual's talents and initiative. Defects of character and skill of the poor themselves are the root cause of their poverty. To the Liberal, poverty is partly the result of failing to behave in an economically responsible manner and partly the result of forces outside an individual's direct control such as racial discrimination, insufficient education, or other characteristics. Conservatives, of course, are content to let the poor struggle out of their condition, whereas Liberals are quick to apply moderately redistributive tax and transfer programs and other social-policy Band-Aids for the economically disadvantaged. By focusing only on the personal characteristics of the poor, albeit in different ways, neither Conservatives nor Liberals recognize that poverty and extreme income inequality are inherent outcomes of the capitalist system.

Demoting the General Welfare

The debate over welfare reform has been almost entirely defined and discussed in profoundly moral terms. Poverty is generally assumed by both Conservatives and Liberals to be the result of an individual's inability to adopt market-friendly habits and attitudes, rather than the persistent failure of an economy that is equally proficient at producing extreme wealth *and* destitution. The Personal Responsibility and Work Opportunity Reconciliation Act (PRWORA) of 1996 began by moralizing that "marriage is the foundation of a successful society" and then went on to blame the growth in poverty, crime, and general social decay since the 1960s on the increase in single motherhood. Left unchallenged was any notion that the lack of employment opportunities and financial resources causes crime and poverty, rather than the reverse. Nor did the legislation acknowledge that white married-couple families were twice as numerous among the poor as families headed by an African American mother. Politicians find it much easier to moralize about the sanctity of marriage than to acknowledge the crushing impact that their so-called welfare reform will have on the economic prospects of the poor.

Under the guise of getting the incorrigible and indigent to adopt behaviors and attitudes that fit into capitalist labor markets, workfare has served a punitive function to lower overall wages and working conditions and break the power of unionized workers. The "successful" meeting of TANF mandates by states (e.g., that half of all single parents and 90 percent of two-parent families have to work thirty hours per week) is glowingly cited by both Conservatives and Liberals. Since areas of high unemployment tend to also have high poverty rates, some states have "privatized" many functions by firing state workers and replacing them with TANF recipients in order to comply with federal workfare requirements. But this is only one of several destructive results from so-called "welfare reform." Profound problems with both the 1996 welfare reform statute and TANF are ignored by the mainstream. First, Congress has fixed the nominal value of total TANF funding for the foreseeable future. Freezing cash benefits at their 1996 value of $16.5 billion guarantees that future job training, childcare, and other discretionary TANF spending will disappear over time due to inflation. Second, the five-year TANF-mandated time limit on benefits has been particularly onerous on poor families and promises only to become more punitive. The previously cited Federal Reserve Bank of New York report on welfare reform stated: "Many studies have shown that a significant portion of the [welfare] caseload spends more than sixty months receiving benefits (the maximum time limit specified under PRWORA), although many states have opted for shorter time limits." Finally, even Conservatives and Liberals admit that the depth of poverty—as measured by families who are 50 percent below the poverty line—has been steadily rising. In 2002, this population increased by 600,000 to about 14 million people. Thus, the "poverty gap" continues to grow rendering the poorest Americans worse off than at any time in the past quarter century. In short, the federal government has not only succeeded in abrogating its responsibility to guarantee some minimum standard of living for *all* its citizens, but states can now balance their budgets on the backs of the poor as they continue to cut social spending with impunity.

While workfare is clearly an attack on the poorest citizens, it also serves to undermine the wages, benefits, and employment conditions of all American workers. By destroying the economic safety net for those at the bottom, welfare reform has ensured that low-wage workers will remain docile with respect to demands for higher compensation and organizing activities. Even higher-paid workers will lower their expectations about pay and job security as they watch workfare recipients replace unionized workers.

In sum, the pacification of the American poor and working class is just one of many consequences of the new welfare reform bill. These changes are not just about economics and government efficiency; they are also about exploiting antagonisms among and between the working poor and the middle class, between whites and minorities, and males and females. Ultimately, this program will serve to polarize and immiserate American society while consolidating and expanding the power of the corporate elite and their minions.

The Legacy and Reality of Wealth Inequality

Reforming the welfare system only serves to draw attention away from the fundamental problem of capitalism's inability to produce an equitable distribution of market outcomes. Adam Smith believed that since growth was an intrinsic feature of capitalism, over time the rewards of the market would spread throughout the economy. While Smith recognized the potential for social conflict, he claimed that competition would prevent the concentration of economic resources and political power. Marx, who very much admired Smith's analysis of capitalism, agreed that capitalism was the only social system capable of generating unparalleled growth; however, it also produced unmatched poverty and inequalities in wealth and income.

While growth in aggregate income, output, and employment has been touted as a long-term feature of American capitalism, inequality in wealth and personal income has also persisted. In fact, with the exception of the early colonial era (through about 1800) and the periods during and around World Wars I and II, American society has been fairly polarized with respect to the distribution of both income and wealth. Although the Depression of the 1930s ushered in a time when incomes at the bottom and in the middle actually rose, since the mid-1960s inequality has steadily increased (see Figure 6.1). Not only do mainstream economists regard this as necessary to spur personal initiative and corporate investment, but each year the business press gloats over the richest people in America. For example, *Forbes* magazine compiles a list of the four hundred wealthiest people in America. In 2003, you needed a net worth of at least $500 million to qualify ($5 billion would have placed you only in thirty-third position). In addition, in 1982, the combined net worth of the *Forbes* 400 was "only" about $92 billion, but in 2003, that figure was ten times higher—a net worth of $955 billion. Finally, it should be noted that rather than being a bunch of Horatio Algers or self-made billionaires, a significant number of the *Forbes* 400 inherited most of their wealth.

While these figures only illuminate the wealth of the super-rich, it is quite evident that the overall distribution of wealth and income remains highly unequal. Table 6.2 provides data on the distribution of wealth, debts, and income based on the Federal Reserve's *Survey of Consumer*

Table 6.2

Distribution of Assets, Liabilities, Income, and Net Worth*

	Bottom 90 percent	Top 10 percent
Assets	30.1	69.9
Home	62.9	37.1
Auto	76.2	23.8
Bonds	4.2	95.8
Stocks	11.9	88.1
Liabilities		
Home mortgage	75.1	24.9
Other real estate	44.4	55.6
Other liabilities	78.8	21.2
Net worth	30.1	69.9
Income	$47,097	$270,000
Average net worth	$133,360	$2,766,673

Source: Federal Reserve Board, *Survey of Consumer Finances*, 2001.

*Figures are percentage shares, except where dollar amounts are indicated. Percentage shares may not sum to 100 percent because of rounding.

Finances for 2001. As Marx would have predicted back in the late nineteenth century, wealth is far more concentrated than income in capitalist America: While the bottom 90 percent garnered a little more than two-thirds of total income, it held less than one-third of total wealth. Moreover, while their net worth was only slightly greater than their income, for the top 10 percent it was more than eleven times as great.

The data also show that the top 10 percent—about 10 million households—owned 90 percent of stocks and 96 percent of bonds (either directly or as part of a mutual fund). On the other hand, it is painfully obvious that the vast majority of Americans have nearly all their assets in a home or car—resources that are not easily deployable to either capital markets or a new business. In fact, the top tenth of households owned over 92 percent of assets held in the form of businesses and well over two-thirds of real estate and other assets.

Rather than showing an evolution toward a more democratic economy, the data underscore how a small class of elites increasingly controls the financial resources that will determine the future livelihoods of most Americans. Moreover, while most of the rich were raised in wealth, more than one in five American children continue to grow up in poverty. Not only does poverty deprive children of a decent standard of living, it also cuts their lives short. Poor children also have a much greater likelihood of dying from diseases and accidents, but even as adults, their longevity is likely to be curtailed by inadequate access to health care.

While "welfare queens" are vilified in the media, little attention is paid to the fact that social service expenditures also subsidize the rich and well-to-do. Welfare dollars buy the goods and services of corporate America. They underwrite the medical-industrial complex that includes hospitals, doctors, drug companies, health maintenance organizations, and a host of suppliers and providers. For example, Medicaid fraud is almost always committed by doctors, hospital administrators, insurance companies, and other well-paid health care professionals. Rarely does an indigent patient ever benefit from such crime. In fact, government expenditures on the truly needy (where income eligibility tests are required) are less than 5 percent of total federal outlays and have been steadily declining for several years. Meanwhile, the wealthy elite and corporations continue to obtain special tax breaks from Congress, which further undermines the revenue base to fund social programs.

A Radical Program to End Inequality

The federal welfare reform program is doomed to failure, especially for those living in states with mean-spirited social policies. As workers and middle-class people continue to be ignored and disaffected by the political system, state and local politicians will continue to hack away at the social safety net. Unchallenged by any threat from either workers or the poor, welfare benefits no longer need to serve the system's need to quell social discontent or legitimate an increasingly inequitable economic system. While AFDC payments and other welfare programs grew after the urban unrest of the 1960s, the current absence of political pressure from the poor and disenfranchised will allow the state to continue to ignore their demands and needs. Meanwhile, following the passage of their welfare reform agenda, corporate interests and their representatives in Congress are actively attacking middle-class entitlements such as Social Security, education subsidies, veterans' benefits, and a host of other programs that benefit both the nonindigent and nonrich.

What can be done to curtail these reactionary social welfare policies and bring about a more equitable distribution of wealth? In the short run, it is crucial that the bottom 90 percent of income earners realize that they must band together with the poor and mobilize around a new political agenda that puts their economic interests ahead of those of the rich. Such action also requires a new political party that can nullify capital's dominance of the current political system. Second, there must be a radical renovation of the tax structure such that taxes on inheritances above about a million dollars would become confiscatory. Third, only *earned* income below a certain threshold, perhaps $40,000, would be free from all taxes. Also, *all* income—from whatever source—would be subject to Social Security taxes. This would allow for a dramatic decline in the payroll tax rate for all workers and insure permanent solvency of the Social Security system. Fourth, social welfare programs would be designed to help families in the most direct manner possible: the government would pay parents to stay home (if they choose) to raise their children. The Scandinavian countries and other Western European nations offer similar benefits to parents irrespective of income. Furthermore, since economists agree that goods and services produced at home are nonmonetary forms of value, such a program would actually have the effect of raising the nation's gross domestic product. Finally, the federal government must get directly involved in providing employment opportunities to the poor and indigent that will be both meaningful and productive *and* pay a living wage. Given the numerous tasks that remain unmet or poorly provided by the free market—such as child and elder care, health care, new infrastructure, pollution reduction and cleanup, along with many other needed goods and services—the federal government will find ample demand for the labor now in their employ.

All of these steps, even though they fall short of the goal of public ownership of capital, would still be unacceptable to the leaders and defenders of the capitalist system. However, the system's failure, indeed its inability, to achieve and sustain some equitable measure of income distribution, along with its chronic problems of joblessness, discrimination, and poor economic growth, must eventually erode popular acceptance of existing arrangements. To be sure, the American dream of equal and unlimited opportunity for everyone has remained a powerful myth promoted by corporate propaganda, and it always has constrained the emergence of a truly Radical political and social movement in the United States. However, as the conflict between the dream and everyday reality sharpens, Radical alternatives to conventional social and economic measures will become matters of public debate and discussion. Just as America has used the promise of equal opportunity as the social glue to hold the nation together, the actual drift toward greater inequality becomes the device that undoes the entire production-for-profit system.

Financing Government

What Is a Fair System of Taxation?

In the most advanced countries, the following will be pretty generally applicable: . . . A heavy progressive or graduated income tax.

—*Karl Marx*, The Communist Manifesto, *1848*

The flat tax is a deeply moral system. Purchase of tax privileges through political influence would end. We accept this social contract: a single tax rate and *no* tax breaks beyond the personal exemption. We will not try to increase government at someone else's expense. Every taxpayer will have to contribute.

—*William Poole, 1996*

This tax relief plan is principled. We cut taxes for every income taxpayer. We target nobody in, we target nobody out. And tax relief is now on the way.

—*President George W. Bush, 2001*

Deficits over the next decade are now projected to be enormous in size. . . . Despite the deteriorating fiscal outlook and the historically low corporate revenue collections we already face, Congress nonetheless seems poised to shower more tax breaks on corporations that would cause deficits to grow substantially larger over time.

—*Center on Budget and Policy Priorities, 2003*

The Problem

In the spring of 2001, the new administration of George W. Bush took up its premier campaign promise: obtaining the largest tax cut ever enacted by the federal government—a ten-year, phased-in reduction of approximately $1.5 trillion, stimulated by the prospect of continued federal budget surpluses. Bush pledged "to give the people back their money." Following the terrorist attacks of September 11 and continued job losses, the White House engineered two more tax cuts in 2002 and 2003 to stimulate a lackluster economy.* However, the combined effects of the tax cuts, declining employment, and growing costs associated with the Iraq war, led to an exploding federal deficit. Despite the tide of red ink, the Bush administration remained steadfastly committed to reducing taxes, especially the dividend and capital gains tax rate. However, the complete impact of the three consecutive tax cuts is a source of controversy. Many of the tax cut provisions in the 2003 legislation that mainly benefited the highest income bracket would not become effective for several years. The use of tax "loopholes" to avoid paying corporate income taxes, including excess depreciation write-offs, offshore tax shelters, and industry-specific subsidies has reduced the corporate tax burden as a share of national income to an all-time low. Thus, the distribution of the tax burden in the face of ever-growing federal deficits and how Americans will pay for mandated tax cuts remains a critical issue. Persistent budget deficits may generate pressure to rescind or reverse the tax reductions.

Whether or not the tax cuts and their consequences will be borne equitably by all Americans is debatable. Indeed, the larger question of whether or not the entire system of American taxation is fair remains a matter of considerably divided opinion. However, before turning to that question, a few general comments on the development of the nation's tax policy are in order.

The American passion for fairness in matters of taxation is a well-established historical fact. Indeed, the very birth of the nation is traceable to this outlook. Taxation without representation, an eminently unfair idea from the perspective of many colonists, led to the famous "tea party" in Boston Harbor in 1774 that directly defied the authority of the British

---

*Economic Growth and Tax Relief Reconciliation Act of 2001, Job Creation and Worker Assistance Act of 2002, and Jobs and Growth Tax Relief Reconciliation Act of 2003.

colonial administrators. That spark was soon fanned into the flame of the American Revolution and, eventually, the birth of the United States of America.

At least through most of the nineteenth century, with the probable exception of the Civil War era (1861–65), the individualistic and anti-central-government temperament of most Americans meant a close eye was kept on the size of the federal government. Indeed, as late as 1902, the federal government's total spending amounted to only $485 million, or about one-third of all governmental outlays in the United States. Reflecting the outlook of Americans toward government in general, local government accounted for nearly 60 percent of all government spending. In any case, government spending of all kinds was equal to only about 7 percent of the nation's gross domestic product (GDP) in 1902.

Events of the twentieth century would greatly alter the anticentrist approach to government and governmental finance. Two major wars and an emerging redefinition of "appropriate" government responsibilities in the economy and social life of the nation not only ballooned the size of governmental outlays in general, but exploded the federal share to nearly two-thirds of total outlays. Such a spending explosion also required a commensurate increase in revenue sources to finance it. Throughout most of the prior century (with the exception of the Civil War years), most federal revenue was obtained from tariffs on goods entering the nation and from sales of public land.

The development of a federal income tax system occurred relatively late in the nation's history. After brief use of an income tax to help finance the Civil War, it was not until 1913—with the enactment of the Sixteenth Amendment—that Congress actually acquired the "power to lay and collect taxes on incomes, from whatever source derived, without apportionment among the several states, without regard to any census or enumeration." The requirements of apportionment and enumeration had restricted the federal government to the option of imposing head taxes—which would have limited the capacity to raise revenue and introduced difficult issues about fairness.

When the new federal income tax was initially levied, the personal exemption was quite generous, such that people earning below $4,000 (about $75,676 in 2004 dollars) did not pay any tax. Beyond incomes of $4,000, the federal income tax was mildly progressive, with tax rates rising in increments of less than 1 percent on those with incomes between $4,000 and $15,000 to a 6 percent rate on all income over $1 million. With family

Table 7.1

Marginal Federal Income Tax Rates on Taxable Income, for Selected Years (in percentages)

Year	$1,000	$5,000	$15,000	$50,000	$100,000	$1,000,000
			Income class			
1913	—	0.4	0.8	1.5	2.5	6.0
1919	—	4.8	11.9	22.3	35.2	70.3
1929	—	0.3	1.9	8.5	14.9	23.1
1934	—	2.8	7.6	17.4	30.2	57.1
1944	11.5	22.1	32.9	55.9	69.9	90.0
1951	8.2	19.3	30.2	53.5	67.3	87.2
1962	8.0	18.9	29.7	52.8	66.8	87.0

Source: "Historical Statistics, Series Y," pp. 319–332 as cited by Albert W. Niemi in *U.S. Economic History* (Chicago: Rand McNally Company, 1975), 121.

income averaging less than $2,000 in 1913, few Americans, even before exemptions and deductions were considered, saw the new income tax as much of a threat. Only 357,000 Americans filed federal income tax returns for 1914. However, as Table 7.1 shows, tax rates soon rose for all levels of income, and they rose quite sharply for higher income levels.

During World War II, the government instituted automatic payroll deductions for federal taxes using a *graduated* schedule in which the tax rate rose with income. At that time, the government also reduced the personal exemption, which had the effect of widening the tax base to include middle- and lower-income classes. *Marginal tax rates*—the rate applied to successively greater increments of earned income—remained relatively high throughout the 1950s. With rising incomes and low inflation during these years, most Americans accepted the *ability-to-pay* principle of taxation. Under this approach, those with higher incomes would be taxed at a higher rate. In reality, however, because of the availability of numerous tax deductions and legal loopholes, few wealthy Americans ever paid the then-existing top statutory rate of 91 percent.

John F. Kennedy, following his election in 1960, undertook the first major change to the federal income tax structure. Faced with a sluggish economy, President Kennedy was counseled by his economic advisers to jump-start macroeconomic growth by lowering income tax rates and granting investment tax credits to the private sector. Although initially reluctant, Kennedy, an astute politician, realized that by tinkering with the tax system he could increase his popularity with both voters and the business community. While some Kennedy advisers believed that manipulating fiscal spending policies rather than taxes was a more effective and equitable means of managing the economy, more conservative advocates of tax cutting prevailed.

The federal income tax system did not change a great deal through the rest of the 1960s and 1970s. Following Kennedy's proposed reduction of the top marginal rate from 91 percent to 70 percent, which was enacted in 1964, not much changed for the average taxpayer. It was not until the early 1980s, following the election of Ronald Reagan, that Congress significantly altered the federal income tax system. First, the Economic Recovery Tax Act of 1981 cut the top rate from 70 percent to about 50 percent. Second, the number of tax brackets was dramatically reduced, and third, many tax loopholes were supposedly closed. Another round of rate changes was undertaken with the Tax Reform Act of 1986, simplifying the rate structure to two basic rates of 15 and 28 percent with the provision that the rate went to about 33 percent for high-income taxpayers.

While the federal tax system remains essentially *progressive,* state and local governments typically use *proportional* and *regressive taxes.* A proportional or flat tax is one that takes a *constant* percentage of income. For example, Pennsylvania has a proportional state income tax. A regressive tax is one that takes a *declining* share of taxpayer income as income rises. Retail sales taxes are regressive because they are mostly levied on consumption items, which tend to claim a larger share of a poor person's total income compared to a wealthy individual. User and registration fees, excise taxes (especially on gasoline), filing fees, and other types of lump-sum payments are all examples of taxes that are effectively regressive. It can also be argued that the Social Security tax is regressive because it applies a 12.4 percent rate (6.2 percent imposed on both the employee and employer) only to wages and salaries under $90,000 (for 2005). Income above this threshold, plus all unearned income (e.g., from dividends, interest, rents), is not subject to the Social Security tax.

In contrast, progressive taxes, as we have seen in the case of the federal income tax, take an *increasing* share of income from higher-income classes. The federal income tax is progressive in that higher tax rates apply to higher income. For example, in 2003 there were six different rates that applied to a single taxpayer: 10 percent on income up to $7,000; 15 percent on additional income up to $28,400; 25 percent on the next slab of income up to $68,800; 28 percent on subsequent income up to $143,500; 33 percent on each dollar of income greater than $311,950; and 35 percent on income above this amount.

Table 7.2

Federal Government Receipts 1950, 1960, 1970, 1980, 1990, 2000, and 2003 (in percentages)

	1950	1960	1970	1980	1990	2000	2003
Current tax receipts							
Personal current taxes	28.6	34.3	36.0	37.5	34.7	39.5	32.9
Taxes on production and imports	34.8	33.2	31.9	25.2	24.9	22.7	26.2
Taxes on corporate income	27.1	16.9	12.0	10.6	8.2	8.2	7.2
Taxes from the rest of the world	0.0	0.1	0.1	0.2	0.2	0.2	0.2
Contributions for government social insurance	8.3	12.2	16.2	20.8	24.0	22.5	25.8
Other sources	1.2	3.3	3.9	5.7	8.0	6.9	7.7
Total	100.0	100.0	100.0*	100.0	100.0	100.0	100.0

Source: U.S. Department of Commerce, National Income and Product Accounts
*Does not add to total due to rounding.

One final point on the federal tax system needs to be made: It has increasingly become a system in which the tax burden falls directly and immediately on *individual* taxpayers. A little over fifty years ago—as Table 7.2 illustrates—taxes collected from corporations accounted for more than 27 percent of all federal tax revenues; by 2003, their share had dropped to about 7 percent. Alternatively, taxes on individual's incomes and employee and employer contributions to Social Security had risen to nearly 59 percent of federal tax revenues. Since deficits are expected to become cumulatively about $5 trillion over the next decade, then the burden borne by individual taxpayers must increase.

It is obvious that the type of revenue system a government chooses to employ—regressive, proportional, or progressive—necessarily says a lot about a nation's sense of fairness. Most economists agree, and have agreed for a long time, that if all taxes paid by all persons to all governmental units in the United States were aggregated, the American tax system could best be described as moderately progressive. Whether a moderately progressive tax system is *fair,* however, remains a matter of debate.

Synopsis

Conservatives generally favor levies on consumption or other activities that will not distort an individual's decision to work or save. On the other hand, Liberals assert that since the level of income and wealth best reflects a person's ability to pay for governmental functions, a proportional or graduated income tax is the fairest system of taxation. Radicals argue that the long-term increase in the share of income borne by wage earners directly reflects the power of business elites to purchase congressional votes to ensure the passage of laws that will lower their share of the tax burden.

Anticipating the Arguments

- Why do Conservatives argue against progressive taxes as a means of financing government?
- What reasoning is employed by Liberals to justify progressive taxes as equitable?
- Why do Radicals advocate a steeply progressive tax on all sources of income?

THE CONSERVATIVE ARGUMENT

Ever since the economist Adam Smith specified the role for limited government interference in a market economy, most Conservative economists have recognized the need for a small public sector. However, the government sector in most advanced capitalist societies has expanded well beyond what Smith ever expected. To Smith, the state should provide for the national defense; educate citizens; administer justice; pay for "public works and institutions for facilitating the commerce of society"; sustain the indigent, old, and infirm; and "support the dignity of the sovereign." Furthermore, government should pay for its provision and administration of goods and services by imposing taxes in an *equitable* and *consistent* manner. Thus, the overall goal of government tax policy should be to (1) devise a system that is fair to all citizens and (2) help stimulate market forces that promote growth and capital formation.

Since the adoption of the federal income tax in 1913, the U.S. tax system has failed to adhere to these two basic principles. Instead, the income tax has been used to redistribute income from productive, hardworking taxpayers and businesses to government programs that support unproductive economic activities or unprofitable ventures. Moreover, onerous redistributive income taxes encourage individuals to avoid paying taxes by either working "off the books" or by seeking employment in the underground economy. The current tax system undermines the work ethic by significantly lowering after-tax wages. This causes workers to reduce their labor effort supplied to the market, often to the point where they choose to avoid work altogether and become dependent upon government welfare. Finally, the design and enforcement of the tax code is unnecessarily bureaucratic and intrusive, and imposes high costs of compliance.

Rather than adhering to Smith's maxim of an "equitable, certain, convenient and efficient" system of taxation, the U.S. government continues to confiscate an increasing share of taxpayers' incomes. Progressive income tax systems are based on the fallacious assumption that wealthy individuals do not gain as much satisfaction from an extra dollar of earnings as do those with lower incomes. Therefore, the government erroneously believes that it is actually improving society's well-being when it taxes away a "hardly missed" dollar from a high-income person and spends it on public goods or redistributes it to the lower end of the income distribution.

Little regard is given to the central role played by the savings and investments of thrifty individuals who provide the funds that ultimately drive growth and job creation. Moreover, since the poor tend to consume all their income, free markets crucially depend upon society's net savers to fund the enterprises (and some government activities) that put people to work. By taxing investors, the government only encourages savers to consume their surplus earnings, invest overseas, seek out unproductive tax shelters, or engage in other tax-avoiding activities.

The Savings Crisis

Adam Smith was one of the first economists to understand that capitalism cannot thrive without the accumulation of a financial surplus for investment. The U.S. economy's ability to provide gainful employment and adequate income for all able-bodied workers is fundamentally determined by its savings rate. American capital markets must be able to harness the surplus funds of households, corporations, and foreigners and deploy them to the private sector for the purchase of new plants, property, and equipment. Thus, it is clear that without savings, the capital stock cannot expand and labor productivity cannot rise, which will ultimately result in a lower overall standard of living.

Unfortunately, the savings rate in the United States has been falling since about 1970. The decline in the personal savings rate is illustrated in

Figure 7.1. Battered by higher personal income tax rates enacted by the Clinton administration, the personal saving rate went into free fall after 1992. In 2002, the savings rate was 2.3 percent—placing the United States on a par with the savings rates of the poorest of lesser-developed nations.

The long-term consequences have been unambiguous: A decline in the savings rate has choked off domestic capital formation, which constrained the growth in overall labor productivity and thus reduced both income and mobility for numerous working people. Economies that cannot sustain an adequate rate of capital accumulation are destined to decline. Moreover, with heightened global competition for limited financial resources, new demands for investment capital can be expected to divert the savings of foreigners (who currently provide about one-third of our domestic savings) from the American economy. Given these dire trends and circumstances, it is essential that federal tax policies be designed to increase capital formation by eliminating taxes on all forms of savings.

The Failure of Progressive Income Taxes

The legacy of progressive taxation has not been good. Since the early 1960s, when the top marginal tax rate was more than 90 percent, both the savings rate and labor productivity have steadily deteriorated while the share of taxes raised from personal income has steadily increased. Efforts to reverse this trend were helped with the passage in 1981 of President Reagan's tax reforms, which were designed to increase federal tax revenues by reducing the top marginal tax rates and by simplifying the federal tax code. The success of supply-side economics is supported by the fact that federal revenues increased by almost 50 percent from 1982 to 1988. While Ronald Reagan's tax policies generated higher revenues, the savings rate has continued to languish because Congress subsequently raised tax rates on the highest-income groups and steadfastly refuses to eliminate taxes on capital gains.

Although Liberals claim that the progressive income tax system helps to reduce income inequality in America, both disparities between income classes and the overall poverty rate steadily increased during the 1970s. This is because our tax laws stifled personal initiative by penalizing those who seek to better themselves. At its core, the old tax system only benefited the very poor—who are exempt from paying taxes—or the very rich who have already amassed their fortunes. For example, a graduated income tax often discourages risk taking by reducing an

172

Figure 7.1   **Personal Saving as Percentage of Disposable Income**

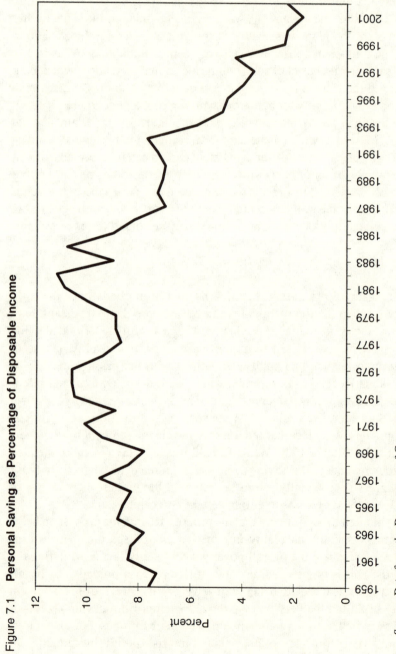

Source: Data from the Department of Commerce.

entrepreneur's net return. This in turn chokes off innovation and competition while acting as a powerful deterrent to others who have the capacity to undertake new business ventures but choose not to for fear of seeing the fruits of their labor taxed away by the state. Furthermore, wealthy individuals living off a flow of unearned income will avoid risky investments in order to cover their ever-increasing tax liability.

Finally, the progressive income tax system is particularly onerous for families with two wage earners. When considered individually, a working husband and wife might not make very much money. However, when their incomes are combined, they are quickly pushed into the highest income tax bracket. In the case where one spouse earns most of the household's income, the less-compensated husband or wife often pays more than half their income in taxes.

Put simply, the prior tax system undermined the free market system by creating powerful disincentives to work, save, or invest. President George W. Bush began to reverse many of these damaging policies with his tax program designed to bolster capital formation and savings. The three tax packages proposed by the administration and quickly enacted by Congress between 2001 and 2003 provided a successful short-term stimulus to the economy while significantly improving the longer-term prospects for growth. The president's strategy of lowering marginal income tax rates, significantly increasing child tax credits, and cutting dividend taxes all resulted in higher inflation-adjusted after-tax income. In addition, business profitability and labor productivity increased as the cost of capital fell assisted by accelerated depreciation rules and a reduction in the capital gains rate.

Despite these short-term successes, the federal income tax code is much too complex, cumbersome, and fundamentally inequitable. Some Conservatives endorse a proportional or "flat tax" on income, which is attractive from the standpoint of practicality and certain equity considerations. However, the superior long-term solution is to adopt a consumption-based tax system.

The Solution—A Progressive Consumption Tax

The Conservative argument for a progressive consumption tax is embedded in the notion that the economy remains fundamentally constrained by insufficient savings on the part of individuals. Moreover, an intrusive and overly complex federal tax system has created perverse incentives that diminish or misdirect investment activities, lowering productivity and encouraging profligate consumption. A progressive consumption tax would simultaneously address issues related to fairness and consistency that plague the current tax system.

Under a progressive consumption tax system, taxpayers would be allowed to deduct *all* funds that are saved or invested from their gross income. Money borrowed or taken out of savings would be included in taxable consumption. Since consumption is defined as income minus savings, computing an individual's tax liability from his or her paycheck would be a relatively straightforward process. There would be no need for investment tax credits or a capital gains tax since the government would allow a single, comprehensive loophole for all earnings not consumed—no matter what the source of those funds. Lobbyists would be banished from the halls of Congress because there could be no gain from trying to get special tax breaks for specific kinds of investments or business activities. Complicated tax formulas to account for inflation, depreciation, and a host of other problems related to capital accounting would be eliminated, as all income from savings and investments would be treated exactly the same—they would *all* be exempt from taxes.

Fairness would improve because tax rates on consumption would increase with higher levels of consumption. This would capture more government revenue from conspicuous and profligate consumption by wealthy individuals. Less affluent taxpayers would have more of an incentive to save because (1) there would be a lower tax rate on the last dollar consumed, and (2) they would gain the benefit of tax-exempt interest earnings. Business people would find it much easier to start new firms because all investments would be made in a tax-free environment. With a greater supply of savings forthcoming, the cost of capital would decline, and riskier and more innovative investment projects would be undertaken. Companies would be much more willing to start up new ventures and/or expand existing operations, thus leading to the hiring of more workers and an overall increase in output, income, and employment.

THE LIBERAL ARGUMENT

Political ideologues of either the Right or Left will eventually come to understand that an optimal system of taxation can never be achieved. Neither a program of "soaking the rich" nor one that primarily taxes consumption can ensure that the collective responsibilities we entrust to government will be funded. Economists have learned that there is no single tax system that can simultaneously achieve an equitable distribution of income, stable growth, high productivity, low unemployment, and a myriad of other policy goals. While economic theories may purport to prove the superiority of a particular tax structure, tax systems—like all governmental undertakings—are *political* institutions that embody social and other noneconomic considerations. This fact cannot be evaded.

Most people would agree that the strength of the U.S. economy and society is largely due to the heterogeneous and pluralist nature of its population. This diversity enables individuals who possess a broad range of talents and abilities to harness America's resources for the betterment of all. However, wealth and skill are not evenly distributed throughout society, so that every individual cannot be expected to succeed solely on his or her initiative and skill. Nor is the private sector capable of insuring society's citizens against uncertainty and calamities of various sorts. Thus, an advanced capitalist economy requires its citizens to pool resources via government in order to offset and ameliorate income and job losses arising from recessions, foreign competition, technological unemployment, disease, natural catastrophes, and a host of other accidental and unforeseen factors. Put simply, the state must find a pragmatic method to raise money in order to undertake the necessary expenditures and projects required to hold a free market society together. The primary problem is to decide how best to obtain the funds needed for the provision of public goods and services.

While Adam Smith was correct in calling for the equitable taxation of those with roughly equal means, the question of how to tax *disparate* incomes is a more vexing issue. For example, a poor taxpayer and a rich taxpayer both receive the same amount of protection from the provision of defense services by the armed forces. Nevertheless, the question remains: Should the wealthy person still pay more for national defense because he or she has more to lose in the event of social unrest, war, or invasion? Alternatively, if a poor person lives in an area with a higher crime rate, should her tax liability be higher to pay for increased police protection? Even if we acknowledge differential abilities to pay, apportioning the appropriate benefits and costs to particular taxpayers cannot be guided by some fixed rule or principle.

Despite these ambiguities, it is quite evident that government revenues should be acquired in such a way as to maximize tax compliance and minimize avoidance and administrative costs. The development of both an efficient and an equitable system of tax collection should be the prime concern of lawmakers, even though the federal income tax system has grown in scope and complexity since its inception in 1913. While tax simplification would likely increase compliance with current tax statutes, the government could also significantly increase its revenues—without raising taxes—if it simply collected all that it was owed. In 2004, the IRS estimated a "tax gap" equal to about $311 billion, a figure equal to approximately one-half of the federal budget deficit. The problem has also been compounded by the persistence of many tax loopholes despite recent tax reform measures to close them. For example, corporations have avoided paying billions of dollars of federal income taxes through the use of various types of domestic and offshore "tax shelters." The Internal Revenue Service estimates that such "abusive" tax shelters are costing taxpayers well over $50 billion per year in lost revenue. Moreover, continued inequities in the incidence and distribution of many state and local taxes have heightened taxpayer frustration.

Nevertheless, the primary justification for the federal income tax rests mainly upon equity considerations. That is, a taxpayer's income is the best indicator of his or her ability to pay for the costs of government. On the other hand, those who are below some minimum income level can be easily excused from paying income taxes. In a similar vein, only the income tax is flexible enough to adjust an individual's personal circumstances to their tax liability. For example, suppose a family incurs substantial medical bills or loses a house to a fire or storm in a given tax year. In the first case, because the family "consumed" a substantial portion of their discretionary income in the form of medical goods and services, that family would now have a substantial tax liability. Moreover, replacing a home or car lost in a fire or accident would also subject a person to substantial consumption taxes. Finally, while many grumble about paying taxes each April 15, taxes fund many activities with significant benefits to all, including police and fire protection, schools, hospitals, sports stadiums, and museums.

The Success of the Progressive Income Tax

While few would dispute the complexity of our federal tax system, it has in fact accomplished its main task of raising government revenues in a generally equitable and efficient manner. Contrary to what Conservatives claim, the top marginal tax rate is one of the lowest among the industrialized nations. Indeed, these same "overtaxed" nations have for the most part reported greater long-term efficiency and growth compared to the United States, thus disposing of the Conservative charge that our "soak the rich" tax strategy is a major cause of our recent sluggish economic performance. We should also remember that we pay taxes other than federal income taxes, for instance, state and local sales, income, property, and use taxes; and, of course, corporate income and other business taxes are to some extent pushed onto consumers in the form of higher prices. When the effects of all of these taxes (many of which are highly regressive) are considered, the alleged "burden" of our progressive tax system is just not true.

What is true, however, is that our federal income tax system has been quite successful in distributing the tax burden: Those with higher incomes *do* pay a greater share of federal income taxes. In 2004, for example, those with incomes exceeding $96,700 pay almost 60 percent of total federal, state, and local taxes. In fact, a key reason why President Clinton was able to achieve a balanced federal budget—without slowing the economy—was that the progressive tax structure permitted a slight tax increase on those with high incomes to generate a greater-than-proportional rise in tax revenues. Unfortunately, President Bush's tax cuts to the wealthiest taxpayers and giveaways to large corporations have caused the federal deficit to escalate at a rate that alarms many Americans. The Bush administration has reintroduced the country to the use of "supply-side" tax cuts to increase tax revenues—a cornerstone of economic policy from the Reagan administration of the 1980s. The balanced budgets by President Clinton during the 1990s should have put an end to this fiction. Thus, instead of accomplishing President Clinton's objective to pay off the entire federal debt by 2010, the Bush administration's tax cuts will likely add $5 trillion to the debt by that year. Although some economists claim that taxes distort an individual's choice to work, consume, or invest, the evidence suggests that only very high marginal income tax rates actually discourage such behavior. Doctors, lawyers, accountants, and stockbrokers continue to supply just as many hours to the market, irrespective of any tinkering that Congress might undertake with regard to the federal income tax law.

A progressive personal income tax also acts as a built-in stabilizer for the overall economy. During business expansions, it allows the government to collect relatively more revenues as output and incomes expand and proportionately less during recessions. Ronald Reagan used tax cuts to stimulate the economy during the 1981–82 recession. Unfortunately, the federal deficit exploded because he did not raise taxes on upper-income individuals, nor cut defense expenditures. This is exactly what is happening again as a result of Bush's tax policies. Nevertheless, fiscal and tax policies—when applied in a reasonable and judicious manner—can be an effective means to maintain a stable balance between the growth of savings and income. While the current federal income tax system is far from perfect, it is clear that it satisfies the range of goals demanded by society.

THE RADICAL ARGUMENT

The development and workings of the American tax system must be understood in the context of its impact on wage earners as opposed to those who obtain their livelihood from unearned income in the form of profits, rents, interest, and dividends. Since the inception of the federal income tax on personal income in the early part of this century, most economists agree that wage earners have increasingly borne a higher share of the national tax burden. Given this trend, mainstream economists either argue for tax simplification—via a single tax rate—or emphasize the need to strengthen tax collection efforts at all levels of government. Alternatively, Radicals analyze the question of a fair tax system by whose interests are being served. For example, lucrative tax credits and esoteric tax deductions were not designed for wage earners who file the standard "EZ" tax form. Rather, our complicated federal tax system and attendant tax laws directly reflect the efforts on the part of rich people, corporations, and other monied interests to reduce their tax burden. The fact that the federal tax liability of capital has steadily *declined* for the past forty years only underscores the success of the richest 1 percent of income earners in shifting the costs of government onto the backs of the vast majority of working people.

Taxes and Accumulation

It has become an unquestioned premise of mainstream economic analysis that savings is the primary determinant of growth and accumulation. According to the Conservative paradigm, government attempts at taxing savings necessarily imply less growth in output, employment, and income. In addition, when the state runs a deficit, not only does it have to raise taxes in the future, but also in the short term it increases the overall cost of capital by bidding up interest rates to attract savings that would normally be allocated to private capital markets.

The logic of the Conservative argument suggests a strong inverse correlation between the top tax rate and the share of income devoted by an economy to investment. However, the economic data for successful advanced capitalist economies do not support this argument. Moreover, the high marginal tax rates of more egalitarian economies do not seem to have a punishing effect on investment spending and savings rates.

The bleating of the "overtaxed rich" is belied by reality, and their seemingly contradictory tolerance for government taxes to fund expenditures for warfare over those to enhance human welfare and dignity cannot be ignored. The federal income tax system initially taxed capital and upper-income individuals while granting generous exemptions to those further down the income ladder. The top marginal income tax rates have remained above the current top rate for most years since the inception of the federal personal income tax in 1913. However, since that time, personal exemptions for most taxpayers have been significantly reduced, as has been the minimum income threshold where one begins paying taxes. Moreover, since 1935, funding the Social Security system has always been borne by workers whose earnings rarely exceed the salary ceiling beyond which no more payroll taxes are due ($90,000 for 2005). Thus, it is no surprise that the Social Security tax is the most highly regressive of all federal income taxes because it is capped at 6.2 percent of salaries up to $90,000. For a person earning $100,000 the Social Security tax is just above 5.5 percent; at a salary above $200,000 the rate drops to about 2.8 percent. Finally, since about 1942, the federal government has reached further and further down the income distribution to find needed revenues. While the exigencies of World War II necessitated emergency taxes and debt financing, the government never returned to the prewar tax schedules that were much less onerous for working-class taxpayers.

The Problem with Flat Taxes

Since the passage of California's Proposition 13 in 1978, the "taxpayer revolt"—primarily against increased property taxes to fund municipal services, especially public schools—has spread to other states. Politicians at the national level have responded to taxpayer frustrations by proposing several changes to the current federal income tax system. Unfortunately, many plans to create a more simplified tax system also include many regressive features that will continue to foster an increase in the share of taxes borne by lower-income workers. There are currently several proposals in Congress to change the current federal income tax system. Most prominent among the Republican initiatives is a *progressive consumption tax*. Let us briefly examine the problem with each of these tax schemes.

Presidents and lesser politicians have often enshrined their names in the history books not by noble deeds but by tinkering with the federal income tax code. The original federal income tax statute enacted in 1913 taxed unearned income (dividends, interest income, and the like) at a higher rate compared to earned (wage and salary) income. In contrast to the current climate, which favors capital income, the first national tax scheme exempted almost all wage earners from federal taxes and permitted more generous personal exemptions. The top marginal personal income tax rate was first lowered by John F. Kennedy from 90 percent to 70 percent in 1964. Ronald Reagan lowered it to 50 percent in 1981 and even further to 33 percent in 1986. In addition to cutting the tax rates, lobbyists and other special interests have spent millions of dollars to induce Congress to include special rules that exempt particular businesses from federal taxes. Over the years, a vast and complicated system of tax laws and administrative rulings has created an unwieldy and highly inequitable tax system. The net result has been a decline in the share of federal taxes paid by large corporations and a notable increase in the tax burden of working people and small businesses.

The Conservative plan for a progressive consumption tax is a clever proposal to reconcile the inherent regressivity of consumption taxes with the current system, which taxes higher incomes at an increasing rate of taxation. To demonstrate its tenability, Conservatives appeal to the logic contained in the following mathematical example: Suppose an individual who makes $50,000 per year is taxed at a rate of 10 percent but also saves $5,000. A tax rate of 11.1 percent on an individual's consumption would be needed to raise the same amount of revenue because taxable income is reduced by the amount saved ($5,000). Though the example appears to be eminently reasonable, a problem arises as we move to higher incomes. Under current law, an individual taxpayer earning $10 million owes about $2.5 million in taxes (an average tax rate of 25 percent). Even if a very wealthy individual could consume $2.5 million of goods and services per year, the consumption tax rate would have to equal at least 100 percent to raise the same amount of revenue obtained from the current income tax structure. The point is that consumption tends to be a rather stable proportion of income for all individuals; however, wealthy people tend to consume a much smaller proportion of each dollar increment of income they earn. Short of forcing rich people to consume more, a consumption-based tax structure is inherently less burdensome for the wealthy compared to those with much less income.

A Return to Progressivity

In recent years, it has become quite unfashionable to argue for a tax system where the rate increases as an individual's income rises. Though Radical policy proposals are rarely put forward with any historical consistency or consensus, Marx and Engels argued for "a heavy progressive or graduated income tax" in their *Communist Manifesto* in 1848. Even Liberal economists have traditionally advocated a progressive income tax system based on the idea that an extra dollar of income for a middle-class or wealthy income earner provides diminishing satisfaction, and thus can be taxed at a higher rate compared to earnings below a mandated threshold. Adam Smith also believed that defense expenditures and education should be funded from "general contributions" and courts, roads, and other social infrastructure should be supported by tolls or fees. Smith also wrote in the *Wealth of Nations* that taxes should be levied in an equitable and consistent manner, *primarily* based upon an individual's ability to pay.

Nevertheless, since about 1981, cutting the top income tax rate while broadening the income range that applies to each rate has reduced the progressivity of the federal income tax system. The net effect of these changes has been to significantly reduce the percent of taxes borne by the upper-income groups. A recent analysis by Citizens for Tax Justice shows that Bush's tax cuts have lowered the overall federal, state, and local tax burden on the richest 1 percent of taxpayers—earnings above $978,000—by 12 percent. The ostensibly small reduction in the top bracket translates into a phenomenal windfall in absolute dollars for those in the top 5 percent of the income distribution. The *Forbes* 400 listing of the richest people in America, whose huge collective wealth multiplied into a megafortune in the last six or seven years (see Issue 6), will beget still greater incomes, now at more favorable tax rates.

While the federal income tax system has become less progressive, state and local tax schemes have also become less equitable. After the Reagan tax cuts of the early 1980s, many states simply adapted the federal tax brackets to their respective tax schedules. Furthermore, most local governments rely upon *regressive* property and sales taxes to fund most municipal activities. Property taxes are regressive because all incomes usually pay the same rate of tax, but the property valuation of the poor, in contrast to the wealthy, is often above its actual market value. Meanwhile, sales taxes are inherently more burdensome to the poor because they tend to spend a higher portion of their income on taxable consumption items. Since property taxes are the major source of funding for public schools, it is obvious why richer communities always seem to have outstanding public school systems, irrespective of governmental tax policies and/or fluctuations in the general economy. Conversely, it is not surprising that poorer communities generally have inferior public schools, particularly when their communities are faced with permanent economic decline.

The Conservative desire for a consumption-based income tax system is part and parcel of their broader program to end all collectively funded social programs. In their view, an individual's ability for pecuniary gain should be the *sole determinant* of personal worth in society. Accordingly, any effort on the part of government to encumber private income is illegitimate and leads to a misallocation of scarce resources. It is only a short leap of Conservative logic to demonstrate how *any* income tax leads to the downfall of capitalism.

A Radical program for a more equitable tax system would start with a steeply progressive income tax system on *all* income. Those who earn less than a government-guaranteed income—say, $40,000 for a family of four—would automatically be exempt from all taxes. Second, most tax loopholes would be eliminated, inheritance taxes would be substantially increased, and a flat tax on all stock market transactions would be imposed. While long-term investors would not be taxed as heavily as short-term speculators, all capital gains would be subject to a highly progressive income tax structure. Under this tax system, no one would be prevented from accumulating wealth; however, wealth would not become the source of dynastic power for those who did not create it.

Finally, all income—both earned and unearned—would be subject to a *progressive* Social Security tax. This would make the Social Security system solvent and eliminate all the inequities existing under current financing methods—especially since about three-quarters of all taxpayers pay more in social security taxes than federal income taxes. Moreover, aggregate demand would grow much faster if payroll taxes on low-wage workers were drastically reduced or temporarily suspended to raise income and stimulate consumption. For far too long, rich corporations and wealthy individuals have been able to use the political system to reduce their tax burden. It is time for the vast majority of Americans to direct their anger not so much at the tax collector but at a Congress that is wholly incapable of creating a fair and equitable tax system. Ultimately, the vast majority of working-class Americans must band together to ensure that there will be an end to taxation without representation.

Part III

Conclusion

The Market Versus Planning and Controls
Which Strategy Works Better?

Whenever the legislature attempts to regulate the differences between the masters and their workmen, its counsellors are always the masters.

—*Adam Smith, 1776*

The world is not so governed from above that private and social interests coincide. It is not so managed here below that in practice they coincide. It is not a correct deduction from the Principles of Economics that enlightened self-interest always operates in the public interest.

—*John Maynard Keynes, 1926*

It used to seem to me that the drift of all Western countries was toward something like socialism. But now, when I reflect on what is happening . . . it is not so clear. There is a sense of return to the market, because the task of planning in a modern economy is so complex.

—*Robert Heilbroner, 1986*

Off-the-shelf utopias may be useful thought experiments, but they're of limited political use, except maybe as long-term inspiration. A future society has to emerge out of this one, on the basis of experimentation and struggle.

—*Doug Henwood, 1997*

The Problem

Throughout our examination of contemporary economic issues, there has been a consistent tension among the Conservative defense of a free and unregulated economy, the limited regulation objectives of the Liberals, and the general assault on free markets by Radicals. At issue has been the question of exactly how free or how planned the economy should be. In our closing debate, it is appropriate to deal with this question directly: Which strategy—the free market or some degree of planning and controls—is more likely to provide desirable outcomes?

Based on recent public opinion surveys, trends in American political rhetoric and practice, and events beyond the borders of the United States, an ordinary observer might quickly conclude that planning is in full retreat. Public support for the Keynesian social-engineering efforts of the 1960s and early 1970s withered by the late 1970s. Between 1980 and 1992, first with Ronald Reagan and then with George Bush, Americans elected presidents who, at least in terms of their public posture, were emphatically promarket. Democrat Bill Clinton entered office in 1992 sporting a sort of moderate Liberal posture, briefly turned leftward, and then, after his party lost both houses of Congress in 1994, moved toward a safer middle-ground position. He was reelected in 1996 after announcing that the era of big government was over. Meanwhile, within the domestic economy, "privatization" became an important new buzzword as extended discussions began to take place about spinning off certain longtime bastions of government power to the private sector. Schools, prison systems, and certain public welfare operations were in fact privatized in some areas of the country, and by 1997 there was serious talk of privatizing the Social Security system. With George W. Bush's election in 2000, the nation's political leadership took an obvious and clearly defined Conservative posture.

Beyond the nation's borders, however, the drift toward privatization and the introduction of market economic policies were much more striking, mostly because these shifts were taking place in economies long in the camp of the central planners. The collapse of the Soviet Union first opened Eastern Europe in 1989 to extensive experimentation with and implementation of a wide variety of market-directed economic policies. By 1990–91, in its reconstitution as Russia, the principal remnant of the former Soviet Union had hired a team of American free market advocates to advise the Russian authorities on the transition from a centrally planned communist state to a more democratically open and market-driven political economy.

However, the perilous decline in Russian living standards and life expectancy has undermined popular support for further privatization schemes. Meanwhile, China introduced *enterprise zones* and some limited experimentation with market economics in some of its southeastern provinces. However, the Chinese effort, promising as it is to free market advocates, remains suspect, still laboring under the cloud of that government's brutal reaction to the Beijing student uprising in the spring of 1989 and the considerable repression that persists throughout most of the nation.

Understandably, promarket advocates are quick to draw final conclusions on the basis of these trends. Yet what can we really conclude with certainty? Seven decades ago, in a world caught up in abject economic depression, the market system stood discredited in the eyes of many. However, market-based economics has obviously enjoyed a rebirth in recent years. The failure of the communist-bloc economies may say more about the effects of poor planning and the shortcomings of imposing ideology through the planning apparatus than about planning in general. After all, economic planning in various degrees remains alive and well in many nations, not the least of which are the highly successful cases of Sweden, France, and Germany. Nor can we ignore the fact that economic planning efforts have deep roots in the American past.

Someone unfamiliar with American history might conclude that current economic trends are a ringing and final referendum against any effort to construct even a modestly planned economy. Such a judgment would likely be premature. Popular political belief in the possibilities of national economic planning has frequently surfaced in the past and has been translated into policy. From Alexander Hamilton's *Report on Manufactures* to Henry Clay's American Plan to Woodrow Wilson's progressive New Freedom to Franklin Roosevelt's New Deal, the United States has undergone a number of periods in which varieties of faith in central planning were applied to the nation's economy. Nor were these experiments with planning mere artifacts of a distant political past.

As recently as the 1980–82 recession, even with a staunch defender of free market economics in the White House, another vision of central planning attracted considerable attention, this time with startlingly strong support in the business community. "Industrial policy," as it was known, promised to revitalize American industry through, among other things, the creation of a federal investment bank that would act as a lender of last resort to businesses, especially those rustbelt industries that were particularly hard pressed. Some industrial policy advocates urged that the United States develop its own version of Japan's then highly successful MITI (Ministry of International Trade and Industry). MITI had operated since shortly after World War II, directing Japanese industrial development and targeting winners and losers in Japan's export and domestic markets through its control over research and development funds, investment sources, and imports. However, industrial policy did have its critics in the United States, and it never developed to the point of proposing specific legislation. At any rate, its attractiveness diminished as the recession of the early 1980s lifted.

While the 1980s and 1990s will doubtless be remembered for the resurgence of market economic philosophy in the United States, some observers can be excused if they wondered aloud just how deep this redirection in American economic thinking really went. After all, the scare provided by the stock market crash of Black Monday, October 19, 1987, produced all manner of pleas from members of the business and financial communities for greater controls over securities trading. Similarly, the savings and loan crisis of 1988–89 triggered calls for greater regulation of American banking. And despite the expansive arguments on behalf of deregulation in general, surveys of public attitudes indicate no diminishing of the general population's support for environmental and consumer protection activities by government. In the fall of 2001, as smoke was still rising from the World Trade Center, the public clamored for "sky marshals" and federalized airport security while the airlines and segments of the tourist industry waited for federal assistance. Meanwhile, the 2001 bursting of the stock market bubble and increasing incidents of corporate fraud among such corporate giants as Enron and WorldCom pushed mindless devotion to market capitalism off center stage.

Given the cyclical nature of economic planning's popularity and its tendency to arise precisely as the general economy's performance sags, it is entirely possible that a national debate about industrial policy, full-employment planning, or perhaps even more radical and far-reaching planning efforts simply await the next significant slump in the economy.

Synopsis

For Conservatives, the adoption of national economic planning would mean the ending of capitalism as a social system and the imposition of an inefficient dictatorship in its place. Liberals, however, see planning as compatible with our mixed capitalist economy, since the essential elements of the system (private property and economic and political freedom) would actually be enhanced by the increased stability that planning would provide. To be sure, Liberals advocate only a limited system of planning. Radicals, meanwhile, see present planning proposals only as efforts to maintain the present inequalities and exploitativeness of the capitalist system. To them, planning is essential, but it must be done at the level of human needs, not those of the corporation.

Anticipating the Arguments

- What is the Conservatives' fundamental philosophical disagreement with centralized planning efforts?
- How do Liberals argue that planning and a basically capitalistic economic system are compatible?
- What do Radicals mean when they call for planning "for and by people"?

THE CONSERVATIVE ARGUMENT

At this stage in our discussion of contemporary economic problems, the Conservative response to the idea of national economic planning should be obvious—or perhaps it would be better to say *familiar*. National economic planning, in the sense that it means nonmarket, administrative decisions on output, pricing, employment, capital, and so on, is to be opposed as vigorously as possible. Planning is the final collectivist victory over freedom and individualism. When economic and political authorities, whether they be fascists or communists or even well-meaning Liberals, have the power to determine all important matters in the economy, there is little else left in life that is beyond their ability to control. The frightening scenarios in such books as *Brave New World* and *1984* are no longer merely science fiction.

The economic criticism of central planning is quickly summarized. First of all, it is profoundly inefficient in terms of theoretical economic principles. Second, empirical evidence on efforts at national economic planning (which is abundant) proves that such planning is ineffective.

National Planning: Theoretically Inefficient

As we know, under a market system prices are the signals for economic activity. The decision to produce a particular good can be calculated both in terms of the actual production costs of labor, capital, or resources and in terms of what that particular good costs compared to other goods. As long as the market designates the prices of the factors of production (labor, capital, and resources) and the prices of final goods, we have a rational basis for allocating resources to their best possible uses. As consumers or producers, we can make choices based on a steady and reliable measure of costs and benefits. This is not to say that prices will not fluctuate. Of course they will. They are supposed to fluctuate to reflect changes in demand and supply and thus changes in the cost structure or in consumer satisfaction.

Far from being anarchy, the market *is* a planning mechanism. The market works like a system and, as Adam Smith observed in an essay on astronomy written long before his *Wealth of Nations,* "a system is like a little machine." Like a machine, a market-planned economy has regulators that keep it in balance.

Administrative planning, on the other hand, has no natural internal or external checks on its effectiveness. In an administered economy, levels of output, employment, and the mix of goods are purely matters of political determination. It is not really important whether these goals are set by commissars, Harvard economists, or the duly elected representatives of the people; they are the result of human judgments. They reflect particular individual or collective biases. Not even a computer can tell what output and employment goals are correct unless it is programmed (by humans) to respond to certain criteria (selected by humans).

Defenders of planning may point out that high levels of growth and employment have been attained in certain planned economies. There is some truth to this, but the argument misses the point. Administrative planning in the Soviet Union during World War II and immediately afterward, and in developing nations more recently, was bound to have some success because of these nations' very primitive level of economic development. When you have nothing and plan something, you can hardly lose, especially if you have authoritarian control over the labor force. It is quite another matter, however, to maintain efficient administrative planning in an advanced, complex economy. This, of course, is exactly what the Russians, the East Europeans, and, to some extent, the Chinese discovered in the 1980s, as decades of inefficient planning brought economic growth to a standstill and discredited communism as an economic and political system.

Like market economies, most administered economies use prices to direct economic activity toward predetermined goals. But it should be remembered that these prices, like the goals themselves, are administratively determined. Prices, therefore, do not reflect costs as we speak of them but are merely a rationing technique used to direct labor, capital, output, and, ultimately, social behavior toward certain imposed objectives.

Space prohibits a more detailed theoretical attack on the output and pricing behavior of planned economies, but a brief survey of some of the problems encountered by such economies may demonstrate the essence of the Conservative critique.

National Planning: Ineffective in Practice

The Soviet Union was a striking example of what can happen when economic mechanisms are subordinated to clearly political objectives. Not unlike legislation American Liberals have sought to pass since the "glory days" of Roosevelt's New Deal, Soviet goals also included full employment, enforced price stability, and specific production targets for certain goods.

In the Soviet case, full employment meant a job for everyone. In an authoritarian collectivist society, this was not a great problem, but there is a big difference between putting people in jobs and having them perform productively. For instance, Soviet plant managers, given output goals by state planners (which were to be met *or else*), often feared a shortage of labor in the future and commonly hoarded workers. On other occasions, they had to hire labor as directed by state authorities, whether or not they needed it. In either case, the workers in question were underemployed. In terms of economic analysis, the result is obvious: inefficiency. Workers were hired without any view to their productivity. Wages were set by state planners, who had little or no knowledge of costs of production at a plant. Thus managers might reach their output targets, with workers *fully employed,* but the actual cost of goods (as reckoned by alternative uses of labor and capital) often were much higher than the planners could cover in setting a price. In real terms this meant that the whole society had to pay the actual costs by forgoing other goods. An inefficiently made tractor often "cost" many thousands of nonproduced consumer items.

The tendency to think only in output (quantitative) terms has qualitative effects too. Production rushed to meet a planner's goal may encourage defective and shoddy manufacture. Quick and flexible adaptation of production to meet changes in goals is very difficult. Planners lack the signals of prices based on supply and demand to tell them when and how to change the production mix. Plans become rigid, at both the plant and planning levels.

In the Soviet Union many of the worst features of central planning were eliminated over time. The introduction of linear programming, in-put-output analysis, and, finally, the computer did improve the accumulation and flow of information. The incredible lapses of mind that earlier had led to the production of motor vehicle engines and chassis but not the needed ball bearings for their wheels had generally disappeared by the 1980s. In fact, Soviet industry had achieved a measure of techno-logical success in some cases (for example, space-related industries). However, as Gorbachev took over, the overall microeconomic decision-making process remained bogged down by the political administration of prices and wages and by mind-boggling distributional inadequacies. Even after years of sacrifice to build the industrial base of the society, ordinary Russians remained as they had always been—the balancing item in the central plan ledger. The errors of planners, even those with computers, were still to be paid for in relinquished consumer goods and in a scarcely improving standard of living. In the end, Gorbachev's timid efforts were his and the Soviet Union's undoing. Racked by strikes, in-ternal economic crises and political disarray, and the secession of key states in the union, the USSR passed into history. Gorbachev was re-moved from power in December 1991, and in the fall of 1992, the Con-stitutional Court of Russia ruled that while communists could still enjoy local political rights and protections, the Communist Party, as a national political party, was illegal. Meanwhile, the party's financial assets and real property were placed under the control of the Russian Federation. The foremost model of the centrally planned, authoritarian state came to an end after a mere seventy-five years of existence.

Putting Planning Within an American Context

Critics will argue that the Soviet case is irrelevant to any planning situ-ation affecting the United States. They will maintain, of course, that American *mixed capitalism*—a combination of a dependence on the market and relevant interventions to correct the market—is much differ-ent from a fully planned, authoritarian economic system. To Conserva-tives, though, the threat of planning is quite real. Talk of national economic planning goes back a long way in American history, and, as is evident in day-to-day government reaction to the issues discussed in this book, the tendency toward collectivist solutions to all economic problems, although diminishing a bit lately, remains strong. History shows that, once commenced, the march toward collectivism is hard to reverse. Today we may be talking merely of obtaining additional data for national planning or making full employment a law. Tomorrow the managed-economy objectives may be more personal to all of us—determining where we live, where we work, what we buy, and so on.

Conservatives are not anarchists. Indeed, they believe in planning, and today we have a high order of acceptable planning in the economy. This planning, however, is a function of *individual choices collectively expressed in the market.* As Milton Friedman has observed:

> Fundamentally, there are only two ways of coordinating the economic activities of millions. One is central direction involving the use of coercion—the technique of the army and of the modern totalitarian state. The other is voluntary cooperation of individuals—the technique of the market place. . . . Exchange can bring about coordination without coercion.*

The present in-between, never-never land of mixed American capitalism cannot continue long. *We must go either one way or the other in the future.*

The Dynamism of the Market

Critics of the market economy have always stressed that the fundamental weakness of a truly capitalist economic system is its recurring propensity toward varieties of instability. Such an idea is both overworked and misleading. As our earlier discussion should have pointed out, the failure of planned economic systems—such as the old Soviet Union—to meet individual needs can be vastly greater than the uncertainties a market order might create.

Yet, the critics do have a point. Market capitalism can be a disruptive system. Indeed, it should be. The driving force of a production-for-profit

---

*Milton Friedman, *Capitalism and Freedom* (Chicago: University of Chicago Press, 1962), 13.

market system is *change*—change in the goods that are produced, change in the way goods are produced and sold, and change from time to time in the distribution of the goods and the distribution of claims to goods produced. The great Austrian economist who for many years taught at Harvard University, Joseph Alois Schumpeter, called this process of capitalist uncertainty and change "creative destruction."

In the very processes of invention, innovation, and the resulting rise of new investment and production opportunities—always events encouraged in a market economic order—the society, said Schumpeter, would be swept by "gales of creative destruction." Perfectly serviceable factories and machines could be rendered obsolete instantly. Old capital investments could rapidly depreciate to scrap. Once-valued skilled labor could become redundant. Great redistributions of income and economic power could take place as new entrepreneurs with new ideas, driven by the desire to profit from their inventions and innovations, turned the old economic order upside down. But, Schumpeter maintained, the resulting destruction was worth the cost to everyone. Better goods, more efficiently produced, provided society with net positive gains even after the costs of destruction were subtracted.

Yet, as Schumpeter knew, there was always a variety of social groups who entrenched themselves against creative destruction. Labor unions, monopolistic business enterprises, bureaucracies of any kind, and their principal agent, government, all stand ready to protect the status quo by controlling, really strangling, change.

Those Liberal and Radical opponents of the market are not just advocates of a different view of economic progress and the benefits that thereby might be accorded. They are, in their hearts and minds, the enemies of progress itself.

THE LIBERAL ARGUMENT

By this point the Liberal propensity to approach contemporary economic problems in pragmatic and nondogmatic ways should be self-evident. Equally, it should be evident that both Conservatives and Radicals, despite their vastly different ideological agendas, share a peculiar tendency: to present economic behavior and economics itself as largely deterministic and mechanistic processes. That is, economic thinking and economic undertakings are viewed not as matters of human choice or as matters of cultural habit but as the unfolding of abstract and eternal verities that, quite simply, exist independently of human beings and of human history. The Radical argument has for the time being been shoved off into history's dustbin as a result of the failure of the Soviet Union. However, and regrettably for the discipline of economics, the Conservative vision has recently come to exercise considerable influence in mainstream American economic thought. It has also been gaining greater influence outside of the United States. Liberals cannot let this development go unchallenged and the debate over the comparative virtues of *the market* versus *employing planning and controls* is a good place to reveal the analytical and practical weakness of the Conservative argument.

The Narrow and Unrealistic Assumptions of Market-Logic Advocates

To see where Conservatives think they are going, it is necessary to understand the logic from which their argument proceeds. The argument, of course, was first set out by Adam Smith a bit over two hundred years ago and augmented and enriched a hundred years later by neoclassical economics. Together Smith and the neoclassical traditions are the foundations of modern Conservative emphasis upon market logic.

Market logic, first of all, presumes the existence of cultural and political stability as a given. Only amid this general external stability is it possible for a market to work according to a fairly consistent and predictable set of expectations. Second, market logic assumes the presence of *rational maximizing* behavior on the part of all individuals as a central element in the popular will of that society. Without social stability and without popular support for individual self-interest, the seeds of market logic cannot take root and give rise to appropriate practices of production-for-profit behavior. A third requirement specifies a *minimum government* condition to be present; in other words, a popular willingness never to tinker collectively with market outcomes. And, although the caveat hardly needs to be added, Conservatives believe the market, left essentially to its own dynamic, will be a competitive market. It should be remembered that all of these conditions are not viewed as mere accidental matters but as normal conditions that will naturally arise over time.

Right away, it becomes evident that a goodly portion of the world's population lives outside the conditions where a truly market-driven economic system could flourish. For instance, consider the problem of rational maximizing. The assertion that human beings are first and foremost acquisitive and self-interested individualists is impossible to prove and is easily disputed by real-world events. It goes without saying that much of the world is ruled by very different outlooks. The dominance of nationalistic, religious, and tribal orthodoxies that militate against individualistic and materialistic values poses an important practical problem in many nations for the development of a personal and social behavior that market-logic theorists describe as "human behavior" and as "natural." Much more troubling to market-logic adherents, however, is the fact that, even in social systems that have been receptive to individualist and materialist values and to the broad outlines of market logic, the tendency to tinker with and try to improve upon free market outcomes has been irresistible. While market-logic advocates rail against big government and its interference in the workings of the market, they offer no convincing explanation for the rise of this clearly *unnatural* tendency in the first place. After all the Conservative arguments against state interference in economic affairs have been reviewed, it still seems fairly obvious that big government with its planning and controls was not invented for the purpose of creating economic inefficiency and dependency.

Certainly in the United States, big government emerged initially as a corrective "political response" to problems viewed as inherent to free markets. It was from practical political experience, not an ignorance of economic logic, that Americans came to understand that a high order of personal freedom entailed much more than just having the right to be a rational maximizer and that individual economic freedom in no way ensured all individuals would enjoy fair and just outcomes in the marketplace.

The principal problem, then, that Conservatives have with regard to the accuracy of their market model and the relevance of its rational maximizer prescription is that none of the world's nations spells out citizens' rights and responsibilities in purely economic terms. The various freedoms and nonfreedoms that individuals have in virtually any society are derived from the prevailing political and social conventions deemed essential by that society to perpetuate and protect itself. Any particular society's taste for economic individualism and for free markets is necessarily constrained by these realities. In any case, the *political* requirements of a social order are set first and the acceptable range of economic behavior follows—a very different reality from the market-logic vision of things.

Putting the Role of the State in the Correct Perspective

Quite apart from the logical problems of Conservatives, there is the practical matter that history offers no convincing example of a successful free market economy. To be sure, there may have been some near misses. Perhaps England of the 1830s, the United States of the 1850s, possibly even Singapore a couple of decades ago demonstrated certain free market characteristics that were reminiscent of market-logic inspiration, but, on closer look, they were pretty pale copies, clearly not meeting the required standards.

With the possible exception of theological belief associated with religious faith, probably no set of formal arguments has endured so long in the absence of any convincing real-world evidence of their practicality and validity as those laid out by the classical advocates of market logic. Even formal scientific postulates in biology, astronomy, and physics have proven to be more adaptive to real-world constraints and the force of empirical evidence. Accordingly, for a very long time now, Conservative economic thinkers have had to spend much of their time explaining why their free market vision has not come to pass. Indeed, these explanations generally occupy more space in Conservative writings than the real body of Conservative analytical doctrine.

Variously over the years, labor unions, monopolistic business enterprise, socialists, communists, intellectuals, and many other groups have been singled out as part of the general "conspiracy" against free markets. And always the device these conspirators have employed to destroy or subvert true economic freedom has been the most malignant of human institutions: government. In any case, it is a heavy burden for Conservatives to bear, constantly having to explain why the "natural" conditions of a free economic order are forever undermined by "unnatural" conspiracies and events.

The Conservative assault on government, apart from its logical irrelevance, as we have earlier noted, rests on a revealing irony. It is true, of course, that Adam Smith intended his articulation of a market economy to free economic thinking (at least English economic thinking) from the hold long imposed by the mercantilist state. But Smith was no anarchist. He continued to assign to government, in his own version of state power, fairly considerable economic responsibilities. These powers Smith's followers ever sought to diminish. Yet, irony of ironies, the English classical economic tradition, the precursor of all market-logic efforts, only gained practical influence through its own, quite unnatural manipulation of government.

In England, as in other nations undergoing industrialization during the first half of the nineteenth century, it was the machinery of government—not the absence of such machinery—that was essential in rolling back the paternalism and protectionism of the feudal and mercantilist past. Repeal in 1846 of the Corn Laws protecting English agriculture, passage in 1832 of a new Poor Law that set aside the social protection of the unemployed in the name of a free labor market, and enactment of the Banking Act of 1844, which set Great Britain upon a gold standard, were efforts *by the state,* supported of course by the advocates of free markets, that paved the way for the temporary flourishing of laissez-faire economic conditions. As Karl Polanyi pointed out many years ago: "Laissez-faire itself was enforced by the state. . . . Laissez-faire was not a method to achieve a thing, it was the thing to be achieved."*

From the beginning, everywhere market capitalism surfaced in its varied forms, the state was the instrumentality through which it came into being. Capitalism was not obtained, as Conservative doctrine might lead one to believe, through evolutionary practice and the "natural" march of economic progress. Indeed, without the state's acting on behalf of a market capitalist agenda, there was no surety that capitalism—or at least capitalism as most Western nations have come to know it—would have emerged at all. And, when the experiments with a laissez-faire market system experienced difficulties from time to time, the state was to be used again and again in either its maintenance or its reform. By regulating away capitalism's more obnoxious social effects, and thereby at least maintaining the basic elements of production-for-profit, practical men of affairs, if hardly ever Conservative economic thinkers, recognized that saving half a loaf was better than no bread at all.

To be sure, many of the market-driven economic tools of Conservative economic theory have been and continue to be useful analytic devices. Liberal economic analysis, as it is known and taught in the United States, is built, after all, on the foundation of classical economics. But the larger vision of Conservatives is another matter. Their faith in the efficient and fair functioning of an economy free of all planning and controls is blind to the flaws of its own logic and overlooks the evidence of history. It is a hopelessly mechanical argument in which iron-clad

---

*Karl Polanyi, *The Great Transformation* (New York: Rinehart, 1944), 250.

economic "laws" can be used to justify great varieties of inequity and unnecessary pain. Capitalism as a system may be able to function and thrive, but only with periodic adjustment and repair.

The Objectives of Liberal Interventionism

A quick review of the Liberal arguments in each of the preceding economic issues provides a range of the types of tinkering Liberals are content to support. The Liberal view is certainly not the collectivist vision Conservatives assign to it.

Contrary to the Conservative outlook, planning is not necessarily communism, nor is it authoritarianism of any special breed. Planning is essential to maintaining the American democratic capitalist tradition. To the Liberal, of course, "democratic" is much more important than "capitalist" in a generic sense. The economic experiences of the United States and all other basically capitalist countries indicate quite clearly that only planning can save the private-property, production-for-profit system from self-destruction.

Although he has not always been in the mainstream of Liberal opinion, John Kenneth Galbraith's observations of over three decades ago fairly represent the Liberal position of today. After weighing the growing problems of American industrial society, Galbraith concluded:

> It is through the state that the society must assert the superior claim of aesthetic over economic goals and particularly of environment over cost. It is to the state we must look for freedom of individual choice as to toil. . . . If the state is to serve these ends, the scientific and educational estate and larger intellectual community must be aware of their power and their opportunity and they must use them. There is no one else.*

THE RADICAL ARGUMENT

Despite the current Conservative celebration of a renaissance of free market thought and practice, capitalism has for a considerable period of time moved inexorably toward greater central control. Although there is much debate on how close we really are to a formally planned and con-

---

*John K. Galbraith, *The New Industrial State* (Boston: Houghton Mifflin, 1967), 335.

trolled economy, Radicals would generally agree that it is the next great leap in capitalist development. From laissez-faire to monopoly capitalism to state-corporate regulation to formal planning, capitalism runs its course in its effort to secure profit and protect itself. The obvious irony, of course, is that planned capitalism is a contradiction in terms. As the basic economics textbooks tell us, capitalism emerged as a philosophy espousing, in theory at least, total economic and personal freedom. Alas, in the practical world, it ends as a statement on behalf of authoritarianism.

From the Radical perspective, it is necessary to get beyond the thoughtless celebration of market economics that presently pervades popular opinion and political rhetoric in the United States. Quite simply, this resuscitation of capitalist ideology has served to obscure the capitalist reality we in fact live in and to mystify for many the actual workings of modern capitalism. Yet the symbiotic relationship between capitalist enterprise and the modern capitalist state persists just below the surface of everyday economic life if only we care to dig beneath the veneer of Conservative ideology.

Capitalism Needs Planning

Ideologies, even after they have proved worthless, die hard, often convulsively. It remains to be seen how the outmoded rhetoric of laissez-faire or even the more sophisticated mixed-economy philosophies will pass into history. They are deeply rooted in the individual practice and thought of American citizens, and their public defenders are still loud and shrill. Nevertheless, as our discussions of other contemporary issues should indicate, the use of government controls and planning in the economy is apparent everywhere.

This process is not really very new. It originated in the late nineteenth-century response to the growing crises of American capitalism. Troubled by periodic panics or recessions (in 1873, 1884, 1893, and 1907), chronic excess capacity and overproduction, and anarchic market conditions, and threatened by increasingly radicalized labor strife, American capitalism depended more and more on state intervention. We have elaborated on these interventions in our discussions of stabilization policy, government deficits, unemployment, and international trade. As the state became a partner in supporting business, American corporations enlarged their monopoly powers through concentration and control.

This growth of state-corporate integration has been euphemistically termed the "mixed economy" in economics texts. Uninformed Conservatives have attacked this integration as the domination of business by the state, without even stopping to ask just whose interests the state has represented. They fail to see that, quite as Marx specified, "the State is the form in which the individuals of the ruling class assert their common interests."

Capitalist production has proved to be extraordinarily rational in a microeconomic sense. The organization of production, labor, and capital for any particular firm is governed by economic rules of behavior (we call it the price system) that, for an individual entrepreneur, give key signals on how best to attain profit objectives. Yet, in totality, the capitalist system is irrational. Though the actions of any given firm are rationally planned or calculated with profit in mind, the actions of all firms taken together produce macroeconomic and social disorder. There is a lack of coordination and integration, even among monopolistic capitalists, in dealing with different industries and different sectors of the economy. Rational control of the whole labor force, of total output, and of investment alternatives is lacking.

The boom-bust rhythm of the business cycle, although recently muted when compared to the past, is still evident—but with a difference. Today's highly integrated and automated production is extremely vulnerable to even the slightest variations in sales, profits, and output. In the past, when industry was predominantly labor-intensive, a business downturn amounted mainly to sending the workers home with empty pay envelopes and waiting until things got better. Today, with greater capital usage and production on an international scale, nonproduction presents a firm with greater losses. These, in turn, adversely affect financial markets and the international structure of business.

Moreover, modern capitalism has so penetrated the world that it is limited in its ability to acquire new markets, so essential to its survival. At the same time, as we have noted repeatedly before, capitalist production can be carried on at higher output levels using less labor power. As a result, the crowning irrationality of the system is that it can produce more and more, but labor becomes increasingly redundant and markets harder to find.

The chronic tendency toward unemployment and excess capacity, the steady threat of inflation, and the worsening balance-of-trade situation leave few options for American capitalism. As the Liberal John Kenneth

Galbraith has argued for years, the next step in capitalist development is to transcend the market and modern Keynesian efforts to correct it and to move straight toward direct economic planning and controls. Only through such efforts can capitalist irrationality be controlled. Planning presents possibilities for reorganizing the capitalist processes of production and accumulation and at the same time can legitimize or bring order to labor markets.

Planning for Profits, Not People

One of the great self-deceptions of Conservative economic thought is the doctrinaire view that planning is inimical to market-based economic behavior. It is wrongheaded as a logical matter and a positively silly notion as a matter of real-world practice. Capitalists, whether we are talking of giant corporations or small mom-and-pop operations, do not earn their profits accidentally. In any case, it would be absurd to suggest that Microsoft, General Motors, and Citicorp do not have a plan for their business operations, that at the end of the year of producing and selling goods and services willy-nilly they are randomly surprised or dismayed when they tally their sales and expenses.

No one in their right mind would seriously argue that planning is not an essential element of every business enterprise's operations. Planning within the modern enterprise is, of course, much more important than it was at the dawn of the capitalist era when Adam Smith and his colleagues were working out the "rules" of a market economy. This does not reflect so much a philosophical change in capitalists' approach to the everyday matter of obtaining profit as it does the vastly increased complexity of the goods they make and the techniques necessary to manufacture and sell these goods.

However, if planning is important as an everyday operational function within a business, why are planning efforts between and among businesses and planning utilizing government not seen as natural progressions for capitalism as a system? Obviously, the Conservative assault upon planning is a spurious argument not taken seriously by real-world practitioners of production for profit.

In fact, business enterprisers—especially large business enterprisers—see real gains and opportunities to be obtained from planning. During the late 1970s and into the 1980s, as the American economy sagged through a particularly unimpressive period of slow growth, high unemployment, and lowered profits, many in the business community flirted publicly with the idea of enlarging the federal government's role as a central planner. Many spoke warmly on behalf of an *industrial policy* that embraced a joint government-business coordination of investment, labor, and trade policies to deal with the then preoccupying concern about the *deindustrialization* of America. To be sure, this enthusiasm for planning has flagged a bit over the past two decades as the American economy's performance and prospects brightened. But when the boom turns to bust, as it surely will and as it always has, it is reasonable to expect that capitalists will rediscover industrial policy.

Regardless of the simplistic Conservative notion that all centralized efforts at economic planning and control are threats to a production-for-profit system, Radicals understand the real issues in any discussion of planning to be very different matters. The crucial question that any inquiry into economic planning should raise is: planning by whom and for what objective? Planning of an industrial policy variety still operates within the capitalist firmament. It amounts to planning by capitalists, or their agents, for the purpose of maintaining profits for business enterprises and profit-making as a social objective. The name of the game in capitalism is still profits, and, contrary to Liberal apologists, the name does not change when essentially capitalist systems adopt centralist planning techniques.

As long as business profitability is the guiding force of planning efforts, Americans will never be able to transcend the limitations of the social order under which they live. Quite literally, all human experience will remain subservient to and positively limited by the eternal quest for *the bottom line*. Radicals have a different prescription for the economic order: Planning should first and foremost be about meeting the needs of real living and breathing people.

The Radical Alternative: Planning for and by People

Although Radicals may be divided on the means by which social planning is to be achieved, there is greater agreement on *how* such planning should proceed once it is established. Most American Radicals would reject out of hand the varieties of social planning demonstrated by such socialist nations as the Soviet Union or China. These efforts at state planning simply lost sight of the major objective of any rational and humane planning: *people*. In these cases, plans were developed and imposed from above by central planning or political authorities whose decisions had no more to do with workers' and consumers' needs than decisions currently being made by Exxon or IBM officials.

The first and unifying rule for Radicals with regard to planning is that the planning process must begin with popular participation and must be conceived to deal with people's problems.

The complexity of modern economies and the immensity of providing people with the opportunities to plan such economies, of course, seem so formidable as to make most citizens believe that popular planning is simply impossible. Radicals reject such a view out of hand. To do anything else would be to submit to the tyranny that is the capitalist mode of production. There are, of course, many levels of planning, from decisions pertaining to a particular plant or factory to broad national output targets. Obviously, the more distant the level of planning, the more difficult individual participation becomes. Nevertheless, society now has the appropriate means of production, such as computer and information processing technologies, to make widespread planned coordination between producers and consumers a reality. Innovations such as bar code technologies and integrated communication and computer networks can facilitate a speed and depth of coordination and allocation that is far superior to anarchic capitalist markets. Recognizing that the Soviet and Chinese communist cases are examples of what can happen when planning lacks the requisite information processing and coordination capabilities and becomes too abstracted from popular input, the object is always to keep as much of the decision making at the lower levels as possible and, when that is no longer a reasonable alternative, to devise the broader elements of the plan through as democratic a means as possible.

Workers or their directly elected representatives must be the basis for local output, pricing, and workplace decisions. Such decisions, of course, must be made with an eye to the general welfare. No worker or group of workers has the right to earnings obtained by sacrificing consumers or some other group of workers. That would merely be capitalism reappearing in the disguise of socialism, and it would lead to the same kind of exploitative conditions we now live under. Thus it is obvious that workers must be joined by consumers in the local or lower-level planning activities. Organizing broad popular participation in the planning process will not be easy, nor is there absolute certainty that a democratically devised plan will not be guilty of error and even failure. It is comparatively easy for Conservatives and Liberals to paint a picture of chaotic planning meetings as various representatives of workers, managers, and consumers determine key economic objectives. However, they miss two very important points. First, the failures of such planning efforts can be little worse than the current private planning "successes." Second, even at its worst, planning based on workers' and consumers' participation *is* democratic planning and *is* consistent with the professed ideals of a democratic society.

Regardless of the precise methods ultimately devised to facilitate participatory planning—and trial and error will certainly play a role in selecting planning goals—the Radical holds to a basic belief that the people must be the architects of their own society. The basic economic decisions of *what* is produced, *how,* and *for whom* must not be entrusted to an elite, whether they be capitalists, political commissars, or excommissars turned capitalist.

The late Radical economic and social historian William Appleman Williams put it this way:

> Hence the issue is not whether to decentralize the economy and politics of the country, but rather how to do so. . . . This literal reconstructing and rebuilding of American society offers the only physical and intellectual challenge capable of absorbing and giving focus to the physical and intellectual resources of the country during the next generation. . . .
>
> Throughout such a process, moreover, the participants will be educating themselves . . . for their membership in the truly human community they will be creating. In the end they will have built a physical America which will be beautiful instead of ugly, and which will facilitate human relationships instead of dividing men into separate functional elements. They will have evolved a political system which is democratic in form and social in content. And they will be prepared . . . to function as men and women who can define their own identity, and their relationships with each other, outside the confining limits of property and the bruising and destructive dynamics of the competitive marketplace. They will be ready to explore the frontier of their own humanity.*

---

*William A. Williams, *The Great Evasion* (Chicago: Quadrangle Books, 1964), 175–76.

Final Thoughts and Suggested Readings

Having reached the end of this volume of debates on contemporary economic issues, it is probable that the reader expects (perhaps even hopes for) the authors to make their pitches—to say straight out which of the representative paradigms is correct and which is not, perhaps each one to unveil his own grand program. Indeed, the opportunity is tempting. For an economist, it is practically a reflex to try to get in the last word, especially one's own last word. However, after much thought, we decided that such conclusions would spoil the entire effort. This book was undertaken to present the differing ideological alternatives as objectively as space and writing talents allowed so that the reader would be free to make personal choices on matters of economic policy.

We can hear some readers complaining: "Cop-out! You're avoiding presenting your own preferences and your own conclusions. You've taken the easy way out of the swamp." Not so. Delivering our own final polemics would in truth be ever so easy. But the book has been about questions and choices. The reader, then, shall be left in the uncomfortable position of making a choice among the paradigms and policy questions surveyed here. And that is the way it should be.

This perspective, however, must not be misunderstood. The authors have not intended to produce a relativistic conclusion in which any choice will do and one choice is as good as any other. The point is for the reader to make a *good* choice, and some policy choices *are* better than others. However, only a reasoned analysis of the facts and a critical study of the truths of this world will permit any of us to make wise choices.

The British economist Joan Robinson has said it best:

> Social life will always present mankind with a choice of evils. No metaphysical solution that can ever be formulated will seem satisfactory for long. The solutions offered by economists were no less delusory than those of the theologians that they displaced.
>
> All the same we must not abandon the hope that economics can make an advance towards science, or the faith that enlightenment is not useless. It is necessary to clear the decaying remnants of obsolete metaphysics out of the way before we can go forward.
>
> The first essential for economists, arguing amongst themselves, is to "very seriously," as Professor Popper says that natural scientists do, "try to avoid talking at cross purposes."*

Before we can "avoid talking at cross purposes" on economic matters, we must understand our fundamental differences in opinion and interpretation. We hope this book has identified some of these important differences for the reader.

In undertaking this task, the authors were sorely tested. While trying to submerge our personal biases, we also had to master the biases of others. Perhaps we have not entirely succeeded on either count. Only the reader can judge. Nevertheless, such an endeavor has been extremely educational.

For readers who desire to dig deeper into economic ideologies and their application to contemporary issues, the following bibliography offers some landmark readings in the respective Conservative, Liberal, and Radical schools of economic thought.

Conservative

Banfield, Edward C. *The Unheavenly City*. Boston: Little, Brown, 1970.
Buckley, William. *Up from Liberalism*. New York: Honor Books, 1959.
Friedman, Milton. *Capitalism and Freedom*. Chicago: University of Chicago Press, 1962.
———. *Free to Choose*. New York: Harcourt Brace Jovanovich, 1980.
Gilder, George. *Wealth and Power*. New York: Basic Books, 1981.
Hazlitt, Henry. *The Failure of the "New Economics": An Analysis of the Keynesian Fallacies*. New York: Van Nostrand, 1959.
Kirk, Russell. *The Conservative Mind*. Chicago: Regnery, 1954.

---

*Joan Robinson, *Economic Philosophy* (Garden City, NY: Anchor Books, 1964), 147–148.

Klamer, Arjo. *Conversations with Economists.* Totowa, NJ: Rowman and Allanhold, 1983.

Knight, Frank. *Freedom and Reform.* New York: Harper and Row, 1947.

Malabre, Alfred E., Jr. *Living Beyond Our Means.* New York: Vintage Books, 1987.

Marshall, Alfred. *Principles of Economics.* New York: Macmillan, 1890.

Rand, Ayn. *Capitalism: The Unknown Ideal.* New York: New American Library Signet Books, 1967.

Schumpeter, Joseph. *Capitalism, Socialism, and Democracy.* New York: Harper Brothers, 1942.

Simon, William E. *A Time for Action.* New York: Berkley, 1980.

Simons, Henry C. *A Positive Program for Laissez-Faire.* Chicago: University of Chicago Press, 1934.

Smith, Adam. *An Inquiry into the Nature and Causes of the Wealth of Nations,* 1776.

Stein, Herbert. *Presidential Economics: The Making of Economic Policy from Roosevelt to Reagan and Beyond.* New York: Simon and Schuster, 1985.

Von Hayek, Friedrich. *The Road to Serfdom.* Chicago: University of Chicago Press, 1944.

Von Mises, Ludwig. *Socialism: An Economic and Sociological Analysis.* New Haven: Yale University Press, 1959.

Liberal

Berle, Adolf A. *The Twentieth Century Capitalist Revolution.* New York: Harcourt Brace Jovanovich, 1954.

Clark, John M. *Alternative to Serfdom.* New York: Random House/Vintage Books, 1960.

————. *Social Control of Business.* New York: McGraw-Hill, 1939.

Friedman, Benjamin. *Day of Reckoning.* New York: Random House, 1988.

Galbraith, John Kenneth. *The New Industrial State.* Boston: Houghton Mifflin, 1967.

————. *The Affluent Society.* Boston: Houghton Mifflin, 1971.

————. *Economics and the Public Purpose.* Boston: Houghton Mifflin, 1973.

————. *Economics in Perspective.* Boston: Houghton Mifflin, 1987.

Hansen, Alvin. *The American Economy.* New York: McGraw-Hill, 1957.

Heilbroner, Robert. "The Future of Capitalism" in *The Limits of American Capitalism.* New York: Harper and Row, 1966.

————. *The Nature and Logic of Capitalism.* New York: Norton, 1985.

Heller, Walter W. *The Economy: Old Myths and New Realities.* New York: Norton, 1976.

Keynes, John M. *The General Theory of Employment, Interest, and Money.* New York: Harcourt Brace Jovanovich, 1936.

Lekachman, Robert. *The Age of Keynes.* New York: Random House, 1966.

Okun, Arthur M. *The Political Economy of Prosperity.* New York: Norton, 1970.

Reagan, Michael D. *The Managed Economy.* New York: Oxford University Press, 1963.

Reich, Robert B. *Tales of a New America.* New York: Times Books, 1987.

Shonfield, Andres. *Modern Capitalism: The Changing Balance of Public and Private Power.* New York: Oxford University Press, 1965.

Thurow, Lester C. *Dangerous Currents.* New York: Basic Books, 1980.

————. *The Zero-Sum Solution.* New York: Simon and Schuster, 1985.

Radical

Baran, Paul. *The Political Economy of Growth.* New York: Monthly Review Press, 1957.

Baran, Paul, and Paul M. Sweezy. *Monopoly Capital.* New York: Monthly Review Press, 1966.

Botwinick, Howard. *Persistent Inequalities.* Princeton, NJ: Princeton University Press, 1993.

Bowles, Samuel, and Herbert Gintis. *Property, Community, and the Contradictions of Modern Social Thought.* New York: Basic Books, 1986.

Bowles, Samuel, and Richard Edwards. *Understanding Capitalism.* New York: Harper and Row, 1985.

Brouwer, Steve. *Sharing the Pie: A Citizen's Guide to Wealth and Power in America.* New York: Henry Holt and Company, 1998.

Domhoff, William. *Who Rules America?* Englewood Cliffs, NJ: Prentice-Hall, 1967.

Dowd, Douglas. *The Twisted Dream.* Cambridge, MA: Winthrop, 1974.

Duboff, Richard. *Accumulation and Capital.* Armonk, NY: M.E. Sharpe, 1990.

Franklin, Raymond S. *American Captialism: Two Visions.* New York: Random House, 1977.

Gordon, David M. *Fat and Mean.* New York: The Free Press, 1996.

Henwood, Doug. *Wall Street.* London: Verso, 1997.

Kolko, Gabriel. *Wealth and Power in America.* New York: Praeger, 1962.

Magdoff, Harry. *The Age of Imperialism.* New York: Monthly Review Press, 1967.

Mandel, Ernest. *Marxist Economic Theory.* New York: Monthly Review Press, 1967.

Marx, Karl. *Capital.* 1867.

O'Connor, James. *The Fiscal Crisis of the State.* New York: St. Martin's Press, 1973.

Robinson, Joan. *An Essay on Marxian Economics.* London: Macmillan, 1942.

Shaikh, Anwar M., and E. Ahmet Tonak. *Measuring the Wealth of Nations.* Cambridge: Cambridge University Press, 1994.

Sherman, Howard. *Radical Political Economy.* New York: Basic Books, 1972.

———. *Stagflation: A Radical Theory of Unemployment and Inflation.* New York: Harper and Row, 1976.

Strachey, John. *The Nature of Capitalist Crisis.* New York: Covici, Friede, 1933.

———. *The Theory and Practice of Socialism.* New York: Random House, 1936.

Sweezy, Paul. *The Theory of Capitalist Development.* New York: Monthly Review Press, 1942.

Williams, William A. *The Great Evasion.* Chicago: Quadrangle Books, 1964.

Index

About the Authors

Robert B. Carson is professor emeritus with the Division of Economics and Business at the State University of New York College at Oneonta. He pioneered the unique approach of teaching economics by addressing economic issues from the Conservative, Liberal, and Radical positions with the first edition of *Economic Issues Today* in 1978. He has authored twelve books on economics, including *What Economists Know* (1990), which has been reprinted abroad in Spanish, Portuguese, Russian, and Arabic editions. Dr. Carson is an expert on the public regulation of American railroads.

Wade L. Thomas is professor of economics and assistant dean of the Division of Economics and Business at the State University of New York College at Oneonta. Dr. Thomas served two terms as president of the New York State Economics Association, and serves as the organization's Web coordinator, and received the association's Distinguished Fellow Award in 2004. In addition to publishing journal articles on the economics of franchising, health care, and antitrust, he coauthored *The American Economy: Contemporary Problems and Analysis* (1993) with Robert B. Carson.

Jason Hecht is associate professor of finance in the School of Administration and Business at Ramapo College of New Jersey. He has published in both academic and business publications including the *Journal of Economics and Business* and the *Cambridge Journal of Economics*. Dr. Hecht previously worked as an economist in the property-liability insurance industry for many years and continues to consult for this industry.